Jungle Bugs

MASTERS OF CAMOUFLAGE AND MIMICRY

Jungle Bugs

MASTERS OF CAMOUFLAGE AND MIMICRY

Bruce Purser

FIREFLY BOOKS

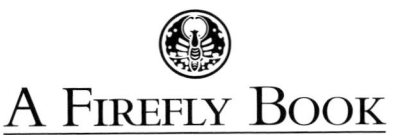

A FIREFLY BOOK

Published by Firefly Books Ltd. 2003

First printing

National Library of Canada Cataloguing in Publication Data

Purser, Bruce
    Jungle bugs : masters of camouflage and mimicry / Bruce Purser.

Includes index.
ISBN 1-55297-671-8 (bound).--ISBN 1-55297-663-7 (pbk.)

    1. Insects--Behavior. 2. Animal defenses. 3. Jungle animals.
I. Title.

QH546.P87 2003   595.7147   C2003-900153-9

Publisher Cataloging-in-Publication Data (U.S.)
(Library of Congress Standards)

Purser, Bruce.
    Jungle bugs : masters of camouflage and mimicry / Bruce Purser. —1st ed.
[128] p. : col. photos. ; cm.
Includes index.
Summary: How insects around the world hide from and defend themselves from predators.
ISBN 1-55297-671-8
ISBN 1-55297-663-7 (pbk.)
    1. Insects. 2. Camouflage (Biology). I. Title.
595.7 21   QL467.2.P87 2003

Published in Canada in 2003 by
Firefly Books Ltd.
3680 Victoria Park Avenue
Toronto, Ontario, M2H 3K1

Published in the United States in 2003 by
Firefly Books (U.S.) Inc.
P.O. Box 1338, Ellicott Station
Buffalo, New York 14205

Design: Jacqueline Hope Raynor
Editor: Charis Cotter

Printed and bound in Canada by Friesens, Altona, Manitoba

The Publisher acknowledges the financial support of the Government of Canada through the Book Publishing Industry Development Program for its publishing activities.

CONTENTS

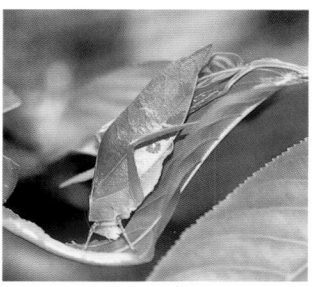

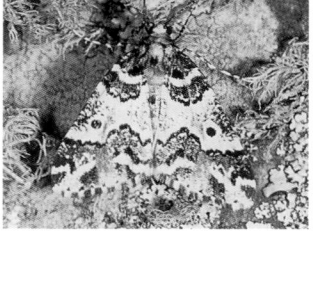

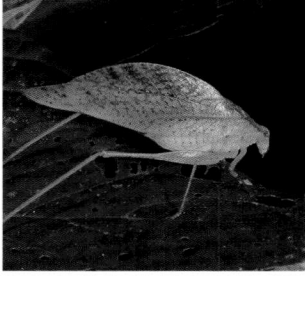

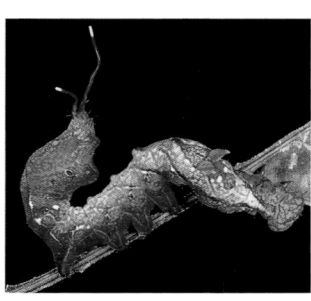

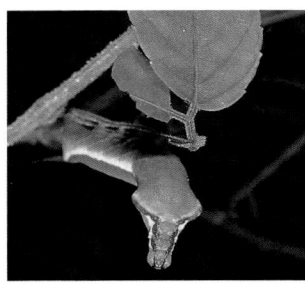

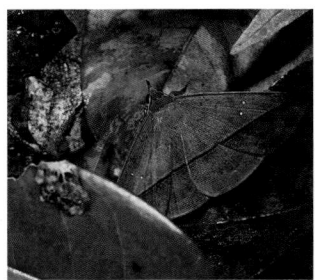

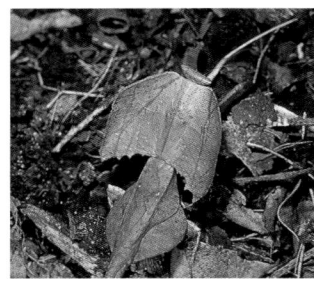

ACKNOWLEDGMENTS

THE PHOTOS PRESENTED in this book have been taken in many out-of-the-way places whose access has been made possible by many people to whom I extend my sincere thanks: the Alfaro family in Chaclacayo, Peru, and Oscar Gonzalez, in Lima, Peru; Michael Guerrero of Quito, Ecuador; Odette Baloup and her husband at Patawa, French Guyana; Michael Hudson of the Ecological Institute at Wau, Papua New Guinea; Paul Zborowski and Anja Bakker at Kuranda, Queensland; and the numerous local guides and drivers in Amazonia, Papua New Guinea, Madagascar, Cameroon, Kenya and Malaysia, without whose help little would have been achieved.

I especially thank my daughter Christine and son Marc, who shared many of my adventures in Amazonia, my wife Marguerite for tolerating my many long absences, and my family in New Zealand for encouragement over the years.

Publication has been greatly helped by Beth Wilson, my business manager, of London. I would also like to thank Charis Cotter, my editor, for her numerous suggestions and corrections that have significantly improved my original manuscript, and Ken Preston-Mafham whose useful scientific criticisms have also helped eliminate many errors. Finally, I am indebted to my old classmate, the novelist Ken McKenney of Comilla, Spain, for literary advice.

No publication is the independent product of its author, for one is always influenced by discussion and, especially, by literature; I am no exception. I have appreciated the works of those great naturalists Henry Bates, Charles Darwin and Arthur Wallace, as well as many others.

The Nature and Significance of Camouflage and Mimicry

THE AIM OF *Jungle Bugs* is to illustrate the many, sometimes incredible, forms of camouflage and mimicry in the insect world. Having had the great luck to work and photograph (and even to live) in many jungles, I now have the opportunity to share something of the boundless variety of the natural world with others through these photographs of living insects and their habitats.

With the possible exception of coral reefs, tropical forests represent the richest biotope (the ecological setting in which plants and animals live) on our planet. In this time of endangered natural environments, it is important to document the life in tropical forests while it is still available to us.

Jungle Bugs invites the reader into the world of bugs in their jungle habitats. The terms "bug" and "jungle" require some explanation here. The word "bug" is a scientific term for a particular order of insects, the Hemiptera, but it is also a word used in the popular sense to refer to virtually all forms of insects, spiders, scorpions and other small invertebrate animals. While the scope of this volume includes several examples from the world of bugs as the word is defined in popular usage, when bugs are spoken of in the text, the word refers specifically to hemipteran insects.

I have used the term "jungle" in *Jungle Bugs* in a rather liberal manner. Strictly speaking, a jungle is a dense, tropical forest. However, the word "jungle" has been expanded by popular usage to include virtually any form of tropical forest. In *Jungle Bugs* I have ventured beyond the popularized meaning of the word by including high altitude cloud forest and temperate evergreen New Zealand "bush" in the jungles of this volume.

Readers may wonder what led to my photographing "bugs" in jungles. The answer goes back to the first ten years of my life, which were spent on an isolated sheep farm in New Zealand where the native forest or "bush" was never far away. I loved the bush, and later, its tropical equivalent, the "jungle." To me, these were friendly environments full of fascinating plants and animals. My particular interest was with the bug life of the forest and, by the age of ten, I had a sizable collection of specimens. At an early age I decided I wanted to be an entomologist.

By the time I was deciding on the university course of study that would determine my future work, I realized that the demand for butterfly collectors was non-existent. I opted for another natural science, geology. When I graduated from university, I was immediately engaged as a petroleum geologist and I traveled to the jungles of Borneo and Sumatra, where I lived for many months deep in the forest. While there, I examined rocks during the week and hunted insects on Sundays, amassing a very large collection.

During my years as a geologist, and, later, as a teacher, I spent my holidays collecting specimens in tropical forests, notably those of South America. In the 1970s I made a major decision. I stopped collecting and took up photographing insects. I realized how important it was to record the more unusual aspects of insect life — such as camouflage and mimicry — that were overlooked by the average person, especially in view of the progressive extinction of insects and the ever-diminishing tropical forests. It has given me great satisfaction to be able to photograph strange bugs from out-of-the-way places, and, especially, to be able to share these pleasures with others.

INSECT NAMES

Every living plant and animal has one or more names. Many have popular, non-scientific, names. For example, the monarch butterfly is readily identified by its popular name of "monarch." To facilitate worldwide understanding, plants and animals also have scientific names based on a system originally proposed by the Swedish naturalist Carolus Linnaeus, in 1735.

Within this system, each distinct type of animal (or plant) has two names. The most important and widely used term is the "species;" this Latin name is always written in italics. Within the species category, the monarch butterfly is termed *plexippus*. But many other butterflies, although distinct species, are very similar to *plexippus*, so they are grouped together under the same "genus," another category. Hence, the full name of the monarch is *Danaus plexippus*. Note that only the generic term (*Danaus*) is spelled with a capital letter.

All butterflies that resemble the genus *Danaus* are grouped within the same family. In the case of *Danaus*, the family is called the Nymphalidae, which is not written in italics. There are about a dozen important families of butterflies and, together with the moths, they are all grouped within an "order," the Lepidoptera. There are different orders of insects, for example, Coleoptera (beetles), Diptera (flies), Hymenoptera (bees and wasps), Odonata (dragonflies), etc.

According to the scientific system of naming, the monarch butterfly is classified as follows:

Phylum: Insecta
Order: Lepidoptera
Family: Nymphalidae
Genus: *Danaus*
Species: *plexippus*

This classification may seem to be complex and confusing at first. However, it is absolutely necessary, not only as a means of precise communication, but also to establish the relationships between the millions of insects that populate our planet.

I have tried to provide the family name of the insects wherever possible.

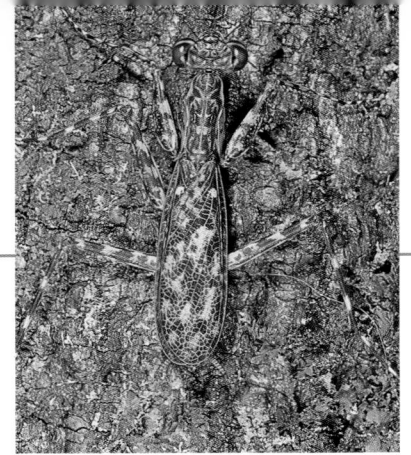

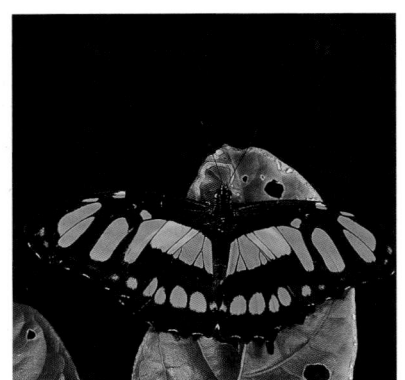

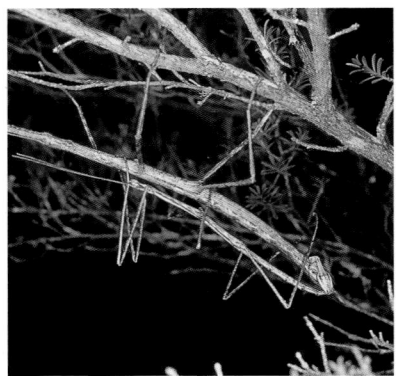

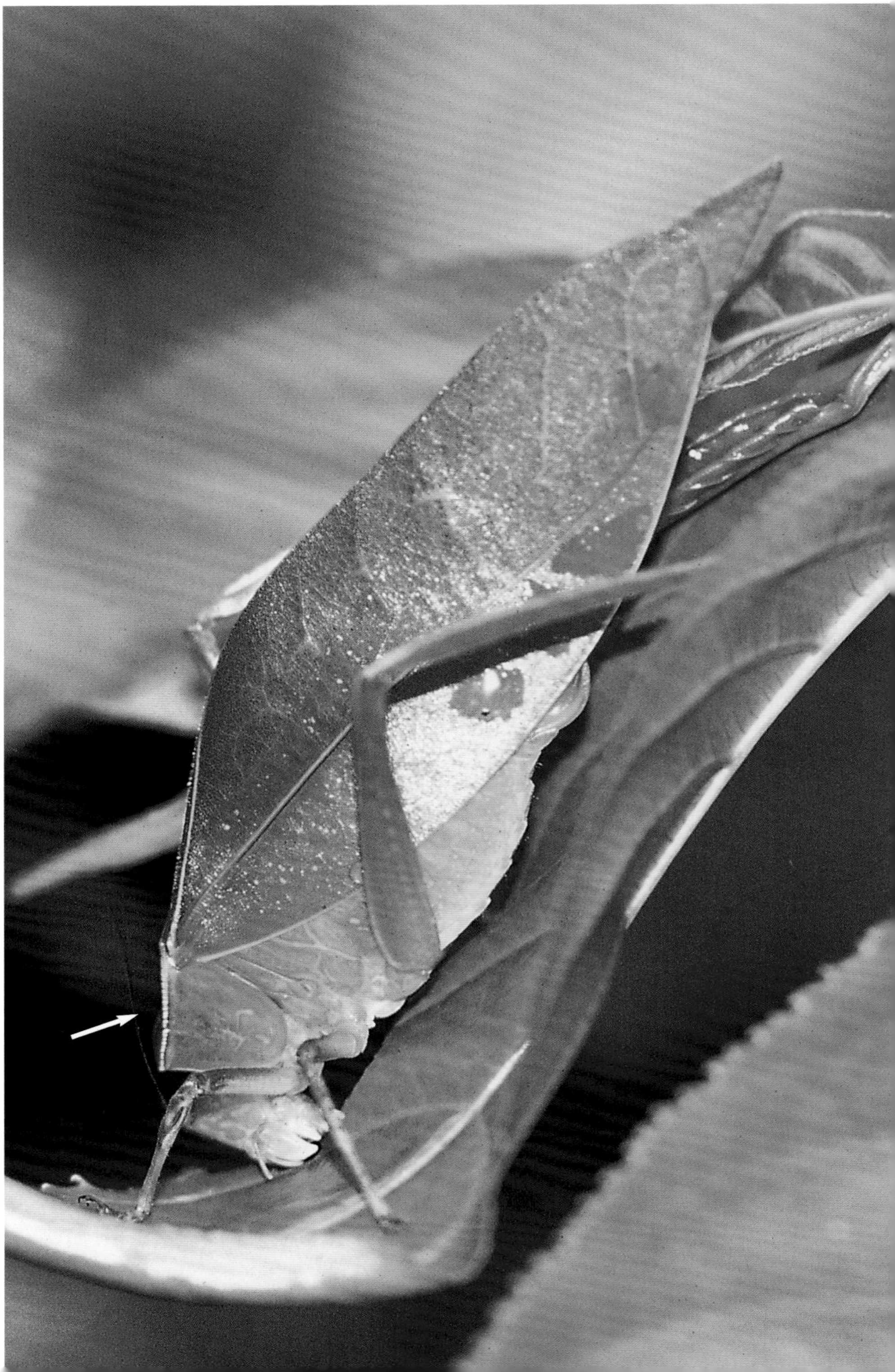

CHAPTER ONE

The Nature
of Insect Disguise

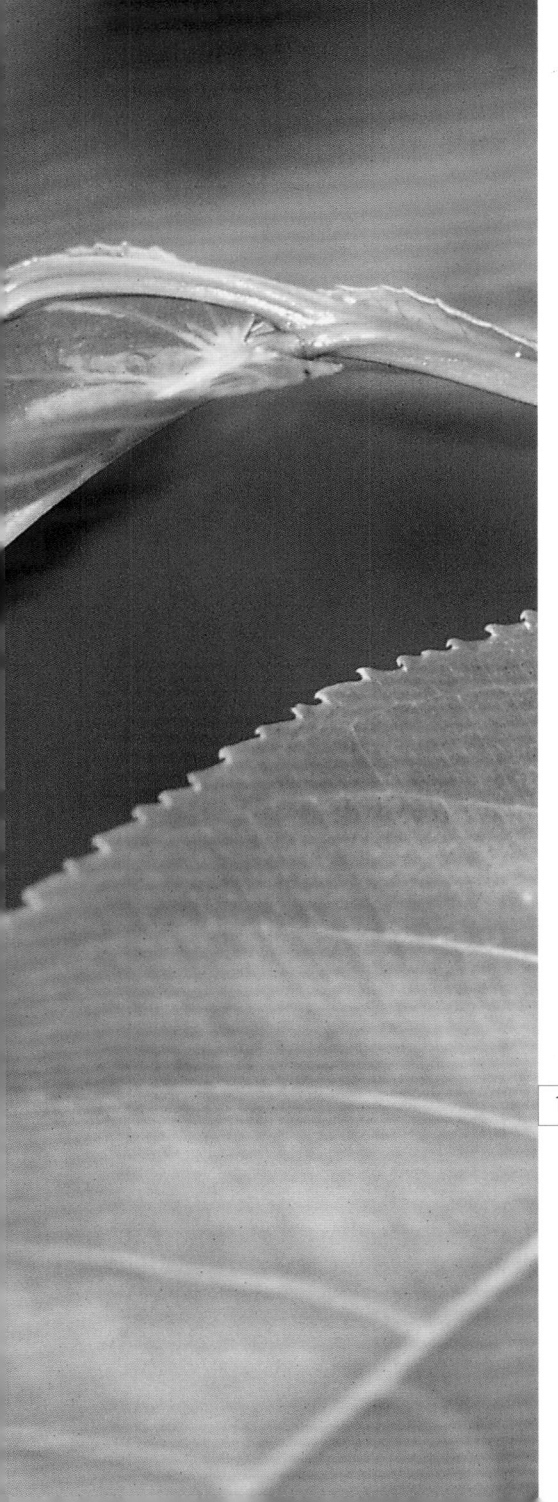

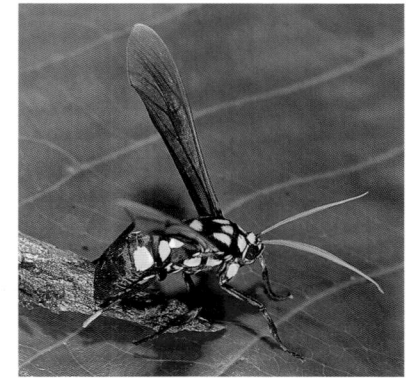

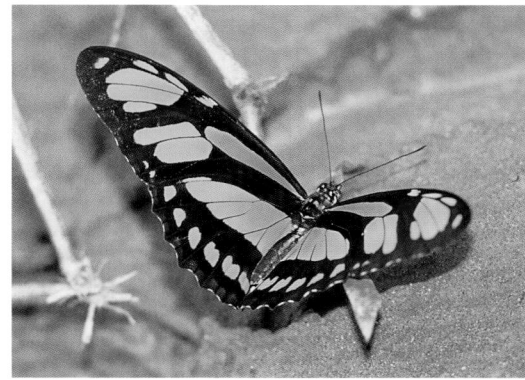

FOR THE LUCKY few who take time to look closely at nature, insects provide a world of wonder and charm. But for most of us, our hurried lives leave little time for these pursuits. Generally speaking, only children, not yet burdened by the superfluous complexity of adult life, will marvel at the colors and behavior of these modest creatures.

Our ignorance of the insect world stems mainly from the fact that most insects are small. They tend to be overlooked — until one is bitten or stung. These unfortunate experiences suggest that insects are horrible little things that are best avoided. Fortunately, we are occasionally impressed, perhaps when on holiday, by the beauty of a butterfly or the unbelievable subtlety of a camouflaged moth. A very small minority of

1 | **Photo 1** Taken in Henri Pittier Reserve in northern Venezuela, this photo demonstrates active camouflage. The green katydid (Tettigoniidae) blends quite well (arrow) with the green leaves on which it sits. However, this camouflage is enhanced by the shape and, especially, by the behavior of the insect; it was sitting on the green branch located near the right side of the photo. When disturbed it walked slowly along this branch to its present position where it lowered its head, adopting an orientation that corresponded perfectly with the adjacent leaves. Length 2½ in/6 cm.

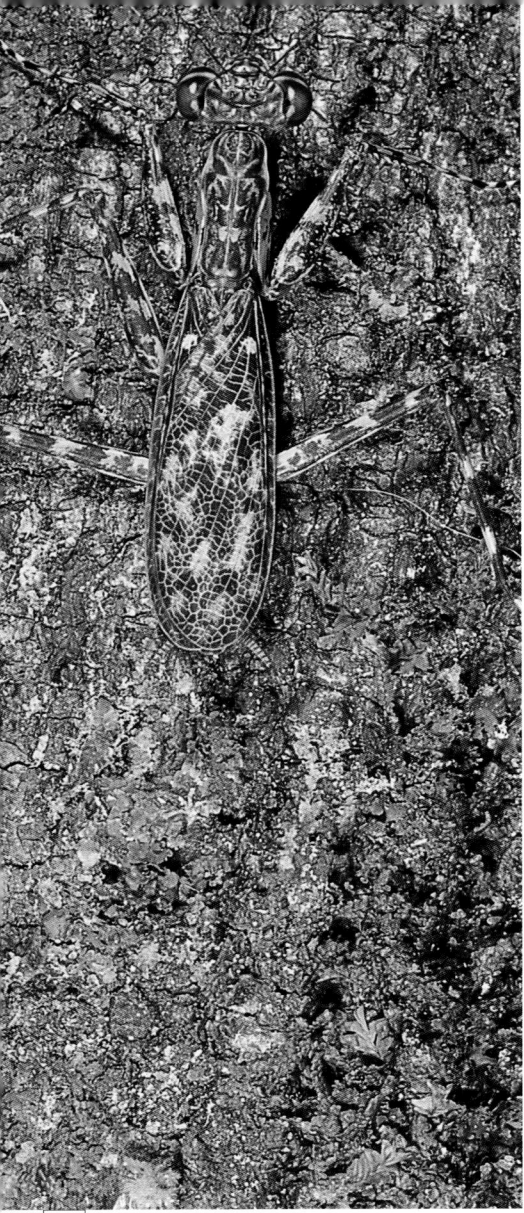

2

Photo 2 This small mantid, *Liturgusa*, lives on moss-covered tree trunks throughout much of tropical America. Its effective camouflage is due to several factors. It remains motionless throughout most of the day, its cryptic coloration matching that of its substrate. But this camouflage is due not only to its color but mainly to a mottled pattern that matches that of the tree trunk. Note also that the mantid is flattened against the tree, its attitude reducing shadow, rendering it less apparent. Photographed in the Kaw Hills, French Guyana. Length 1 in/2.5 cm.

us, often influenced by our early encounters with nature, have graduated progressively into the fields of entomology and other natural sciences. These lifelong studies are never to be regretted, for they amply confirm the endless beauty of plants and animals.

To most naturalists, perhaps the most basic conclusion of their experiences is the great diversity of the insect world. A rapid examination of the many books devoted to insects reveals that there exist at least one million different species. But this is a minimal estimate based only on the species described scientifically, which are those that have been given scientific names. Most specialists agree that there exist between three and five million species of insects, while some experts argue that there are more than ten million. The importance of insects relative to other forms of animal life is overwhelming: there are only 10,000 species of birds, 5000 species of mammals, and only 250,000 species of all known plants. In other words, there are more beetles alone (350,000) than plants.

So why this great diversity? There are, naturally, a number of reasons. To diversify, there must be a need or stimulus. Insects, being relatively small creatures, tend to be preyed upon by higher vertebrates and by other insects. Therefore, insects are obliged to seek protection, this being facilitated by their modest size. Through geological history (usually measured in millions of years), their shapes and colors have

Rough Breakdown of Insect Species*

Beetles	350,000
Flies	185,000
Moths	130,000
Butterflies	20,000
Ants, bees, wasps	150,000
Bugs and cicadas	75,000
Grasshoppers, mantids and phasmids	20,000
Others	70, 000
TOTAL	1,000,000 species

*This table shows a rough estimate of the numbers of species in the various orders of insects, based on figures from *Alien Empire*, by C. O'Toole, 1995. Because at least seven thousand new species are discovered each year, these numbers are a rough estimate only, but they do indicate the relative proportions of each of the major groups. The total number of insect species is a figure that cannot be accurately determined, but it may exceed 5 million.

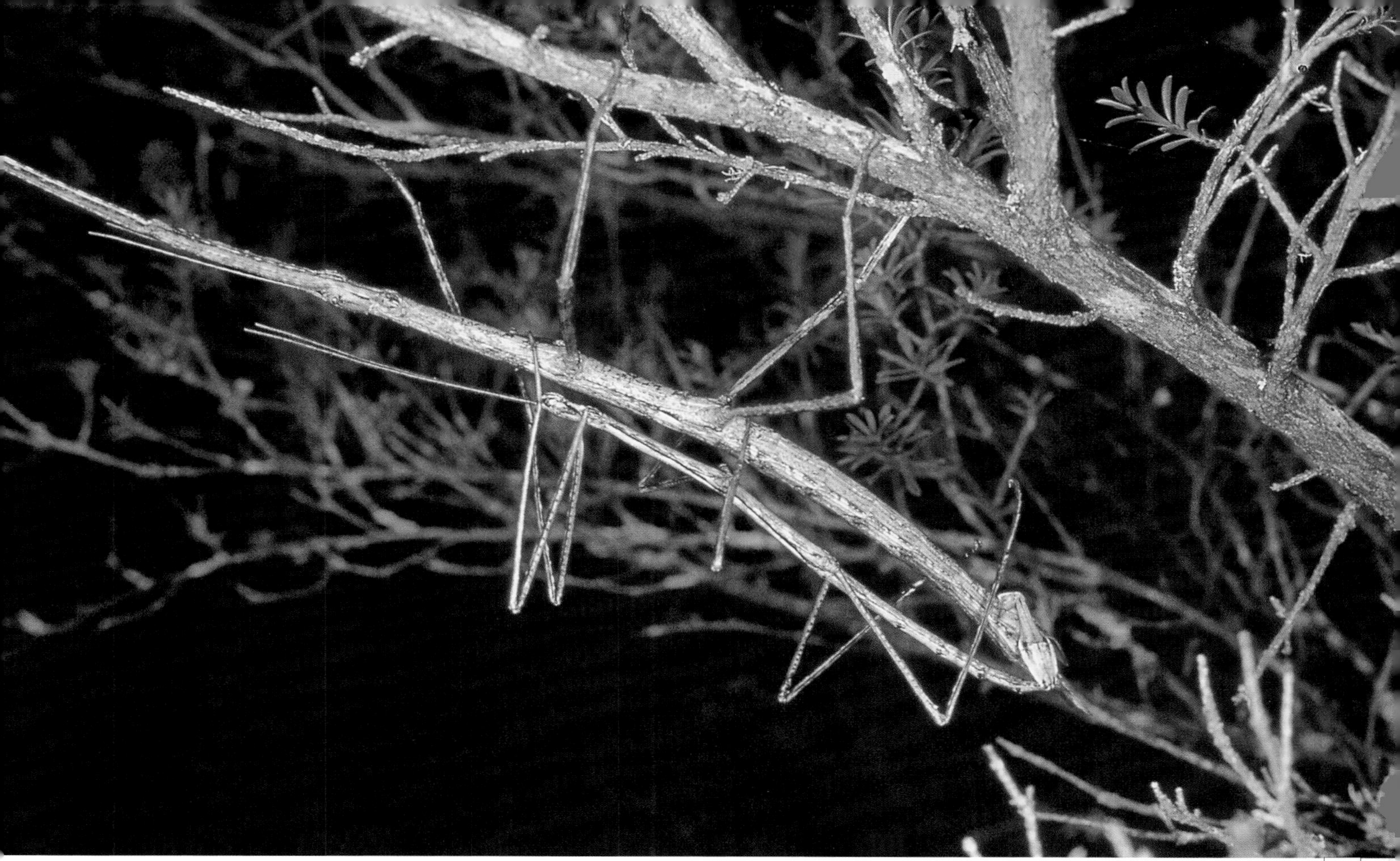

evolved to best conform with their habitats. And because there is such an endless variety of habitats, especially considering the great climatic spectrum that characterizes the planet, insects have had a limitless choice. Insects have evolved over a very long period — about 450 million years. They lived on Earth before the dinosaurs and long before humans, and may well persist long after! Curiously, many of the insects we know today already existed in the distant geological past. Time has favored the insects, preserving many and enabling the development of new forms, so that today, as far as sheer numbers go, they dominate our planet.

Insects have evolved many subtle ways of hiding to escape predators. These include their amazing ability to camouflage themselves. Who has not been impressed by a perfectly camouflaged moth or mantid, perhaps wondering whether the insect was conscious of its act — an enigma to which we shall return. Perhaps even more astounding is the ability of many insects to mimic other, quite unrelated, insects and even vertebrates. In so doing, they appear to be seeking protection from predatorial menace — for the models are generally unpalatable or dangerous insects such as bees or wasps.

Camouflage results when an object, insect, bird or even human being merges optically with its surroundings, often to facilitate escape or

Photo 3 A pair of mating phasmids suspended below a branch in secondary forest near Rotorua, New Zealand. Their camouflage involves both color and, especially, shape. This photo clearly shows why these phasmids are commonly called "stick insects." Length of larger insect 4 in/10 cm.

aggression. It may be calculated or accidental. However, when examined closely, this loss of identity is seen to comprise a number of properties that are not immediately evident. For example, camouflage involves both color and form. The basic prerequisite for effective camouflage, seemingly, is that the insect concerned sport the same color as the material on which it rests. While this is essentially true, a monochromatic insect, whatever its color, does not merge well with its surroundings. To be effective, the insect (or other animal) must have a color pattern that matches that of the "substrate" (the underlying surface against which an insect is camouflaged), as demonstrated in Photo 2. Lacking mottled or other patterns, the outlines of the insect generally remain visible and its future limited.

Camouflage is very dependant on shape; a stick insect (a phasmid) is shaped like a stick (Photo 3) and a leaf butterfly (*Kallima*) is shaped like a leaf. As we shall see, camouflage may involve even stranger forms. But the most convincing ingredient of camouflage is behavior. There are many examples illustrated in the following chapters where camouflage is effective only because the insect has made a seemingly conscious effort to position itself in order to best conform with its surroundings.

Although not the major form of protection among insects, their multiple systems of camouflage and mimicry are more sophisticated than those of any other animal group. A moth perfectly imitating a wasp, not only in color and form but in its behavior patterns, gives rise to wonder and speculation (Photo 6). The reasons for this are not clear. Obviously there is a necessity or stimulus, for, as we have already noted, insects as a whole are preyed upon.

Admitting that certain insects exhibit a remarkable degree of camouflage and mimicry, the logical question is how have they managed to acquire

Photos 4 (top) **5** (bottom) An example of mimicry. These two almost identical butterflies, both common throughout tropical America, are only distantly related. Photo 4 shows a model, *Philaethria dido* (Heliconiidae), a butterfly protected from predators by its noxious body fluids. Photographed in Tambopata Reserve, Peruvian Amazon; wingspan 3¼ in/8 cm.
Photo 5 is of a similar butterfly, *Siproeta stelenes* (Nymphalidae), is edible and thus is liable to be eaten by birds or reptiles. It gains protection by mimicking *Philaethria*, tricking predators into believing that it also is inedible. Photographed near Patawa, French Guyana; wingspan 2¾ in/7 cm.

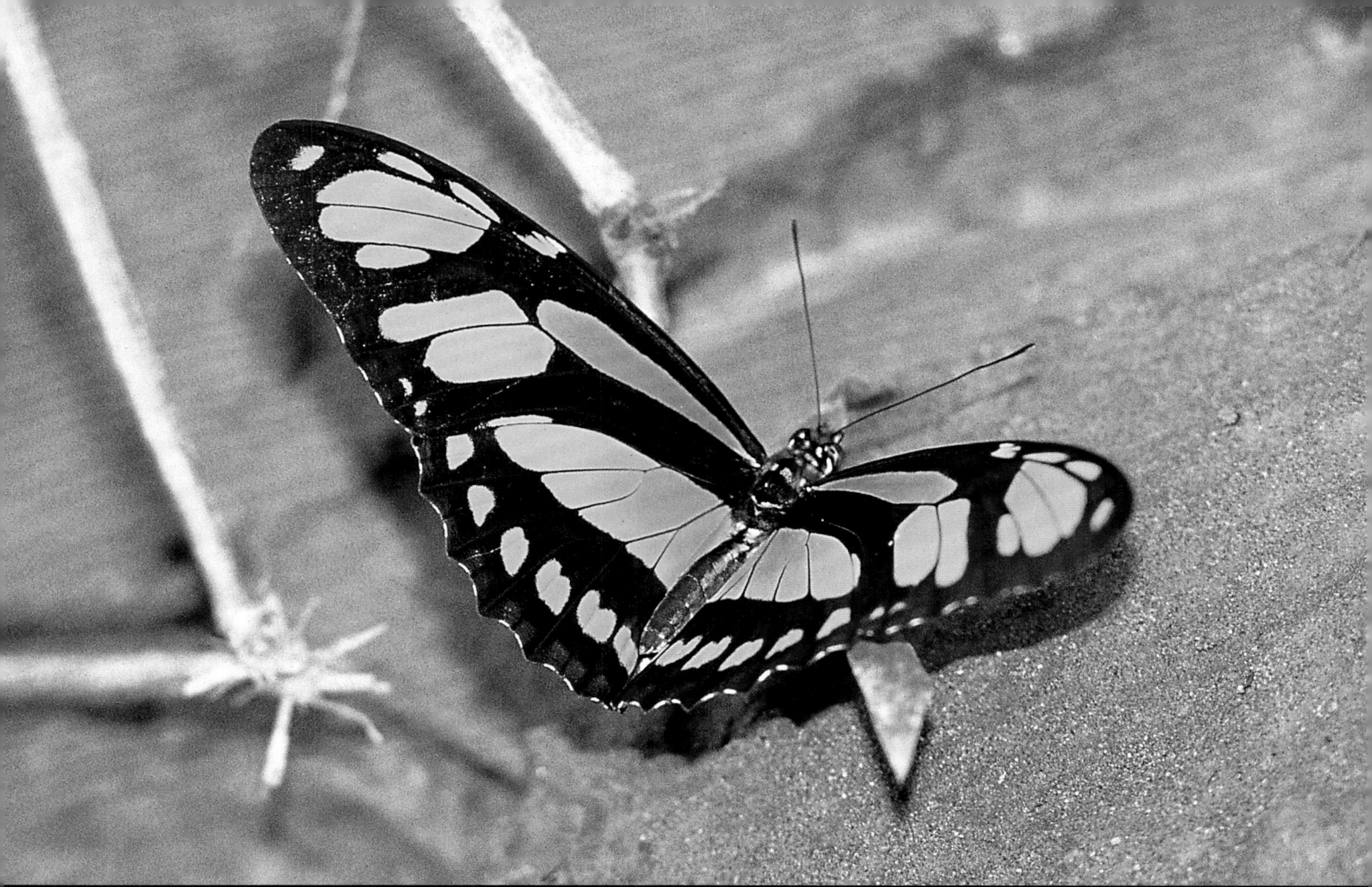

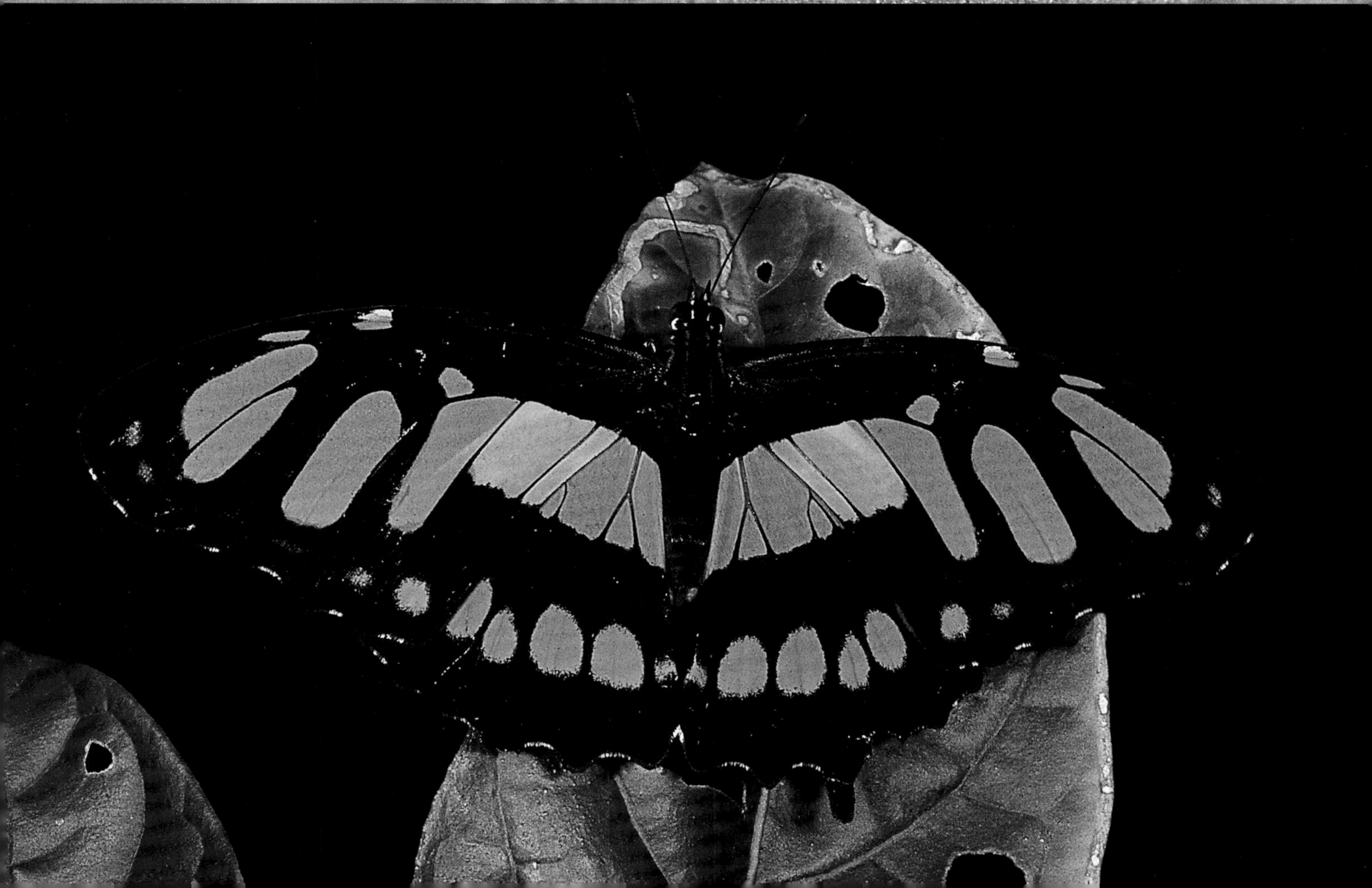

what seem to be very sophisticated systems of protection? Observing an insect perfectly camouflaged on a moss-covered tree trunk, one is tempted to assume that the creature has deliberately chosen its surroundings. However, systematic search may well reveal that the same insect sits on many different substrates; camouflage may be purely coincidental.

Other examples of active camouflage require deeper consideration, for some insects, notably the grasshoppers and mantids, make a deliberate effort to camouflage themselves, their astute maneuvers proving extremely effective, as seen in Photo 1. One can not escape the conclusion that many forms of camouflage and mimicry are not coincidental. Thus, the problem remains: by what mechanism have insects acquired these seemingly intelligent properties?

Sophisticated insect camouflage and mimicry, illustrated in the following chapters, present one of the most intriguing aspects of the natural world. Their refinement is the consequence of organic evolution. Indeed, insect mimicry, observed by Bates, Darwin and Wallace during the nineteenth century, is one of the foundations for the theory of natural selection. In other words, the deliberate efforts of certain insects (and other animals) to camouflage themselves or to mimic others, is predetermined, being governed by their genetic template. Perfection has been attained by the "fittest" insects: those variants (mutants) that are best suited to certain selective aspects of their environment. *Genetics proposes, environment selects.* This is the basic premise of the theory of natural selection.

However, when we examine more critically the factors that are supposed to govern organic evolution we are soon faced with contradictions. For the moment, it is sufficient to note that neither camouflage nor mimicry are necessarily successful. Examination of the contents of birds' stomachs reveals the remains of many insects, including those that appear to be well camouflaged. And if camouflage and mimicry are the result of natural selection and, therefore, by definition, advantageous, this is not clearly expressed in the numbers of living insects concerned. Although we must admit that camouflage and mimicry exist in nature, the origins and causes of these phenomena remain enigmatic. We should, however, be realistic when attempting to understand them. Our logic is not necessarily that of the insects. One simple example: the color spectrum visible through the eyes of an insect tends to favor the extremes (ultraviolet and infrared), which are not available to human beings. Insects, literally, see things differently. And in our search for understanding of the natural world, we often inject a fairly massive dose of imagination into the process. Admirable as this may be, there is little guarantee that nature obeys the logic of humans.

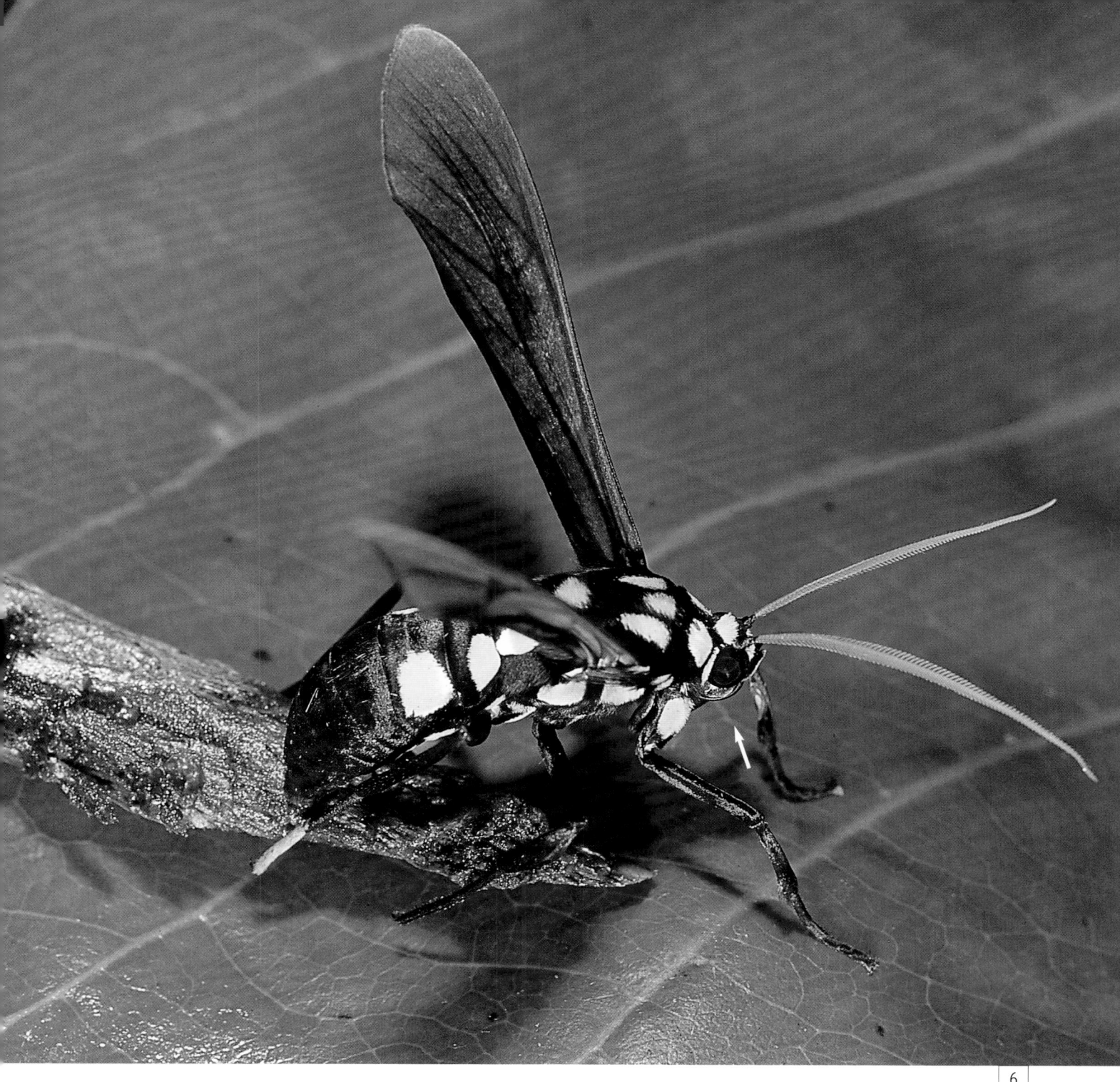

6

Photo 6 Another example of mimicry: This wasp-like insect is in fact a harmless moth (Ctenuchidae) mimicking a stinging wasp in an attempt to trick potential predators. This masquerade is further enhanced by the behavior of the moth; generally, moths fold their wings in a horizontal manner but this one holds its wings obliquely, like a wasp. Furthermore, when handled, the moth curves its abdomen, giving the impression that it is about to sting. Finally, the moth cleans its antennae with its front legs in a very wasp-like manner. But careful observation reveals that its antennae are finely branched like those of moths, while its true affinities are confirmed by its proboscis (arrow), since wasps have biting jaws. So I would award this insect "9 out of 10" for its mimicry, which is very good, but not perfect. Cacao, French Guyana; length 1 in/2.5 cm.

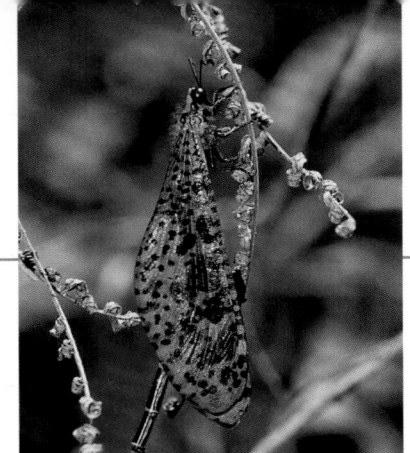

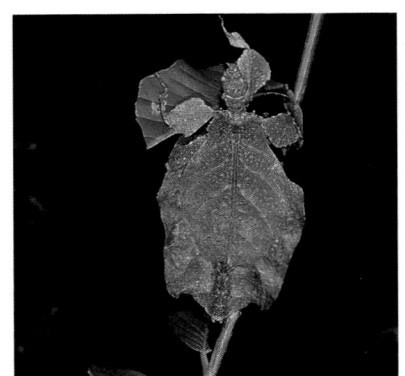

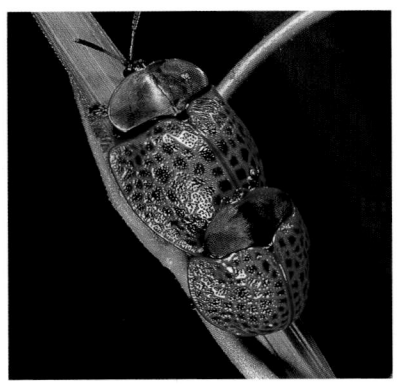

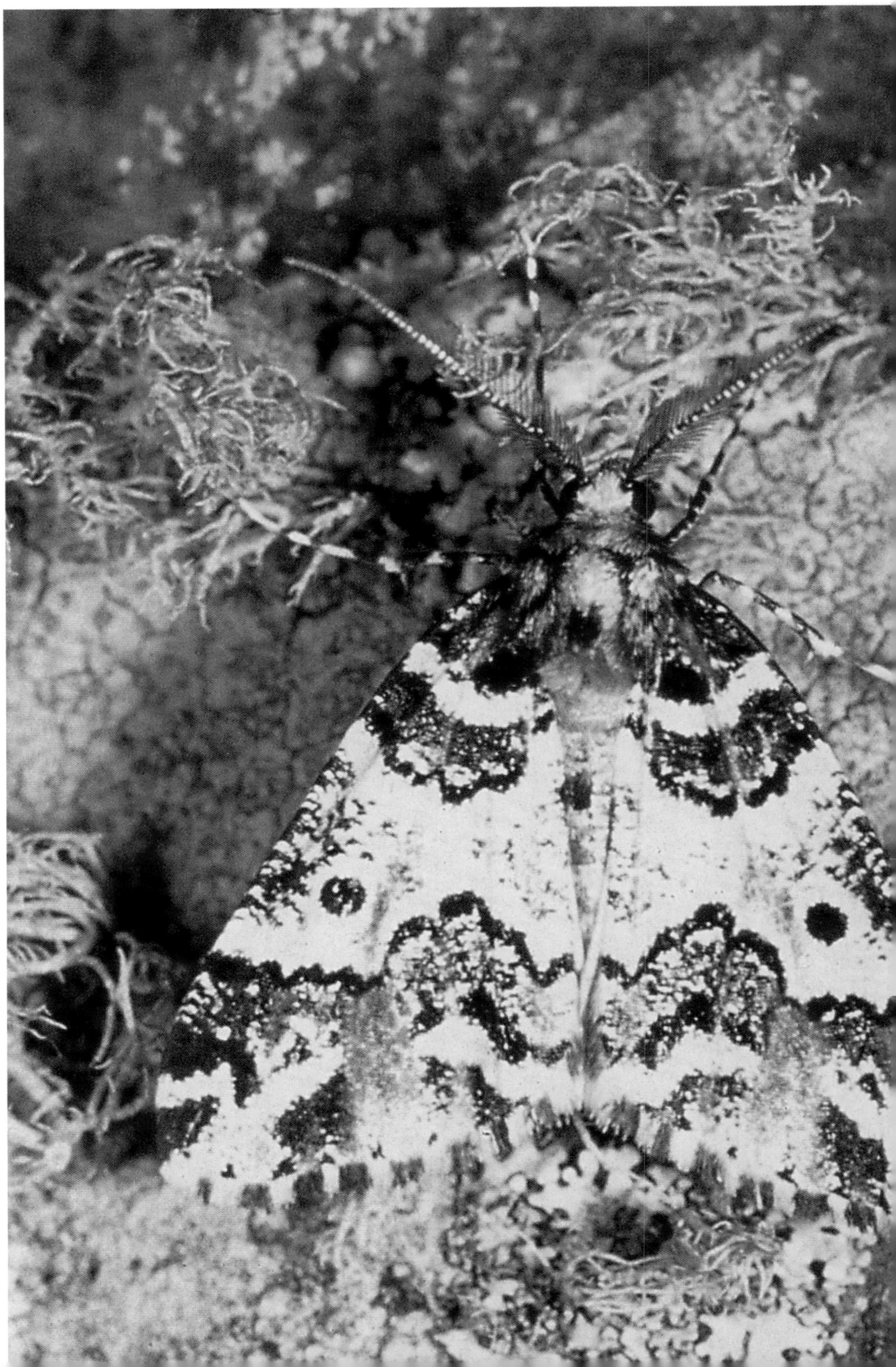

CHAPTER TWO

Passive Camouflage

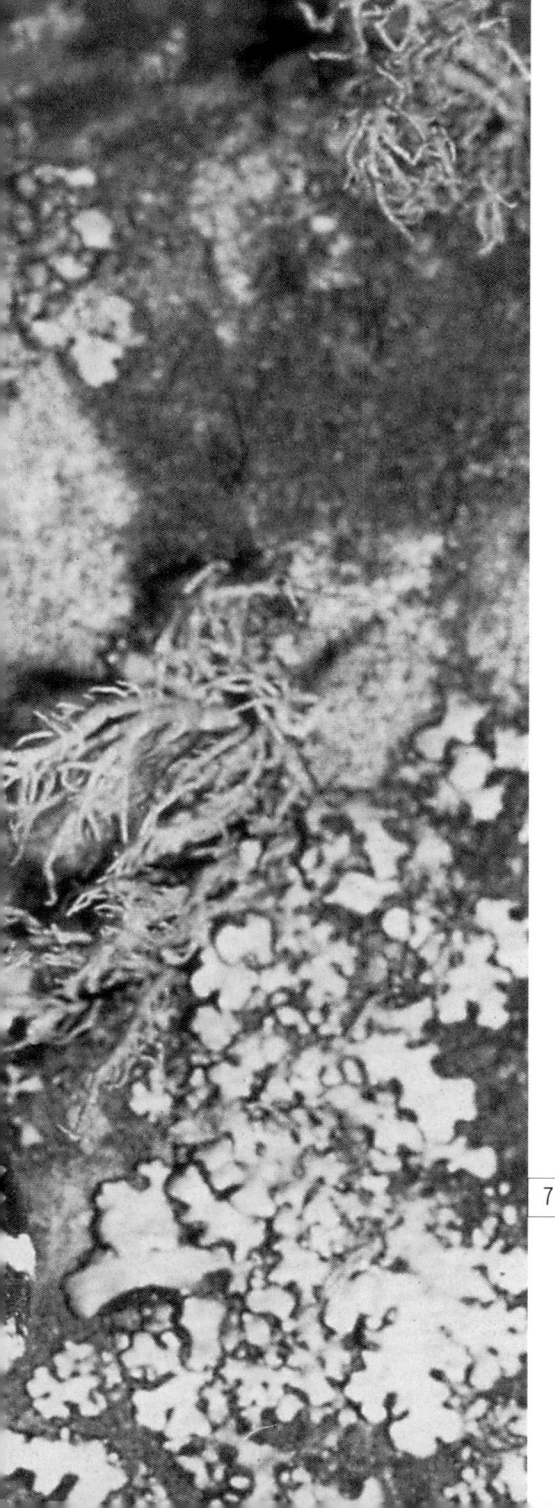

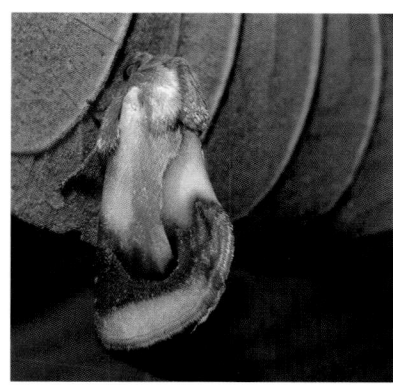

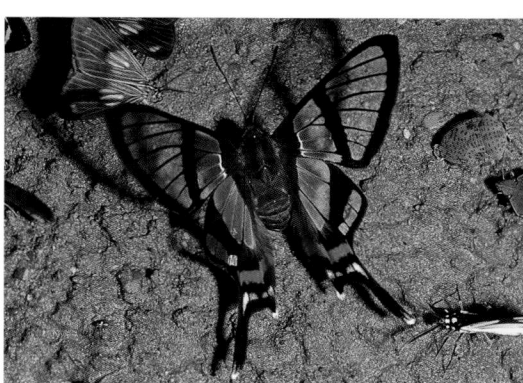

AN INSECT MIGHT spend the day sitting quietly on a tree trunk where no effort is required to blend with its immediate surroundings. It thus "disappears." A grey moth might rest on grey lichens (Photo 7). Both of these are examples of passive camouflage.

Camouflage has two important objectives. Because it tends to render the insect less visible, it is an important means of protection. However, camouflage also facilitates aggression; many spiders and certain mantids have evolved color patterns resembling flowers from which they prey on visiting insects, including bees.

If camouflage is an effective means of protection — and this is not necessarily the case — one may ask "why are most insects *not* camouflaged?" As already noted, only a small minority of insects seem to adopt

7

Photo 7 A geometrid moth whose wing pattern and coloration blend well with the moss and lichen-covered tree trunk. Photographed at 9840 feet (3000 meters) above sea level in the Upper Urubamba Valley, Peru; wingspan 1 in/2.5 cm.

CAMOUFLAGE: A VISUAL SUMMARY

1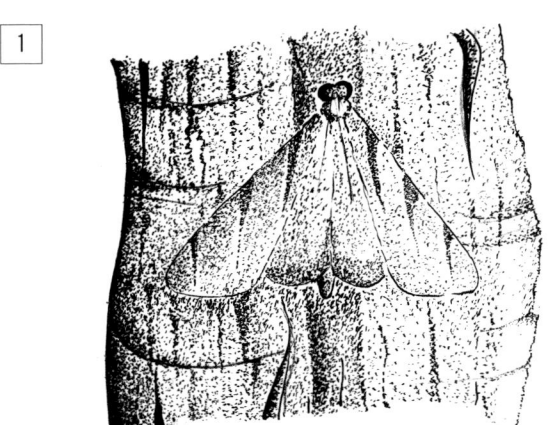

2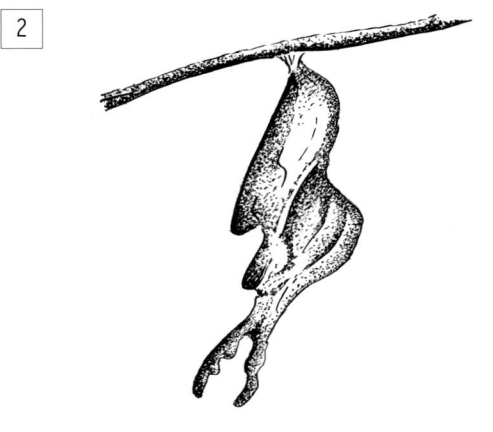

3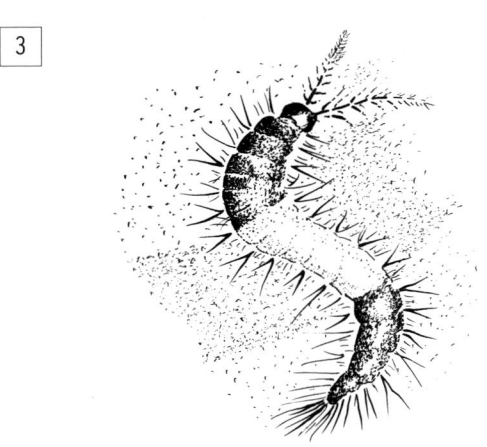

4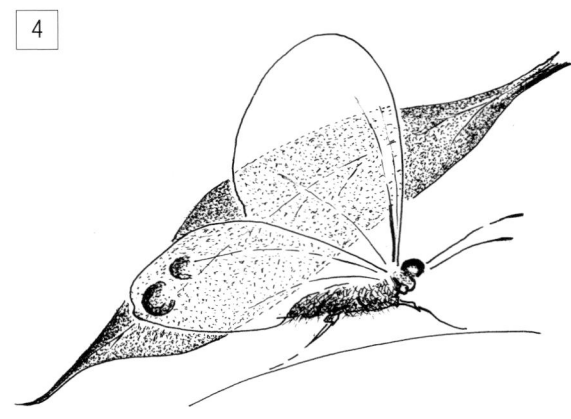

5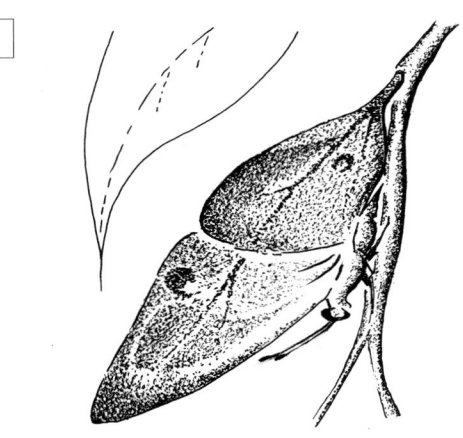

6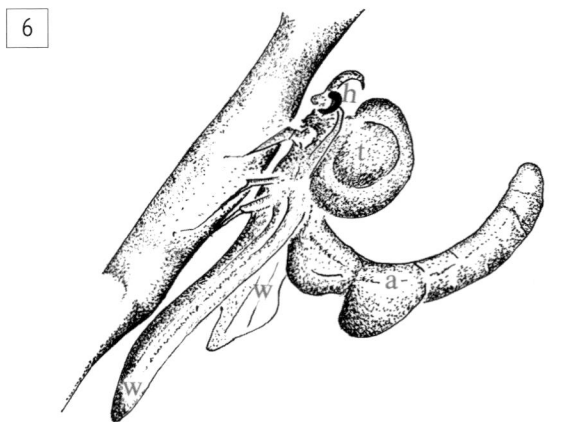

1. *cryptism:* a moth has the same color pattern as the bark of the tree on which it sits
2. *protective resemblance:* a chrysalid closely resembles a dead leaf
3. *disruptive coloration:* the oblique color bands on a caterpillar disguise its true shape
4. *transparency:* a butterfly lacking color is difficult to see

5. *active camouflage:* a butterfly places itself to conform with nearby leaves
6. *gymnasty:* a moth adopts an unusual shape, thus disguising its identity (w = wing, a = abdomen, h = head, t = thorax)

Note that the level of complexity rises from relatively simple, #1, to relatively complicated, #6.

this ruse. There are several replies to this question. The first, a fairly obvious one, is that most insects have no need to camouflage themselves; many are hidden under stones or in the earth and other protected habitats where camouflage would be superfluous. To camouflage there must be a need. Many insects are protected by other mechanisms, notably noxious body fluids, stings or spines. These insects run little risk of being preyed upon. Nevertheless, these noxious insects often sport red or yellow *aposematic* colors, which act as warnings for predators; "red for danger" applies here.

As already noted, the term *camouflage* is a general term involving color, shape and behavior, the latter being either passive or active. The simplest form of camouflage, *crypsis*, involves only color, as demonstrated in Photos 7, 8 and 9. Crypsis may be passive when the insect seems not to make any deliberate attempt to choose its background. In fact, this type of camouflage may be quite accidental, the grey moth having settled on a grey tree-trunk, not by choice, but by pure coincidence. Nevertheless, it is camouflaged. Active camouflage can be demonstrated only occasionally when one has the great luck to observe an insect adjust its position, seemingly to conform better with the color of its immediate surroundings.

A more sophisticated form of camouflage involves both color and shape. As shown in the following illustrations, many insects, notably the grasshoppers and their relatives, the katydids, phasmids and mantids, closely resemble leaves or stones. This type of camouflage is commonly referred to as *protective resemblance*. And, once again, this resemblance may be passive or active. A desert grasshopper may land, by chance, among beige limestone gravels that closely resemble the grasshopper, both in color and in shape. But I have had the opportunity of watching grasshoppers "choose" their surroundings: grey grasshoppers congregating among grey volcanic gravels and pinkish-colored grasshoppers of the same species frequenting pink granitic detritus.

Passive camouflage involving a color correspondence between the insect and its substrate (the material it is sitting on) is particularly frequent among moths but much less so among butterflies. The main reason for this is that most moths do not fly during the day, remaining immobile on tree trunks and other vegetation, where they are vulnerable to predatorial attack. Therefore, camouflage is essential. Butterflies, on the contrary, are mobile insects and thus do not conform with the basic requirement of effective camouflage: immobility.

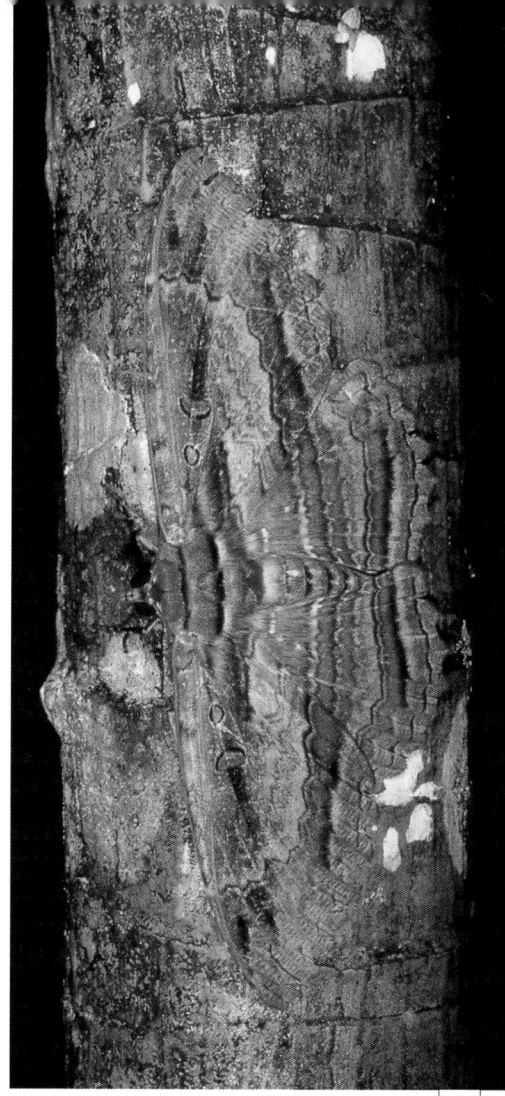

8

Photo 8 Camouflage may be coincidental, as shown in Photos 8 and 9 of two noctuid moths. The well-camouflaged moth in Photo 8 was located only because I saw it settle on a tree trunk, in Costa Rica. Wingspan 4½ in/11 cm.

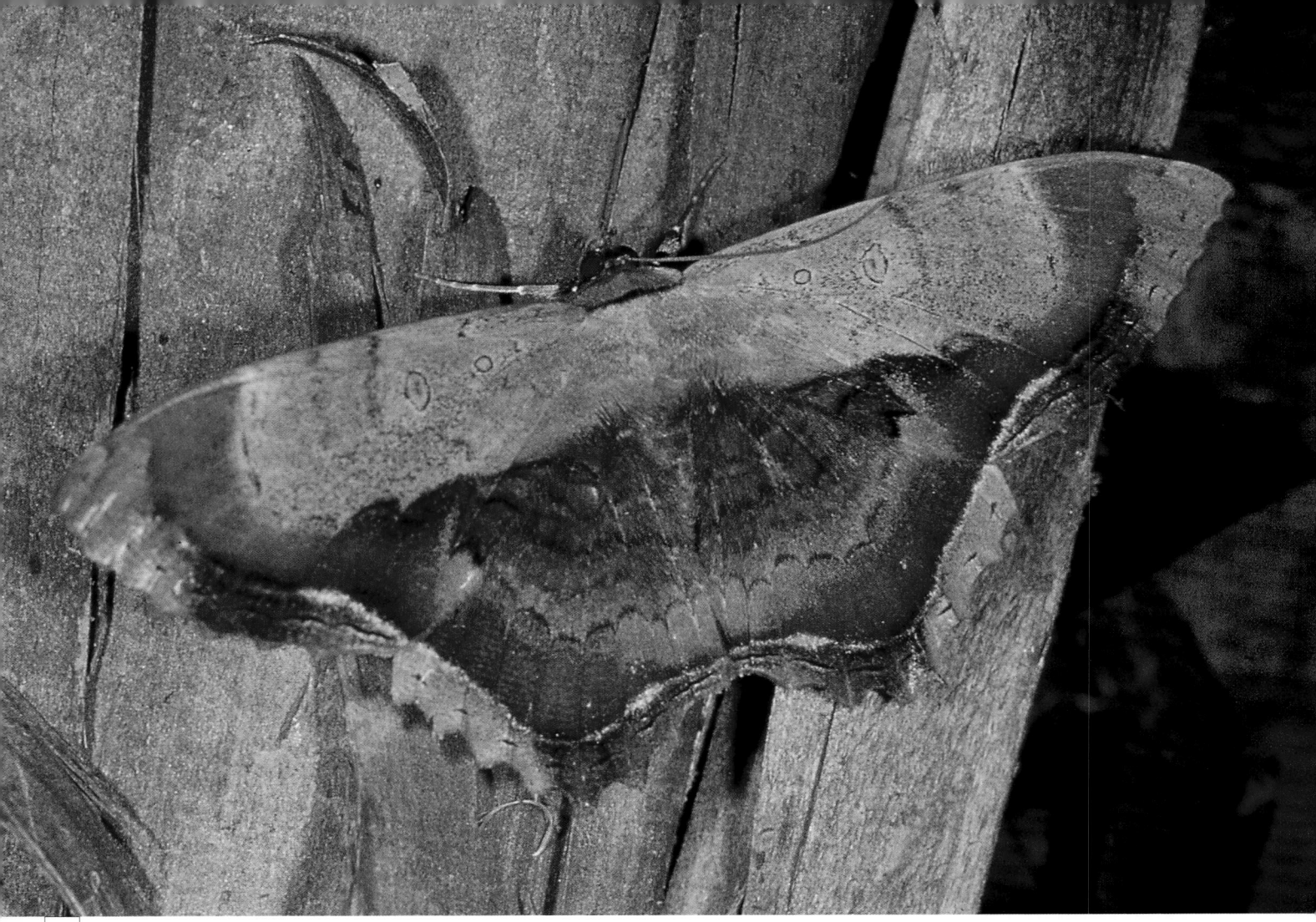

9

Photo 9 This moth, photographed in the Urubamba Valley of Peru, is oriented in a haphazard manner resulting in poor camouflage. Wingspan 4 3/4 in/12 cm.

HAPHAZARD CAMOUFLAGE

Camouflage may be passive, active or completely haphazard, the distinction often being difficult to establish. Photos 8 and 9 show how camouflage may be haphazard. These two moths both belong to the same family, the Noctuidae. In Latin America, these moths can be quite large. Although photographed (at night) in two widely separated localities, both moths have very similar habits, facilitating their comparison.

Photo 8, taken in Costa Rica, illustrates cryptic camouflage, the wing pattern conforming perfectly with the vertical pattern of the bark on which it sits. Camouflage is enhanced by the lack of shadow, with the moth flattened against its substrate. Is the camouflage calculated or coincidental?

Photo 9, taken in the Urubamba Valley of Peru, shows a rather similar moth that has settled on a dead tree. However, its wing pattern is not oriented parallel to the structure of its substratum; it is not camouflaged.

These two photos demonstrate the haphazard nature of certain types of camouflage, in which luck may play an important role.

PASSIVE OR ACTIVE?

It is not always possible to distinguish between active and passive camouflage, as illustrated in Photo 10. A rust-colored grasshopper was photographed among rust-colored quartzite gravels, among which it was perfectly camouflaged. The grasshopper may have settled by accident among these favorable settings and the resulting crypsis would be *passive*. But, because I did not actually observe the grasshopper settle, it is possible that it chose these favorable circumstances deliberately — in which case the resulting camouflage would be *active*. In this particular case we will never know. Fortunately, in many cases the distinction is possible, as described in the next chapter.

Photo 10 A well-camouflaged acridid grasshopper (arrow) hidden among quartzite gravels on the Masai Steppes, Tanzania. There is an almost perfect correspondence between the color pattern of the grasshopper and the rust-colored pebbles between which it sits. Length ½ in/12 mm.

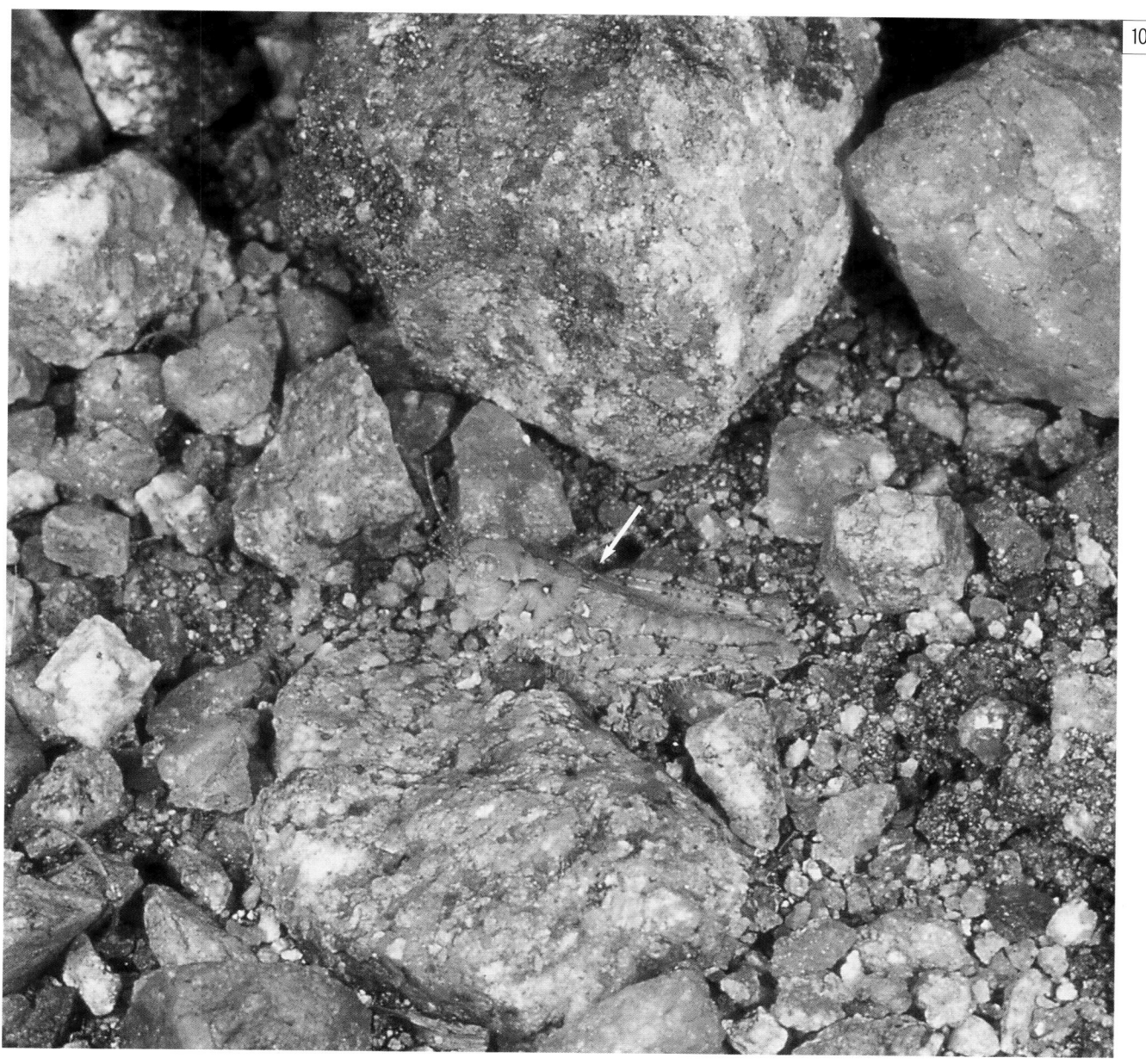

10

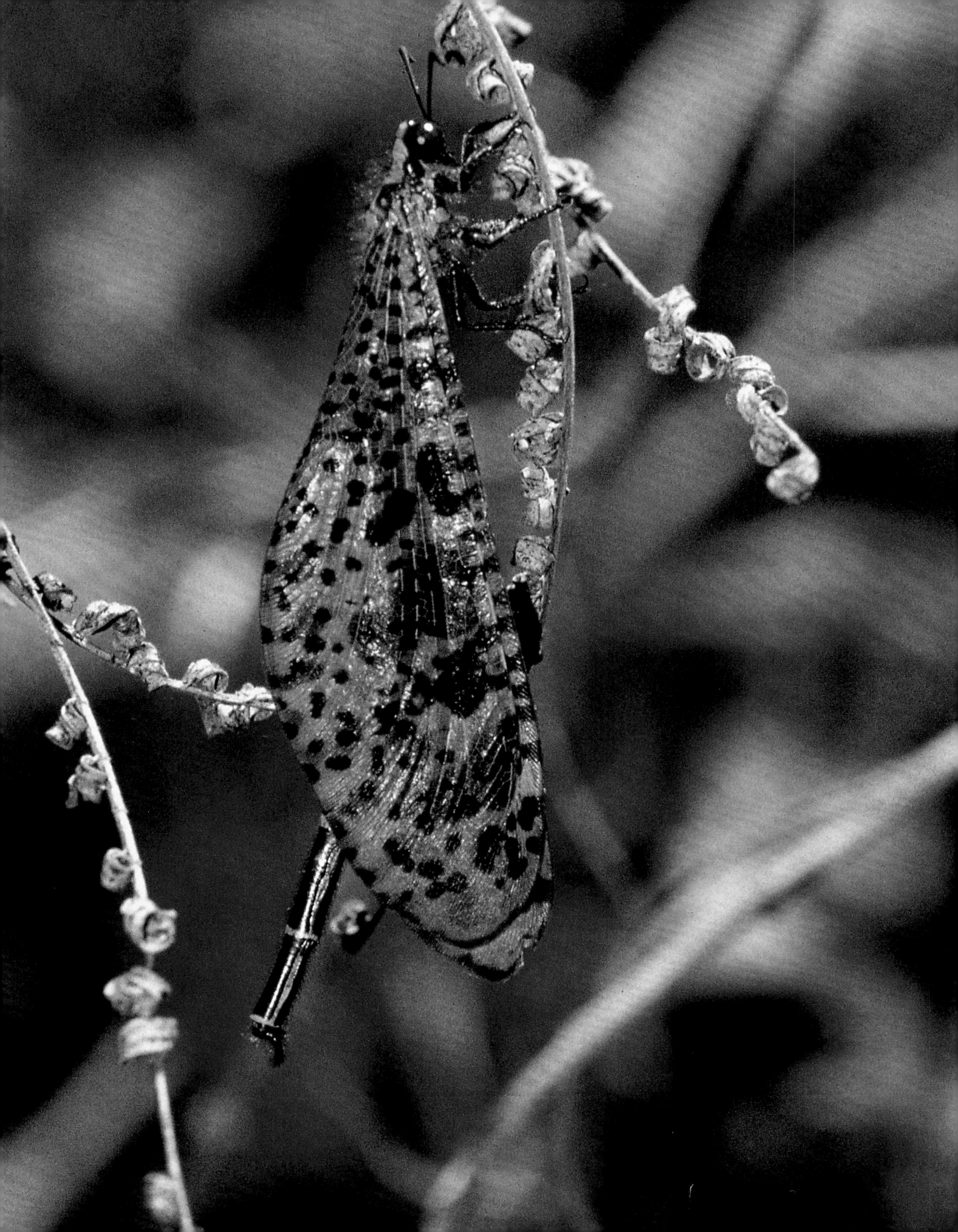

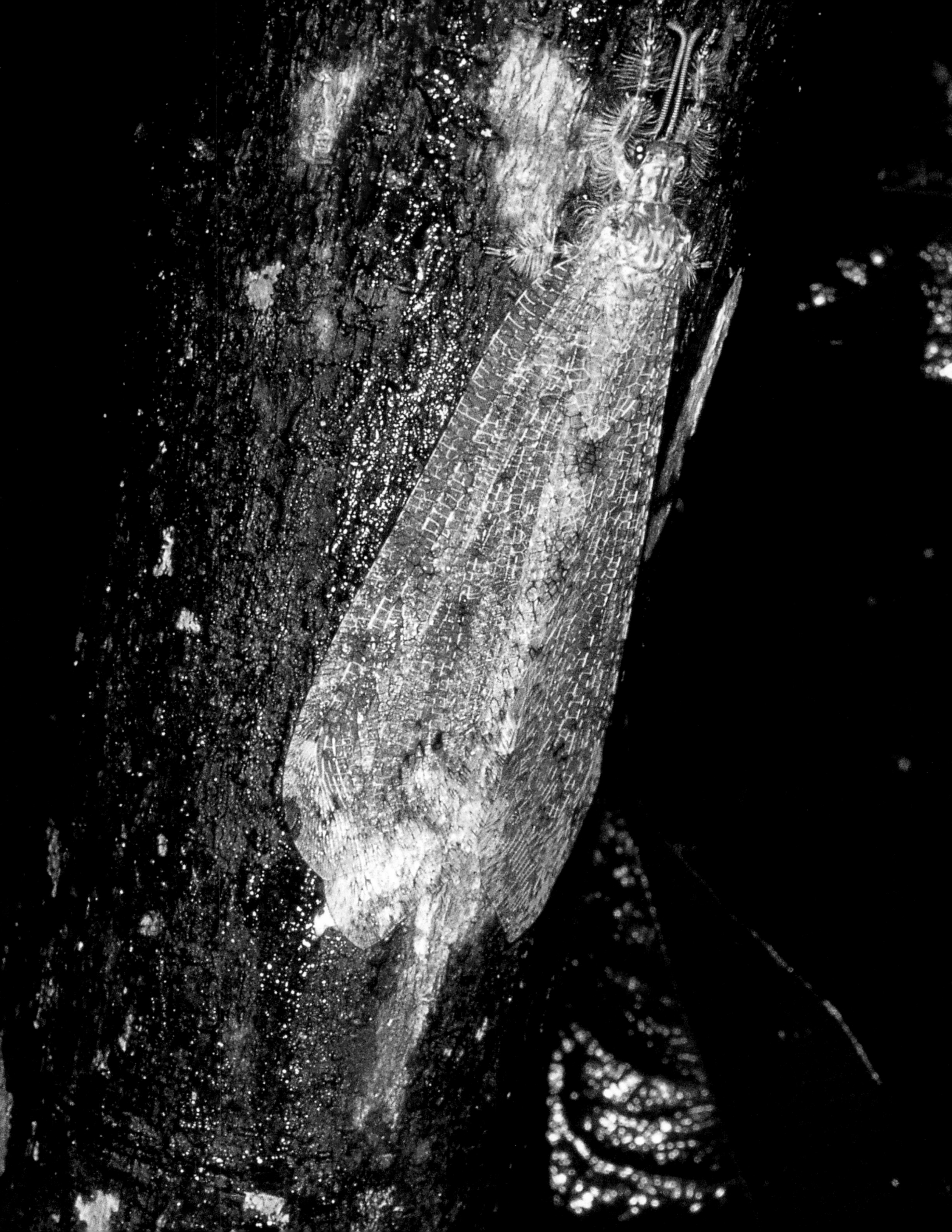

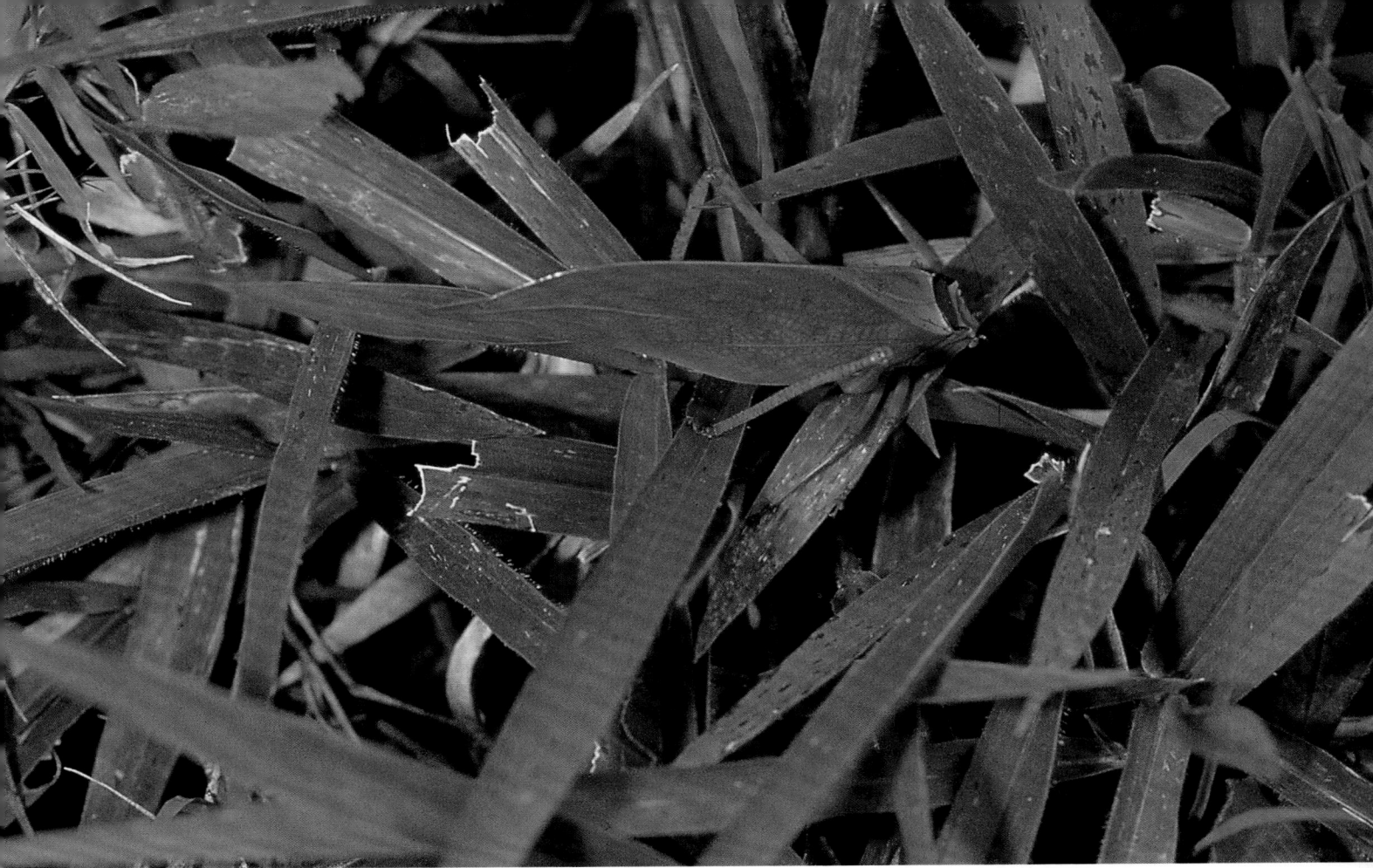

13

Photo 13 A green katydid (Tettigoniidae) in roadside grass. The shape of the insect's wings matches well with the grasses in which it sits. Pozozu Valley, Central Peru; length 2½ in/6 cm.

Photos 11, 12 (left and right, previous 2 pages) These two antlions (Myrmeleontidae), although basically similar, have quite different colors. The insect in Photo 11, photographed on the dry central plateau of Madagascar, has a mottled pattern that blends moderately well with the dead vegetation where it lives. Length 2¾ in/7 cm. The antlion shown in Photo 12 lives in dry forests in northern Costa Rica, where it sits quietly on tree trunks. The differences between these two closely related insects reflect the predominant colors of their respective habitats. Length 2 in/5 cm.

ANTLIONS

These rather strange insects generally live in fairly dry regions, being very common around the Mediterranean. Their rather unusual name derives from the fact that their larvae are sometimes aggressively carnivorous, constructing conical traps in sandy soil and frequently devouring ants.

PHASMIDS AND KATYDIDS

An insect may resemble an object, often a leaf or a stick. This protective resemblance adds another dimension to camouflage. Although immobility is essential, there is no longer a problem of shadow. On the contrary, shadow may improve the matching of the insect and its substrate. Photos 13 and 14 clearly show how different insects may resemble quite different forms of living leaves. The "stick insect," (Photo 14) in fact, would be better termed a "grass insect," for its form and colors are almost identical with those of the spiny grasses on which it sits. Grasshoppers are aptly named for they often resemble green grass. This similarity is enhanced by the veined structure of the grasshopper's wings, which closely resembles the veins of a blade of grass.

LEAF INSECTS

Probably the most convincing example of protective resemblance is offered by the Asiatic phasmid Phyllium. There are about twenty species of *Phyllium*, found from the Seychelles to Australia. This particular species, from Malaysia, is a very friendly insect and is frequently kept as a pet. Living specimens are bred in Europe for this purpose.

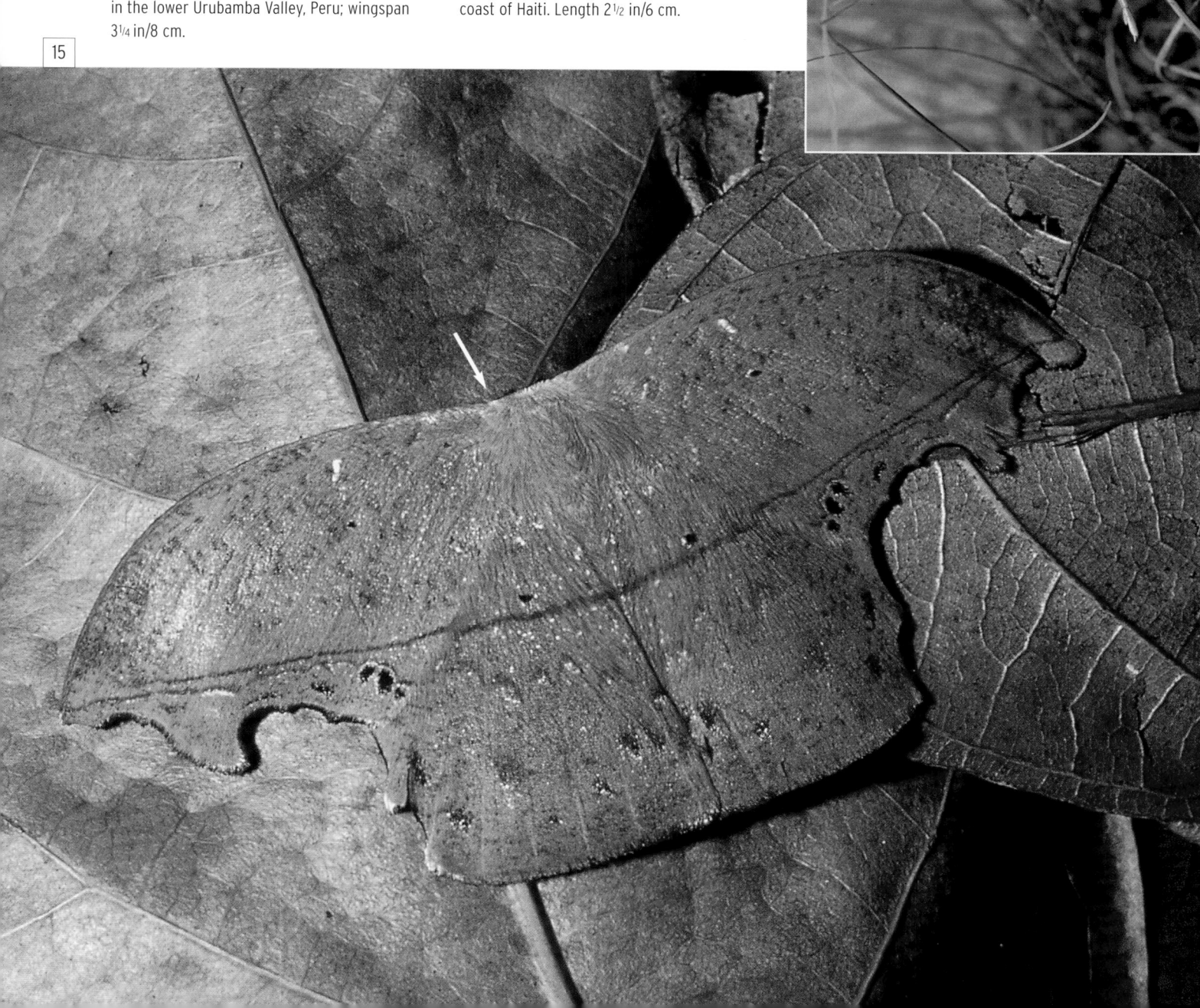

Photo 15 Other insects, such as this large moth (Saturniidae), hide among leaves, which they closely resemble. The arrow indicates the head of the moth. Photographed at night in the lower Urubamba Valley, Peru; wingspan 3¼ in/8 cm.

Photo 14 Passive camouflage may involve shape, as shown by this wingless phasmid, whose color, shape and orientation blend well with the dry grass of the arid north coast of Haiti. Length 2½ in/6 cm.

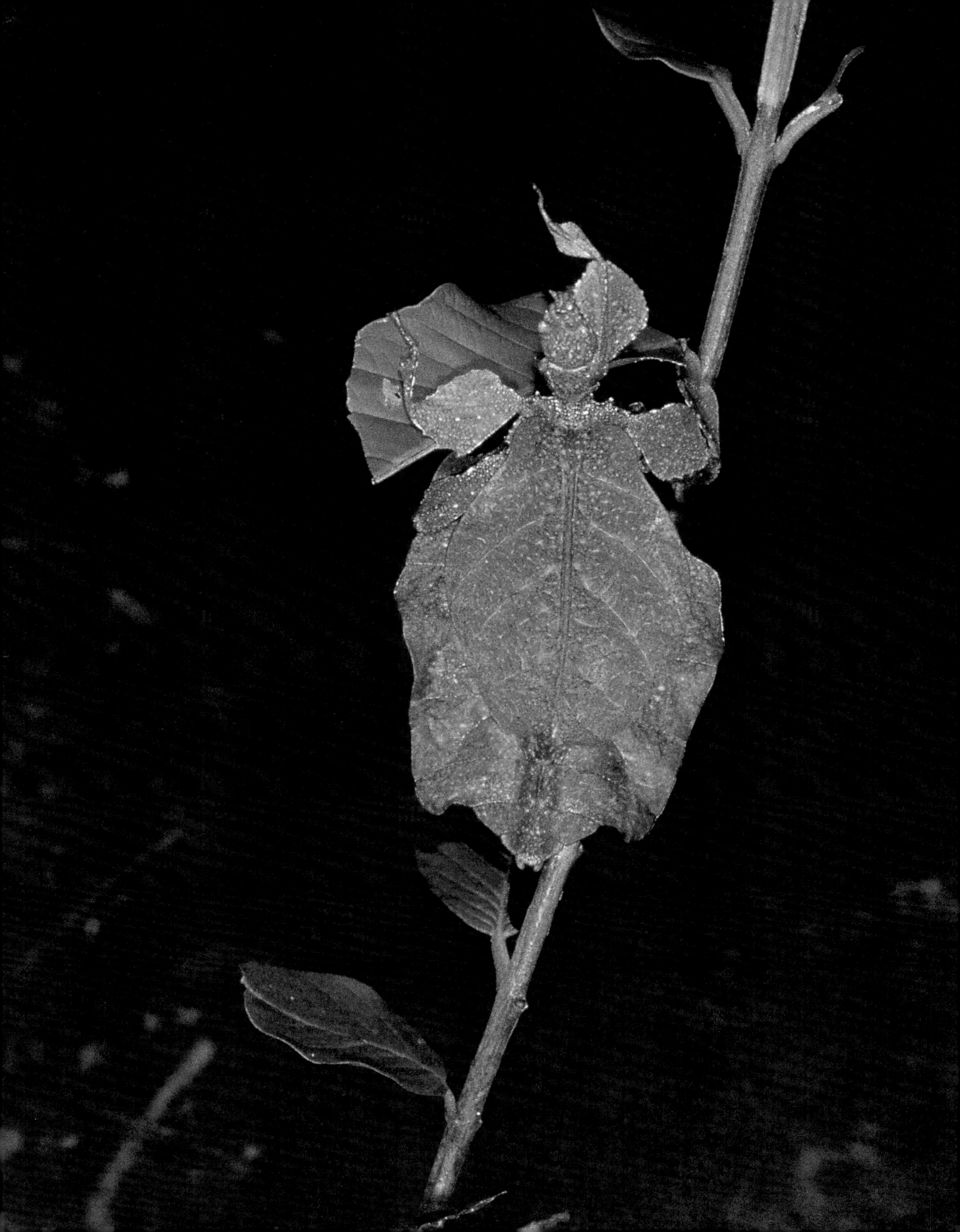

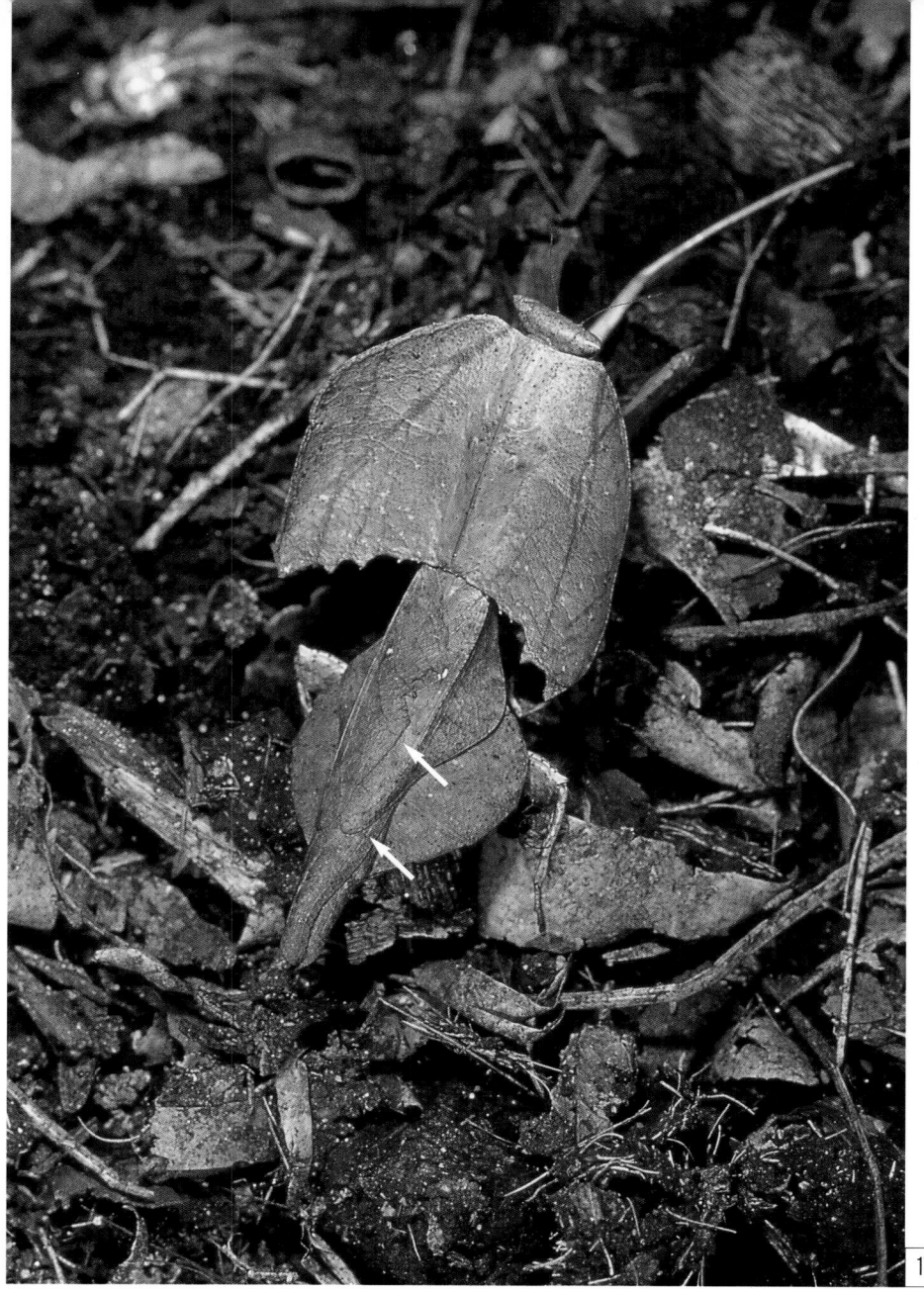

Leaf insects may resemble green, living vegetation, as in the example at left, while other brown varieties resemble dead leaves. These photos illustrate rather unusual insects whose irregular shapes and colors blend well with the dead vegetation on which they have been photographed; they combine crypsis and protective resemblance. However, it must be admitted that the situation is not completely natural: the moth in Photo 15 was attracted by my strong lamp and landed on dried leaves below it, while the mantid in Photo 17, scared by my presence, jumped from a branch onto the ground before running away.

Photo 16 (opposite) The phasmid *Phyllium* closely resembles a living leaf, with its branching vein structure. This individual was photo-graphed on a guava shrub, on which it feeds. Central Malaysia; length 3¼ in/8 cm.

Photo 17 This mantid *Brantsikia*, which lives in dry secondary forests (new growth of low trees and shrubs where the primary forest has been cut or burned) in Madagascar, has curious leaf-like appendages that enable it to blend with dead vegetation. Its wings (arrows) are folded over its abdomen. Length 2 in/5 cm.

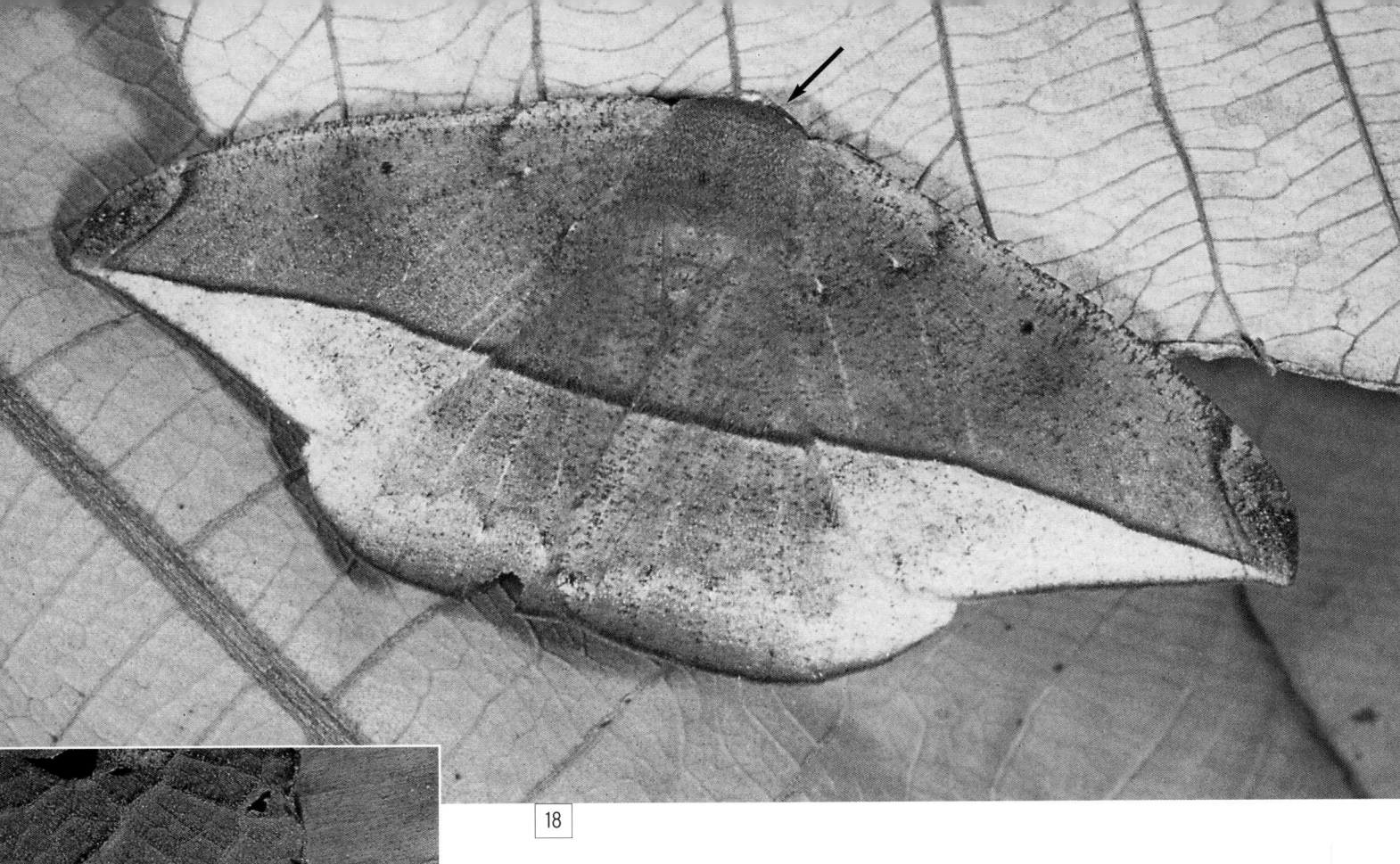

18

19

MOTHS

Forest-dwelling moths spend the daylight hours immobile among various forms of vegetation, where they are susceptible to predatorial attack. Possibly for this reason many have evolved color patterns that blend with those of the adjacent vegetation. And because the majority sport fairly somber colors, they tend to resemble dead leaves. This resemblance is often accentuated by the presence of a dark line that traverses both pairs of wings, as seen in Photos 18 and 19. These lines tend to resemble the mid-rib of a leaf. Note that this median line is continuous across all four wings (which are very difficult to distinguish in these photos). Therefore, to be effective, the moth must remain in a natural position. In museum collections, however, the wings of moths and butterflies are spread in an unnatural position and the natural wing pattern is disrupted. To appreciate nature one must observe it *alive*!

The tropical forest comprises an almost unlimited number of habitats, this variety being expressed by a corresponding variety of insects and spiders that have adapted to these habitats. Because much of the forest is either green or brown, evolution of its insect fauna has resulted in the predominance of these two colors. However, many dead leaves are suspended temporarily among green, leafy branches, so brown insects, such

Photos 18, 19 (opposite) Moths from the forests of the Peruvian Amazon have shapes and colors that closely resemble dead leaves. This protective resemblance is further enhanced by the disruptive color pattern. Arrows indicate the head of each moth. Wingspans 2 3/4 in/7cm (18), 3/4 in/2 cm (19).

Photos 20, 21 This unusual moth was photographed at seven p.m. in the dry forests of the Santa Rosa Reserve in northwest Costa Rica. Attracted by the lamp, it settled on the dry leaves below. Its colors and its very irregular shape closely resemble those of dead leaves. Protective resemblance is further enhanced by the transparent patches shown in detail in Photo 21. Each transparent patch is interlaced by an intricate pattern that looks like the veins of decomposing leaves, as seen on the right side of Photo 20. Wingspan 2 1/4 in/5.5 cm.

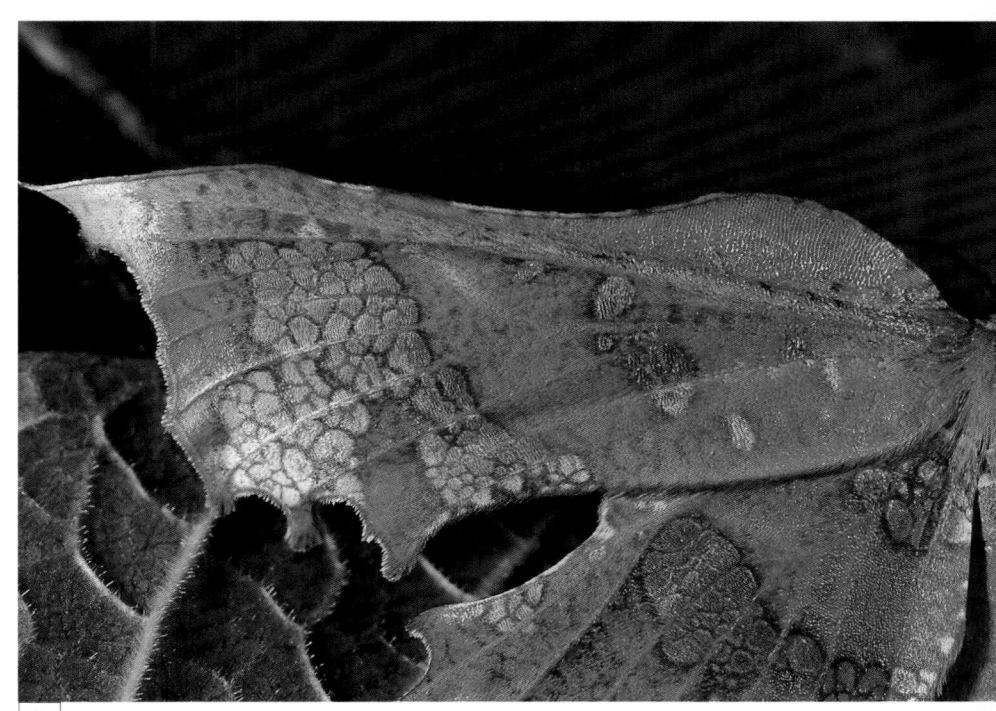

21

20

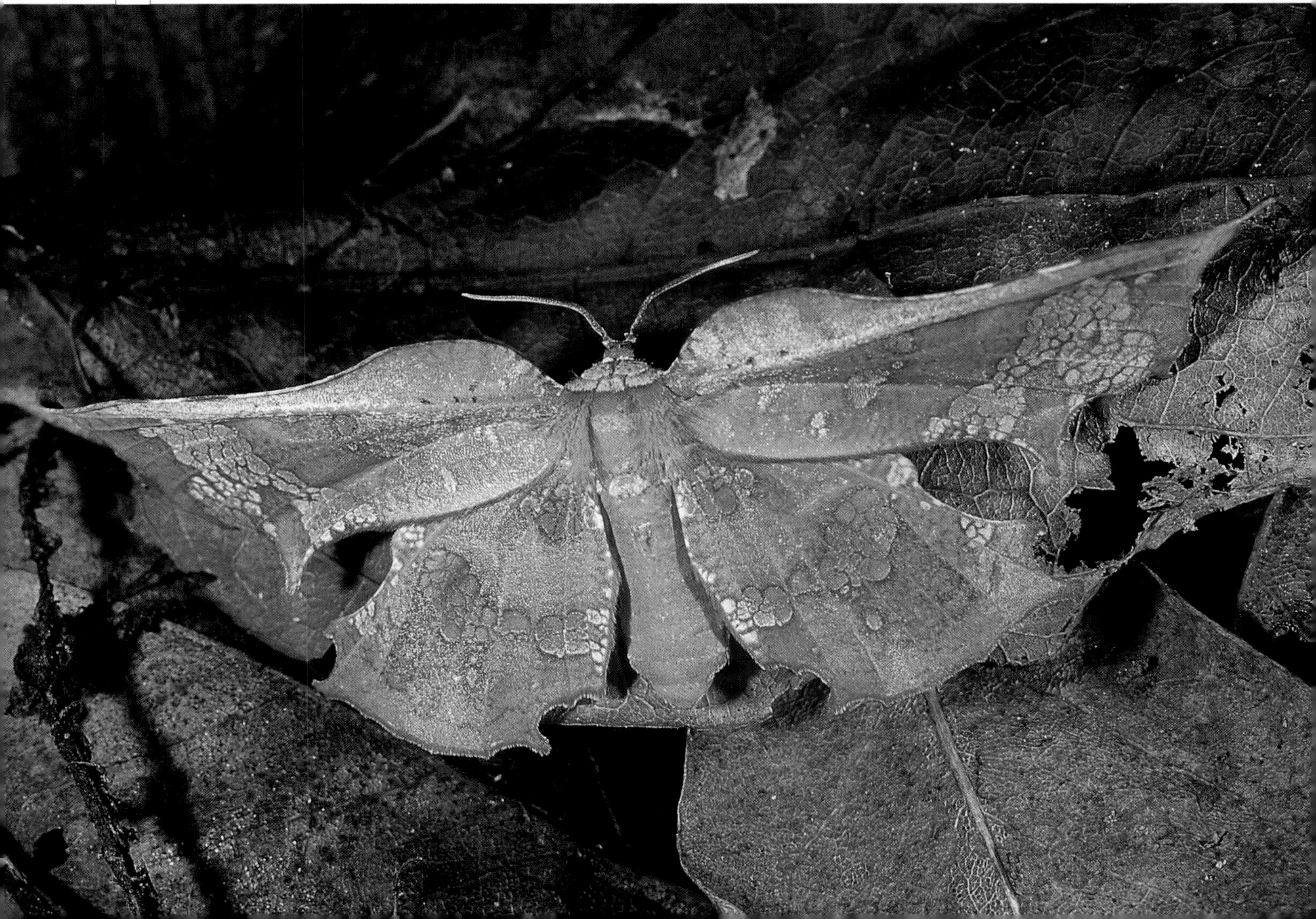

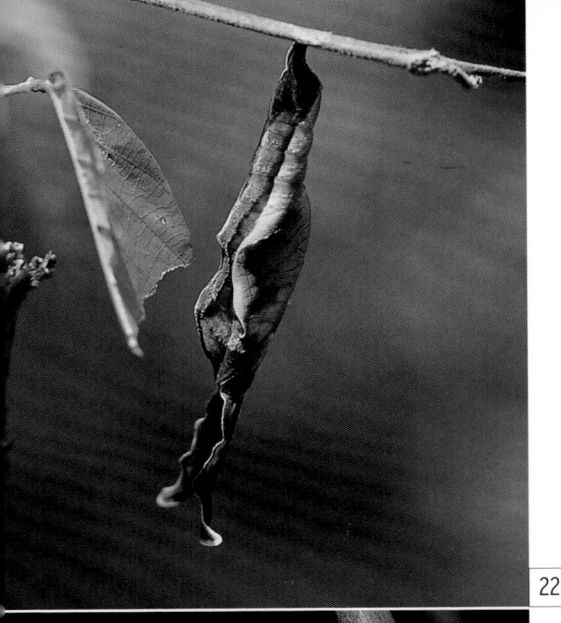

as moths and mantids, which resemble dead leaves, may not necessarily live on the ground, but may hang among green leafy branches, looking like dead leaves that have fallen and are temporarily suspended in the tree.

CHRYSALIDS

The similarity between insects and leaves attains near-perfection among the chrysalids of butterflies. While chrysalids of moths are usually hidden in the earth or enveloped in cocoons, those of butterflies are unprotected, suspended below twigs or leaves where they may spend many months at the mercy of parasitic wasps, ants and other predators. The majority fail to mature.

The only protection available to most chrysalids is camouflage and, because the chrysalid can not move about, this must be effective. Indeed, their resemblance to dead leaves or other vegetation is staggering. This is born out by the fact that I have only a limited number of photos showing chrysalids. Under natural conditions, most are impossible to find. With luck, one can search in the vicinity of the caterpillar's food plants, if these are known. The alternative is to collect the caterpillars, which are generally easier to find, and rear them in captivity. This was the case with the chrysalids shown in Photos 22, 23 and 24.

While chrysalids are usually highly camouflaged, there do exist a fair number of brightly colored caterpillars and chrysalids. These chrysalids have no need for camouflage because they possess other means of protection, often in the form of noxious body fluids.

22

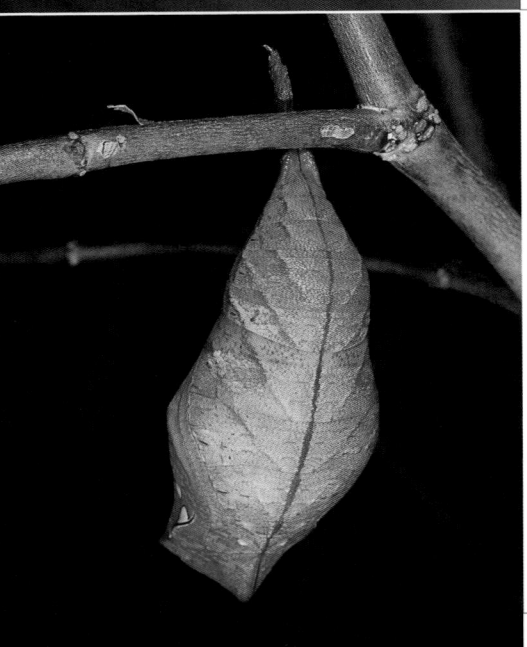

23

Photos 22, 23, 24 Chrysalids generally are very well camouflaged and because they frequently resemble dead leaves they are excellent examples of protective resemblance.

Photo 22 shows the chrysalis of a tropical American butterfly *Hamadryas arinome* (Nymphalidae), whose shape is almost identical to a shriveled leaf. Cacao, French Guyana; length 1 in/2.5 cm.

Photo 23 shows the chrysalis of a large (6 in/15 cm) butterfly, *Caligo atreus* (Brassolidae), photographed in Costa Rica. Its resemblance to a leaf is enhanced by the pattern of brown lines similar to a leaf's rib and veins. Length 2 in/5 cm.

Photo 24 shows the chrysalis of a common African butterfly, *Papilio demodocus* (Papilionidae), which resembles the spiny vegetation of citrus trees on which the caterpillar lives. Mandraka, Madagascar; length 1 in/2.5 cm.

Photo 25 (right) Spiders offer some of the best examples of camouflage. Like the insects, they are not always easy to find. Those who inhabit webs are easily seen and thus susceptible to attack. They are obliged to adopt many ruses. Many of these web-builders venture onto their webs only to snatch unfortunate prey, following which they retreat to the adjacent vegetation.

This photo shows an araneid spider hidden within a crack in the bark of a living tree. Camouflage is effective partly because of its color pattern; the brown and green abdomen (upper half of the spider) matches well with the adjacent blue-green lichens. Puerto Ayacucho, central Venezuela; length 1¼ in/3 cm.

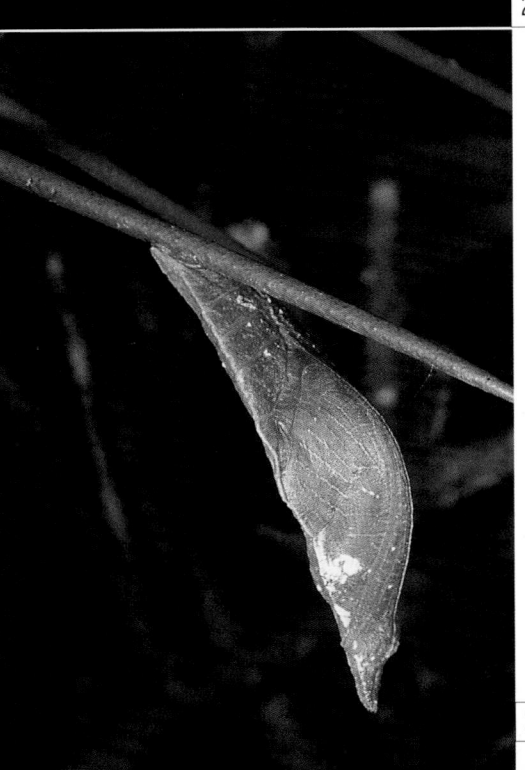

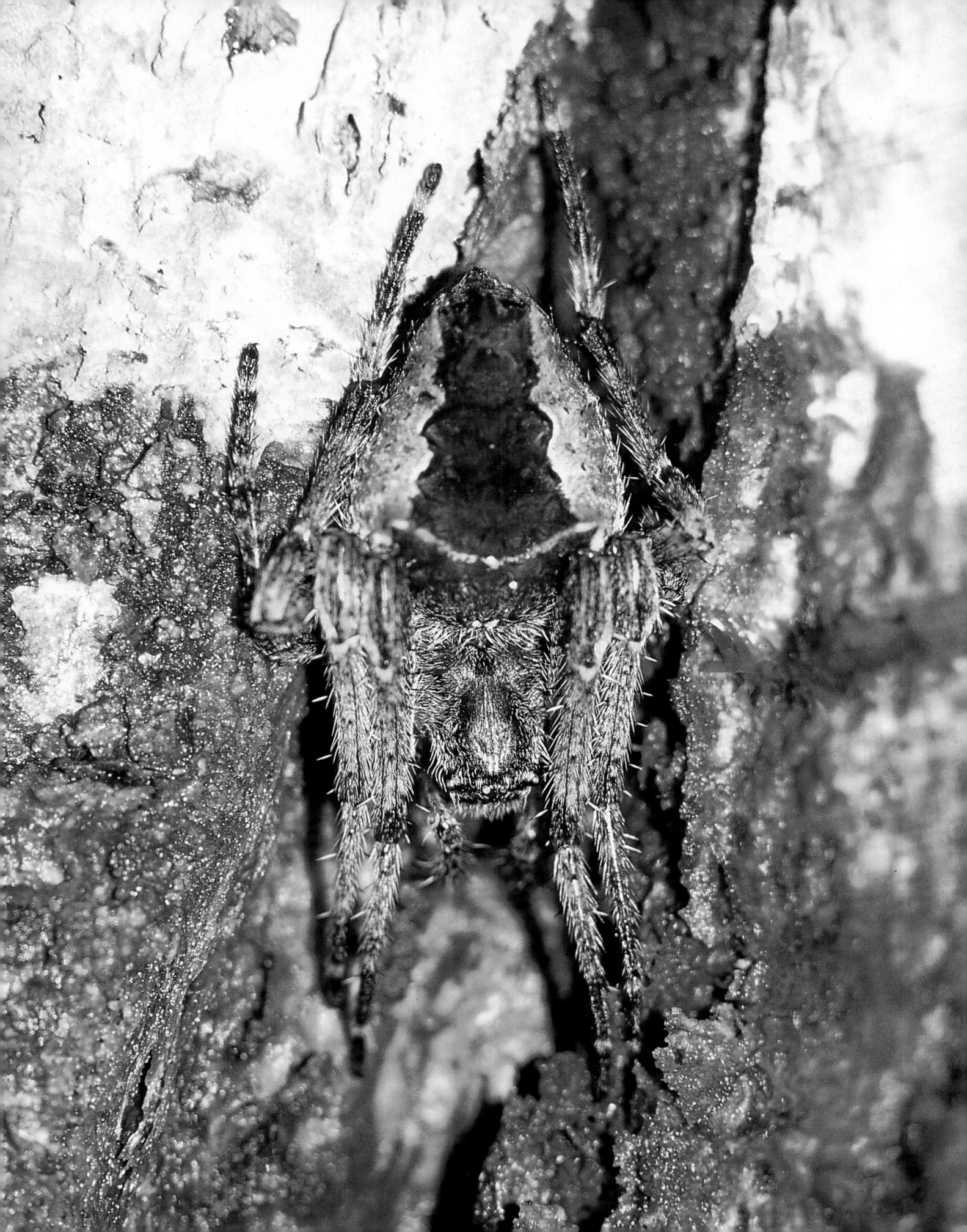

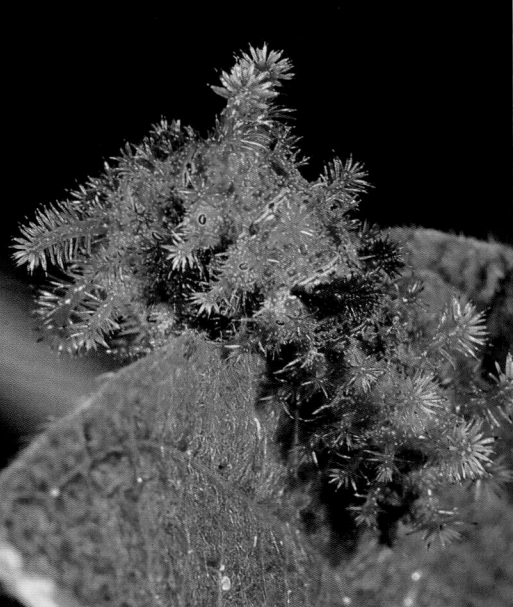

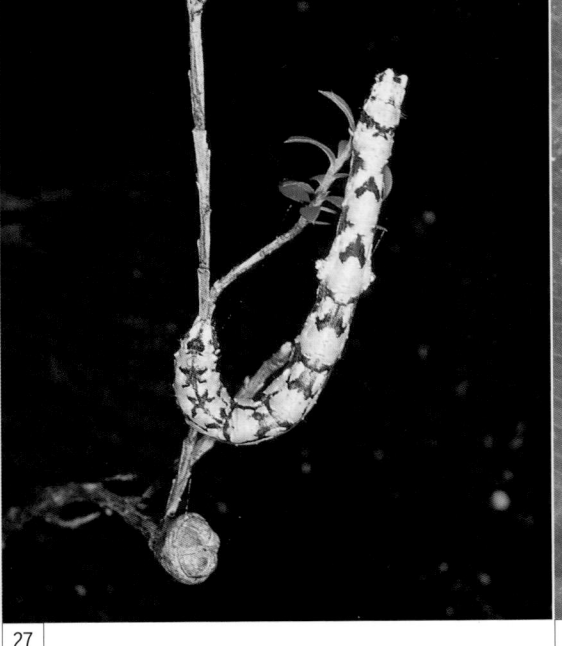

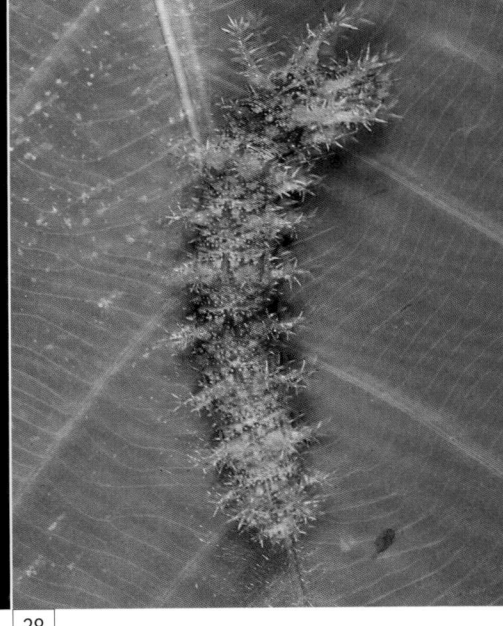

26

27

28

Photos 26, 28 Caterpillars often blend with the plants on which they live. In Photo 26, a caterpillar photographed in the forests of French Guyana resembles a piece of fallen moss (length ¾ in/2 cm). An almost identical caterpillar (Photo 28) was observed in the small forest reserve of Bukit Timah on the island of Singapore. Although they look like finely branched moss, these decorations are poisonous spines, which provide a second line of defense.

Photos 27, 29 Another caterpillar whose color and body texture are very similar to the lichens among which it lives. Probably the caterpillar of a geometrid moth. Rotorua, New Zealand; length 1¼ in/3 cm.

CATERPILLARS

Caterpillars with very similar forms of camouflage occur on widely separated continents; they may resemble lichens in New Zealand and in Europe, or moss in South America or Asia.

MANTIDS

Camouflage involves loss of identity either when the insect blends with a substrate with the same color pattern or when the insect resembles a natural object such as a leaf or a twig. In the latter case, the color of the insect does not necessarily blend with the colors of its immediate surroundings. On the contrary, it may be clearly visible (Photo 30).

29

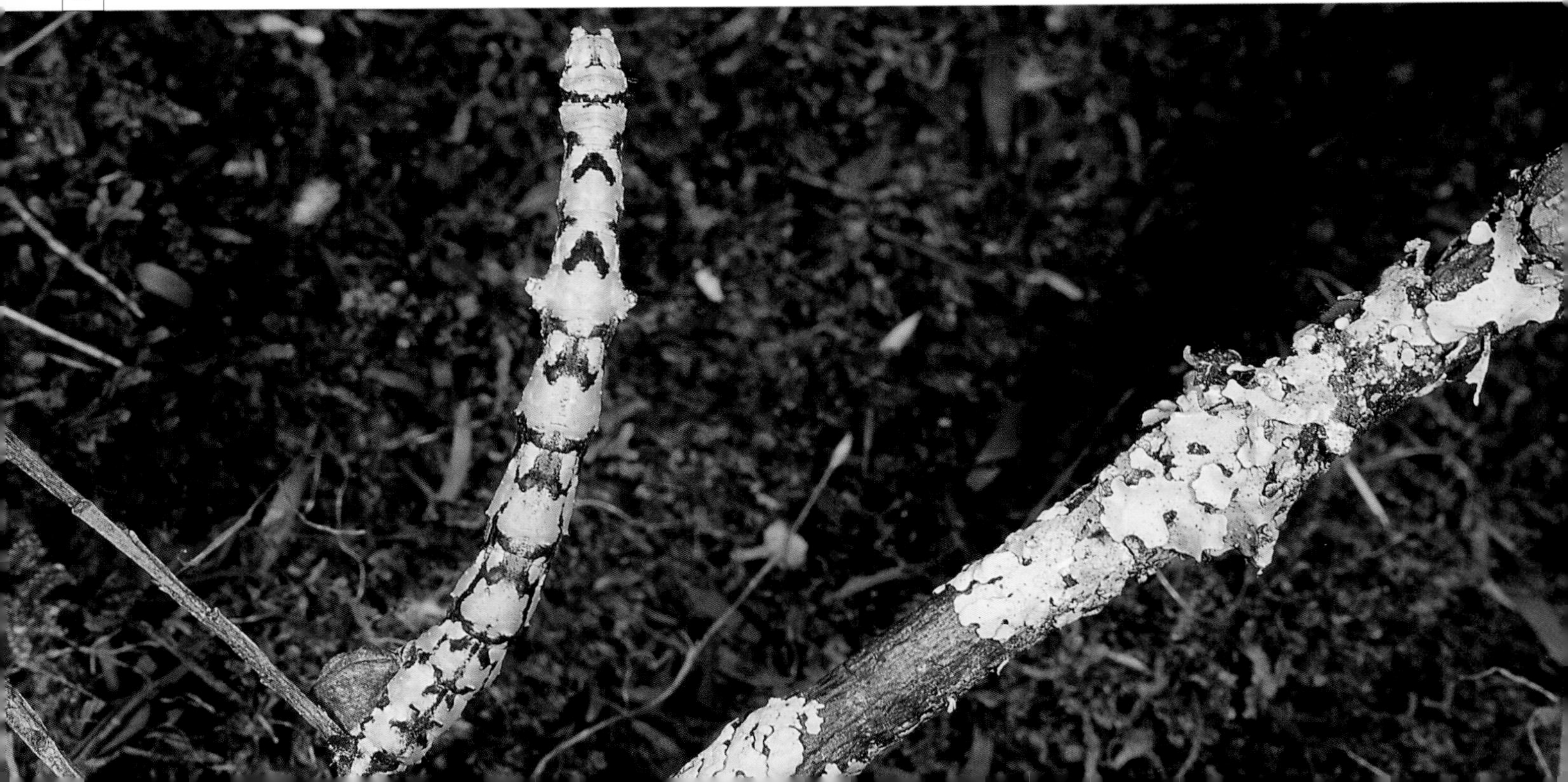

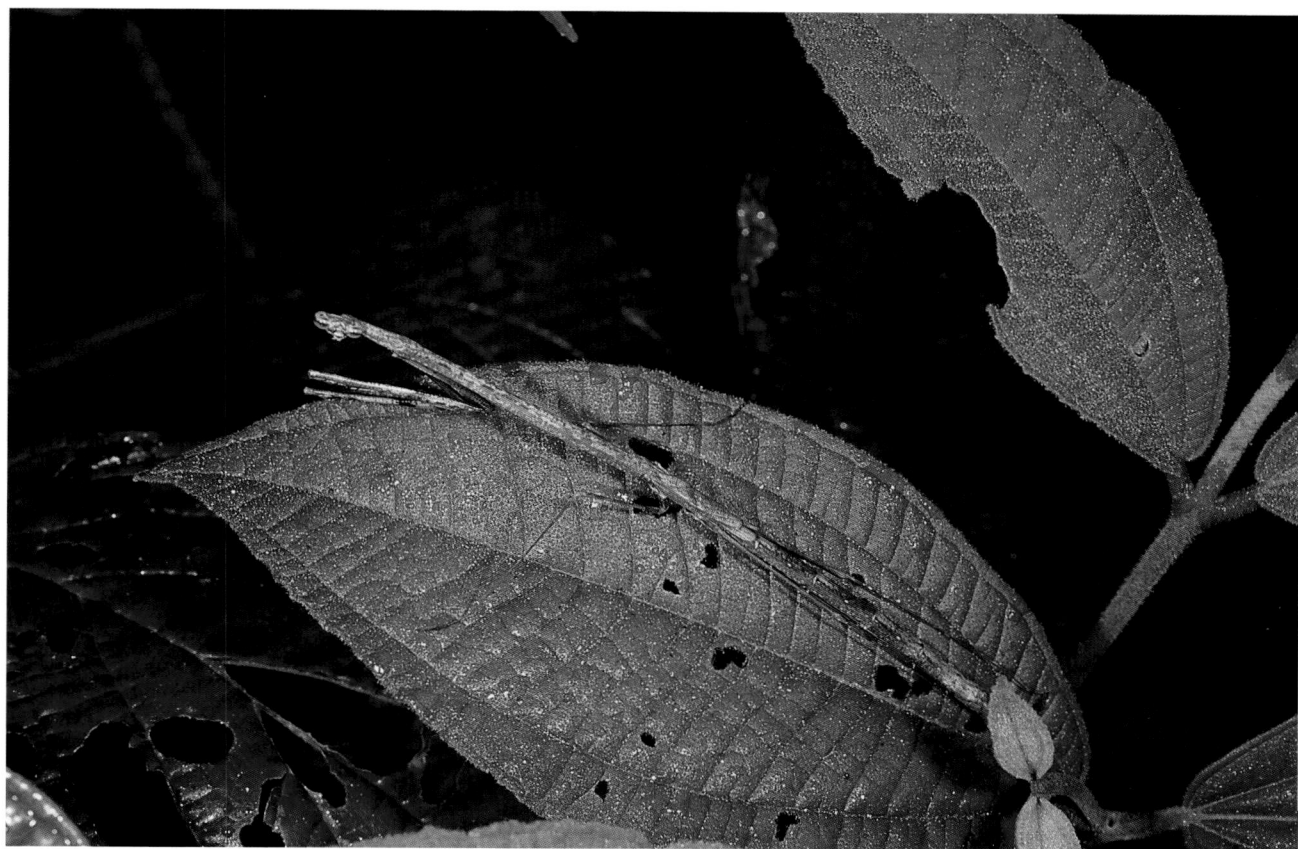

The insect escapes only because it is mistaken for an object other than an insect. The efficiency of this type of ruse is difficult to estimate and probably varies according to the insect concerned.

The protective resemblance shown by the curious mantid above should not be confused with the notion of *mimicry*; the mantid is not mimicking a fallen twig. The term mimicry expresses a sophisticated relationship in which the mime actively imitates both the form and the *behavior* of the model. Because the model is usually another insect or an animal, mimicry is more dynamic than camouflage, which involves the relationships between insects and vegetation.

The forest floor is covered by a relatively thin (4 in/10 cm) layer of detritus, dead leaves and twigs in varying states of decay that have dropped from the trees above. Many insects, including hordes of ants, inhabit the forest floor. While the ants are in constant movement and do not require camouflage, the grasshoppers, mantids and certain moths are motionless. Because they are all brown, they are extremely difficult to find against the brown forest litter, and successful photography is a hands and knees job, requiring much patience.

Photo 30 An unusual mantid lying quietly on a forest leaf in the Peruvian Amazon. Its color, long thin body and its flat disposition give the impression of a fallen twig, another example of protective resemblance. Tambopata Reserve; length 4 in/10 cm.

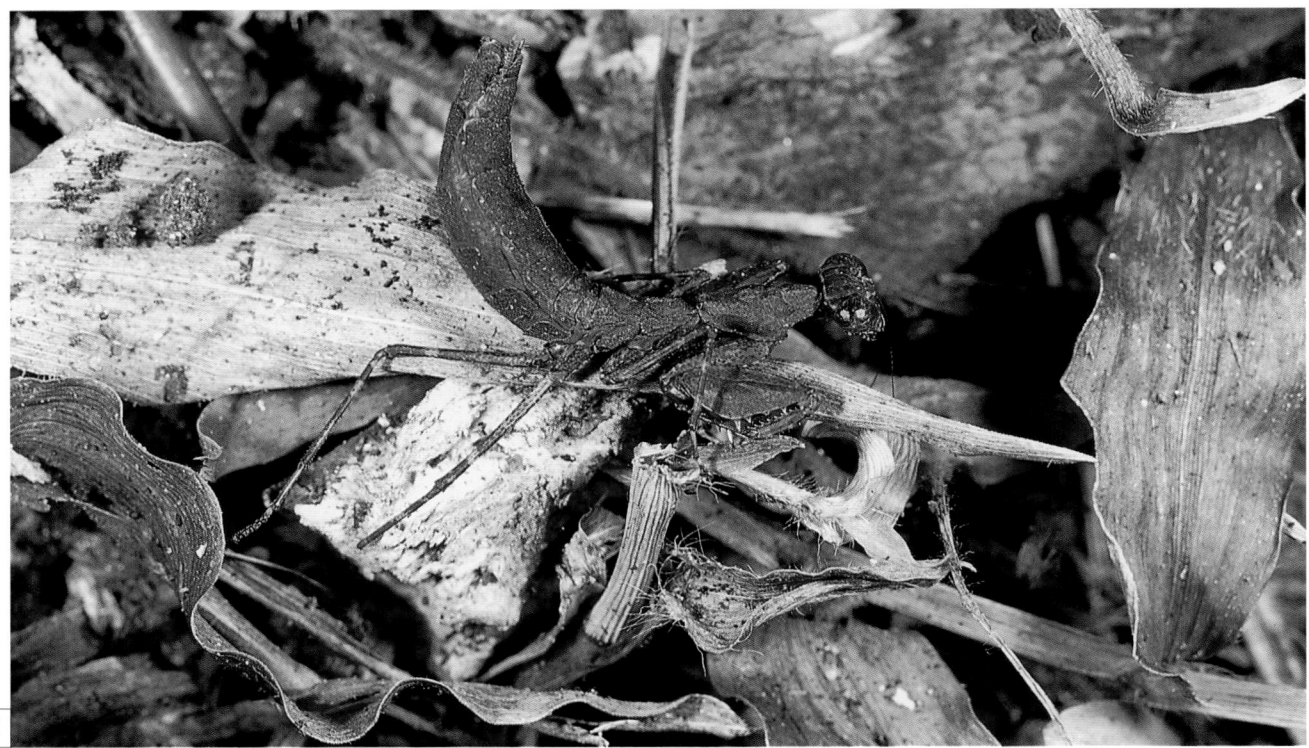

31

Photo 31 A wingless mantid hidden in dry litter on the forest floor. The mantid remained motionless and thus was very well camouflaged here among the brown detritus on the forest floor, where it lives and hunts ground-dwelling insects. Shimba Hills, coastal Kenya; length ¾ in/2 cm.

EVOLUTIONARY CONVERGENCE

Photos 31, 32 and 33 show insects that inhabit the forest floor and exhibit a certain homogeneity: all are brown. The reasons for this are fairly evident for, as already noted, the habitat is dominated by this color. But perhaps the most remarkable aspect of these photos is that each represents a quite different type of insect. Mantids and grasshoppers from these same families that inhabit living vegetation in these forests are often green. Color alone does not necessarily identify the true affinity of the insect. Color convergence, brown on the forest floor, results from natural selection, since the brown insects are best suited to this particular habitat, and species with other colors have been eliminated by predators. This process, where unrelated insects grow to resemble each other, is termed *evolutionary convergence*.

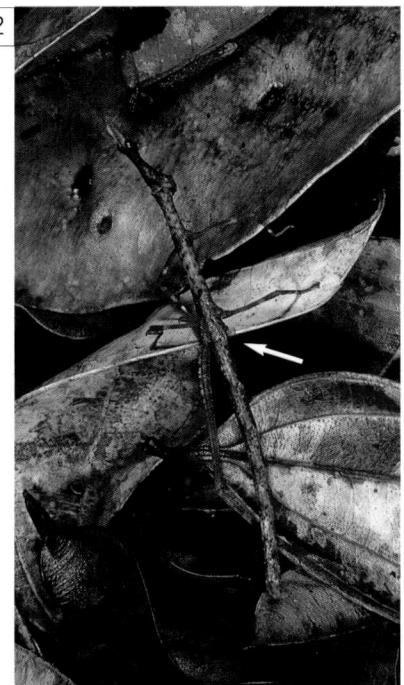

32

Photo 32 This unusual *Proscopis* (Proscopidae) also resembles a rotting twig lying among dry leaves. Although found on the forest floor, it probably spends most of its time on green vegetation, upon which it feeds. Length 3½ in/9 cm.

Photo 34 (opposite) What appears to be a small dry leaf is in fact a moth, whose head is indicated by the arrow. It flew away when touched. Saül, French Guyana; length ¾ in/2 cm.

Photo 35 (opposite) A false flower: this rare white orchid mantid was sitting motionless on a broad green leaf, where it closely resembled a fallen flower. Gopeng, central Malaysia; length ¾ in/2 cm. Both insects are excellent examples of protective resemblance.

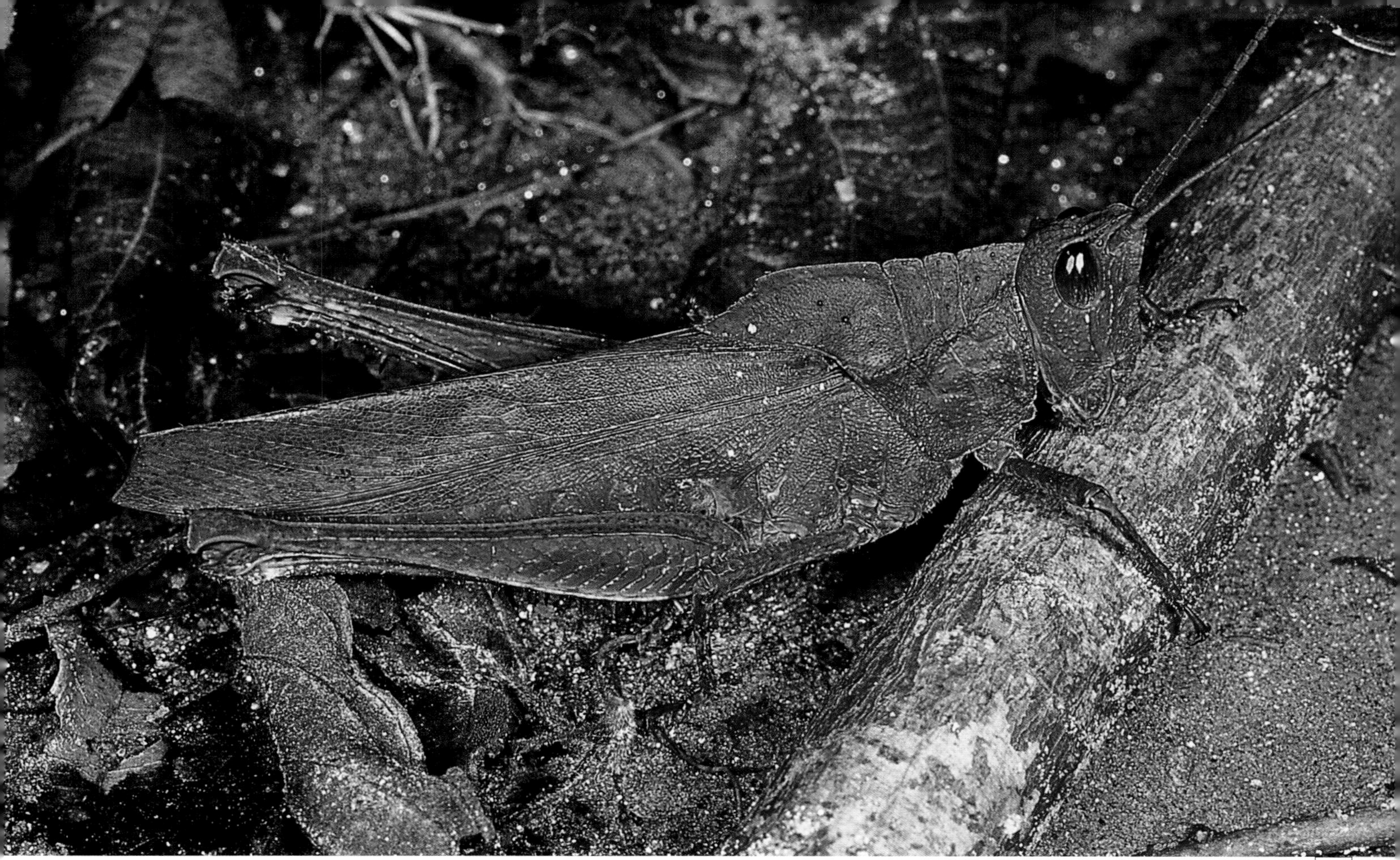

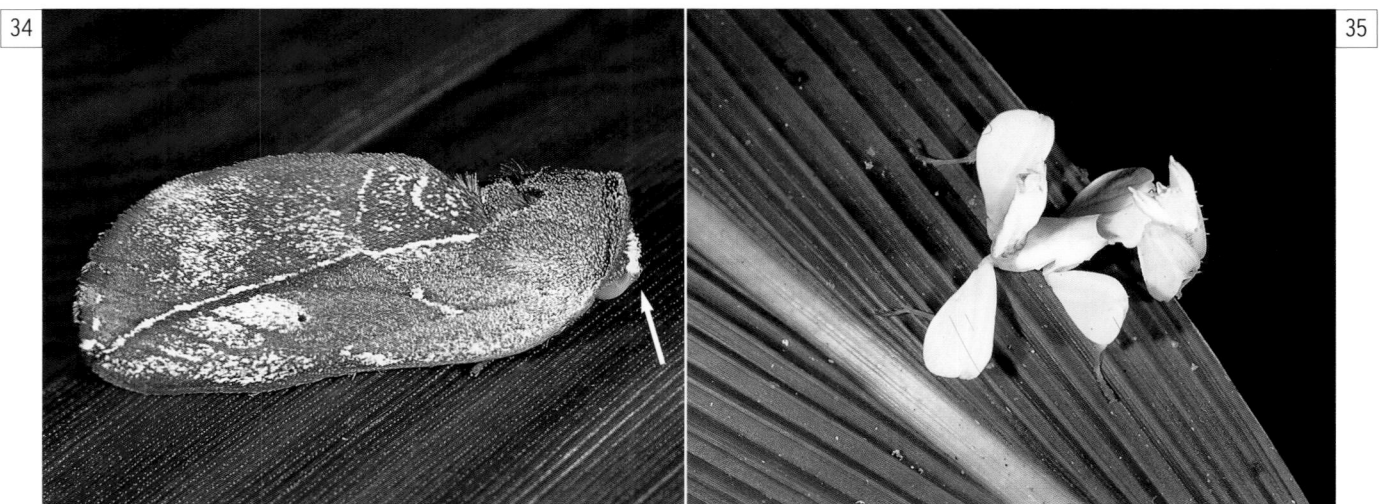

PROTECTIVE RESEMBLANCE

Protective resemblance may attain surprising forms, as shown in Photos 34, 35, 36 and 37. Although quite different, each insect closely resembles a specific fragment of vegetation. It is interesting to note in each case that the "vegetation," although dead, is not located on the forest floor but is suspended on green leaves, where a dead leaf or a flower might fall naturally.

Photo 33 This brown grasshopper (Acrididae) is easily confused with the brown leaves littering the forest floor. Henri Pittier Reserve, Venezuela; length 2 in/5 cm.

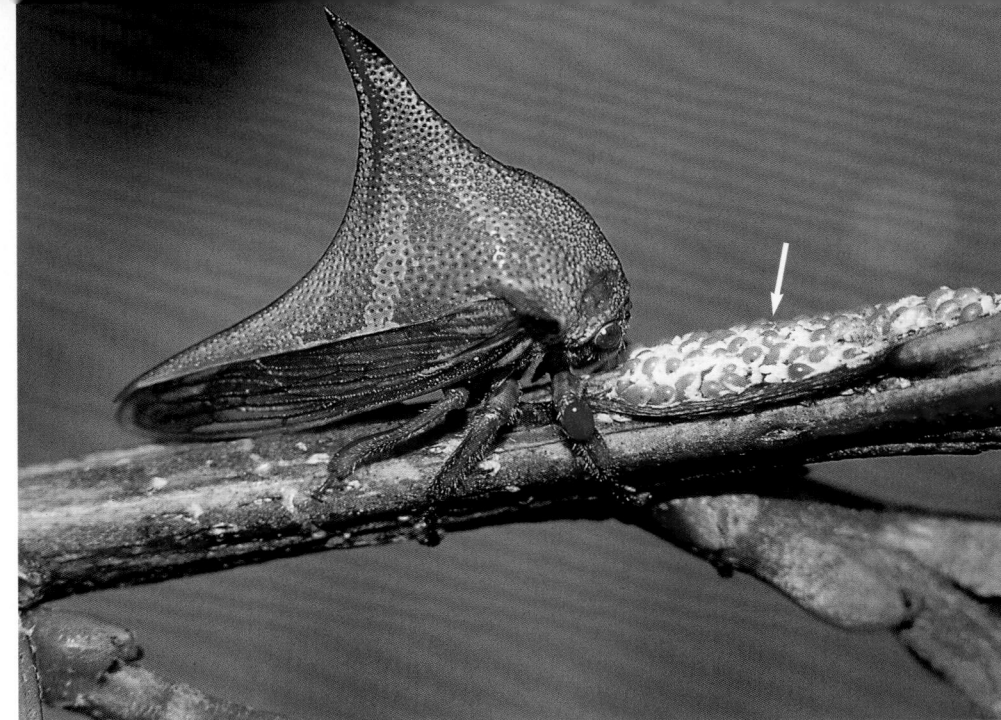

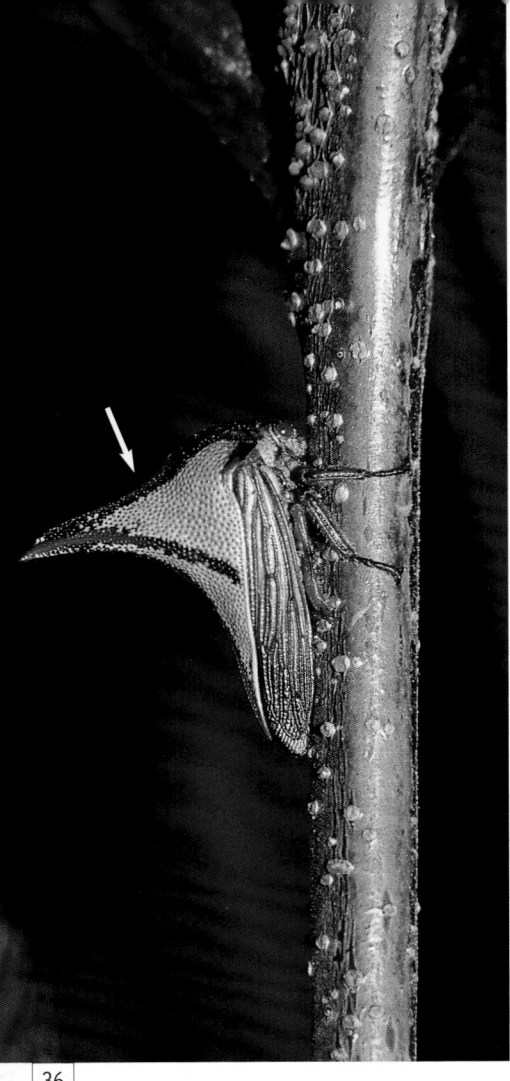

Photos 36, 37 Tree-hoppers, minute cicada-like insects, assume many strange forms. This little creature, *Umbonia* (Membracidae), indicated by the white arrow, closely resembles a thorn. Photo 37 shows a slightly different species of the Membracidae family guarding a batch of eggs (arrow). It is burdened by a small red parasite attached to its front leg. Secondary forest, central Guatemala; ³⁄₈ in/1 cm.

Photo 38 (opposite page) This bunch of spiny fruit is actually a group of caterpillars sitting quietly on a roadside shrub near Roura, French Guyana. Length of each caterpillar: 2 in/5 cm.

The photo of the white orchid mantis also illustrates how protective resemblance may serve a double purpose. Although it may escape its predators by resembling a flower, this ruse may also be designed for aggression. This carnivorous mantid may attract unsuspecting prey, who would be attracted by a white orchid flower.

Tree-hoppers or membracids are strange little creatures closely related to cicadas. They usually carry an unusual protuberance or pronotum, which may take the form of branched horns or spines, as seen in Photos 36 and 37. While the utility of these decorations is not yet understood (by humans!), some may possibly serve as camouflage. This is the case with *Umbonia*, which closely resembles a thorn. However, this similarity may be coincidental, for the owner does not always sit on thorny bushes. The very unusual shape of this small (³⁄₈ in/1 cm) insect may render it difficult to swallow and thus dissuade predators. Common throughout tropical America, where it lives on small shrubs from which it sucks the juice, it is capable of jumping and flying with considerable efficiency, in spite of the cumbersome horn.

BUGS OR BIRD-DROPPINGS?

Caterpillars, especially those eaten by birds, are often well camouflaged. While most blend with the vegetation, either in the form of leaves or branches, others seem to resemble fruit (Photo 38). But perhaps the most bizarre form is found in caterpillars that become swallowtail (Papilionidae) butterflies. These are sometimes smooth, shiny, slug-like creatures (Photos 39, 42) sporting a splotchy-white and brown pattern. The overall

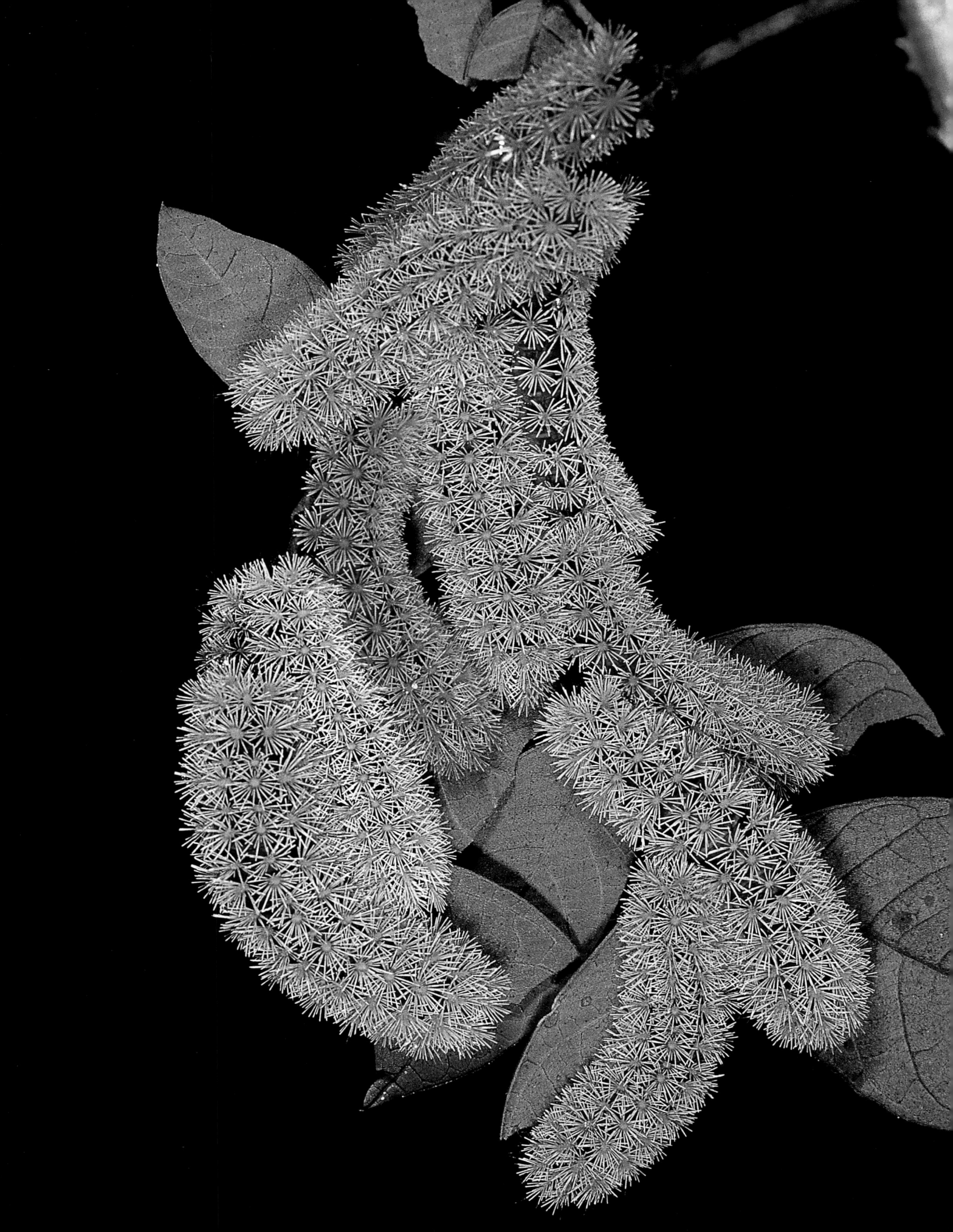

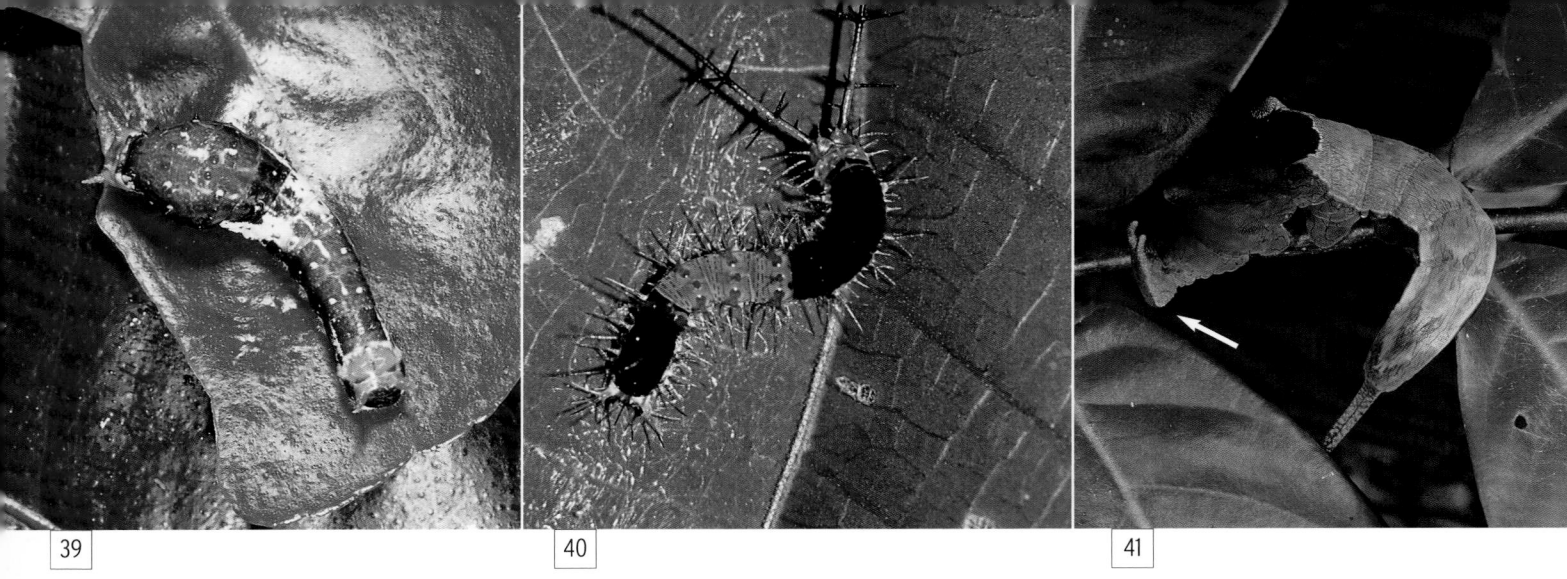

Photos 39, 42 Certain caterpillars tend to resemble bird droppings. These two caterpillars both belong to the same family of papilionid (swallowtail) butterflies; Photo 39 was photographed near Cairns, in Queensland, Australia; the other (42), on the edge of an Amazon forest near Atalaya, Peru. Respective lengths ¾ in/2 cm (39) and 2 in/5 cm (42).

Photo 40 The green-colored middle segment, which separates the two black extremities of this caterpillar, forms a color pattern that disrupts the general shape of the insect. This disruptive coloration makes it more difficult for predators to identify a potential prey. Saül, French Guyana; length ¾ in/2 cm.

Photo 41 The overall shape of this *Prepona* (Nymphalidae) caterpillar, whose horned head is on the left (arrow), is disrupted by its marked color contrasts. Cacao, French Guyana; length 2½ in/6 cm.

Photo 43 (opposite) The small weevil (Curculionidae), firmly clasping the leaf of a cecropia tree sports a highly contrasting color pattern that, when seen from a distance, tends to dissimulate the overall shape of the insect. Route de Belizon, French Guyana; length ½ in/12 mm.

appearance is rather repulsive and this may discourage predators. It has been suggested that these caterpillars imitate bird droppings and, indeed, certain examples are very convincing.

Furthermore, these caterpillars are nearly always found on the upper surfaces of leaves, where they are immediately evident. In spite of their edible qualities, they make little attempt to hide, having confidence in their rather unusual camouflage. This form of disguise can also be found in some adult beetles and moths. As already noted, many insects have evolved very unusual shapes and behavior, presumably as a defence against their predators. However, in interpreting the meaning of these "bird droppings," leaves and other objects, we may be exerting our human imagination.

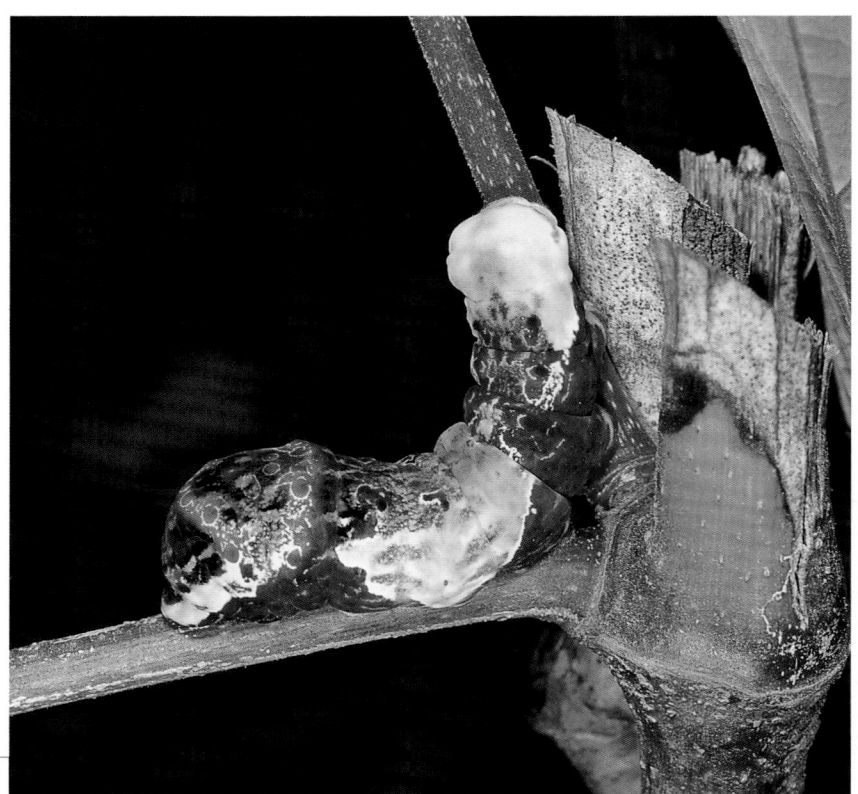

DISRUPTIVE COLORATION

Passive camouflage most frequently concerns either the blending of an insect with its immediate surroundings, or its close resemblance to a natural object. There is another form of camouflage in which the insect seems to combine these two basic traits, called *disruptive coloration*. The insect, although readily visible as a discrete object, nevertheless looses its identity via a color pattern that modifies its overall appearance. This pattern, generally a fairly simple one, consists of two fairly contrasting colors, often in the form of distinct patches or bands that traverse the body of the insect. Because these colors are fairly distinct, their oblique disposition tends to optically disrupt the overall shape of the insect, thus complicating its identity. In many cases, one of the colors is green (Photo 40). Because this green band tends to match the green vegetation, the insect appears as two or more distinct segments. In other cases, the color pattern may involve light grey or even white bands that match the under surfaces of the leaves on which the insect lives (Photo 43).

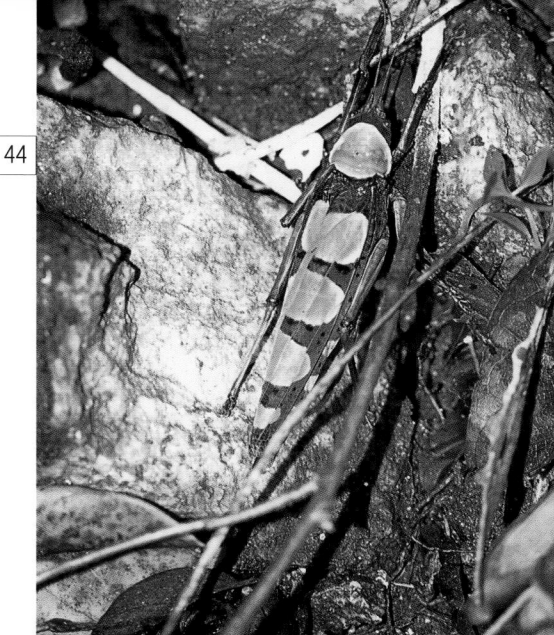

Photo 44 The discontinuous nature of its bright green colors tends to disrupt the shape of this katydid (Tettigoniidae), especially when it is sitting on green vegetation. Pai, central Thailand, length 2 3/4 in/7 cm.

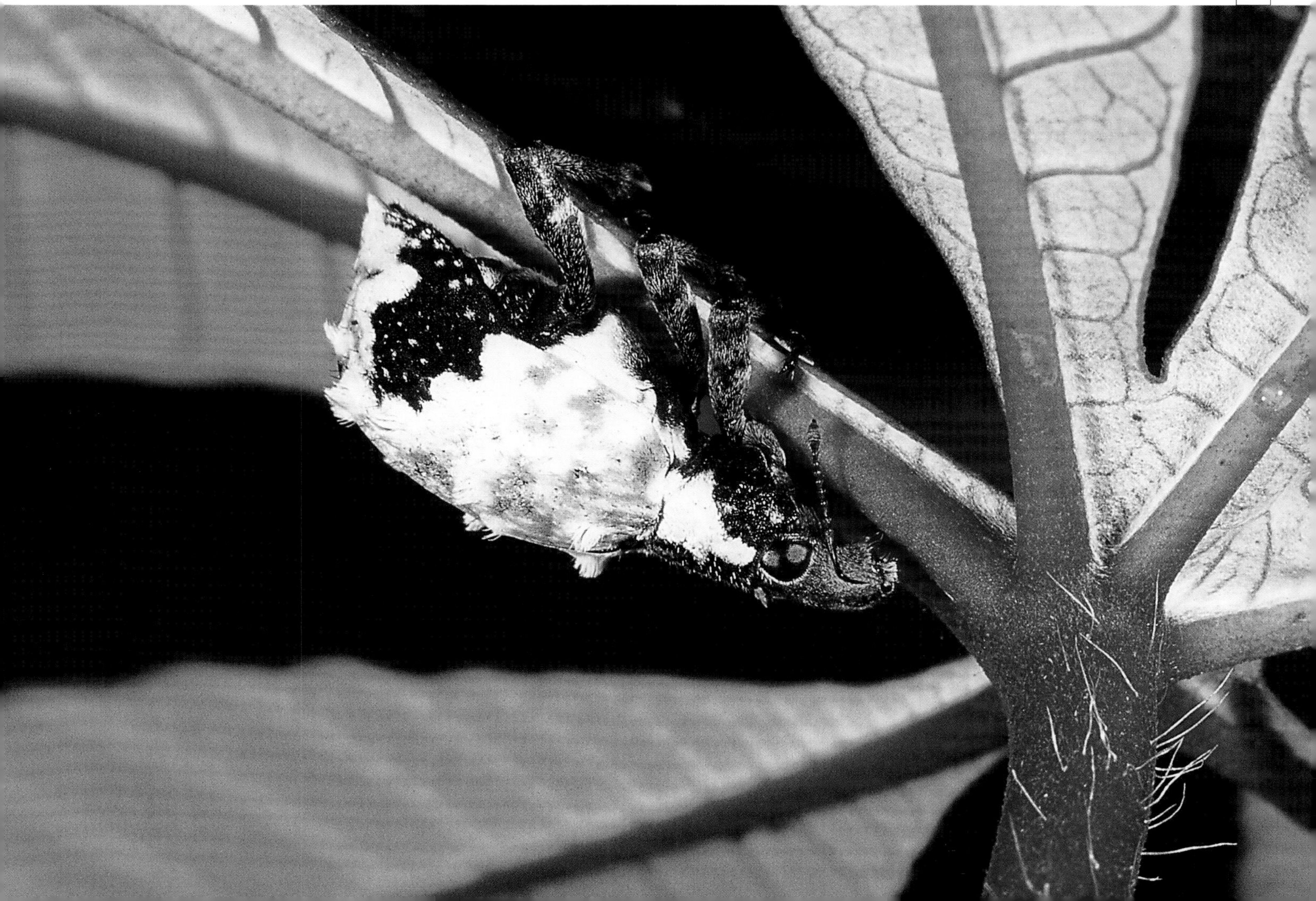

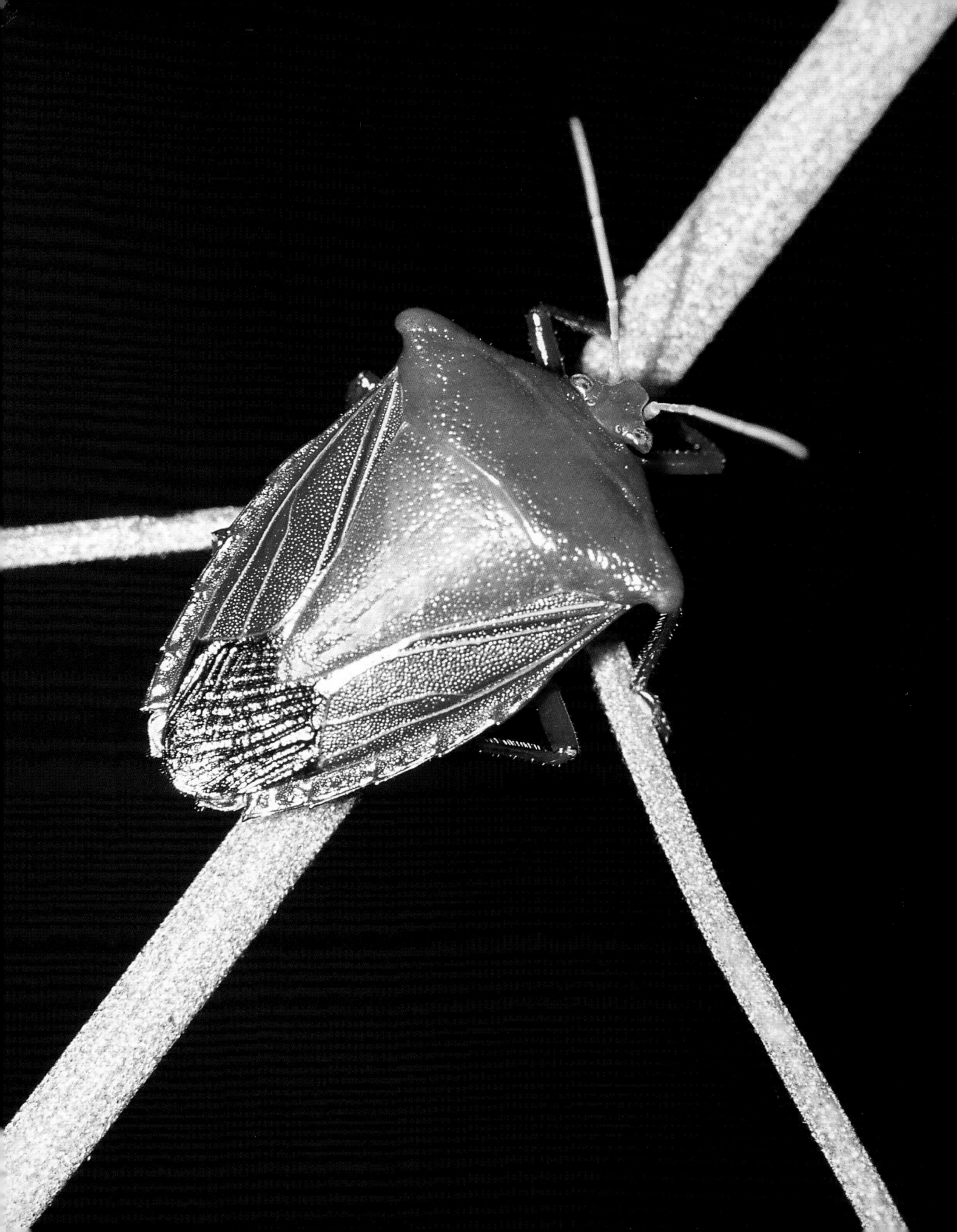

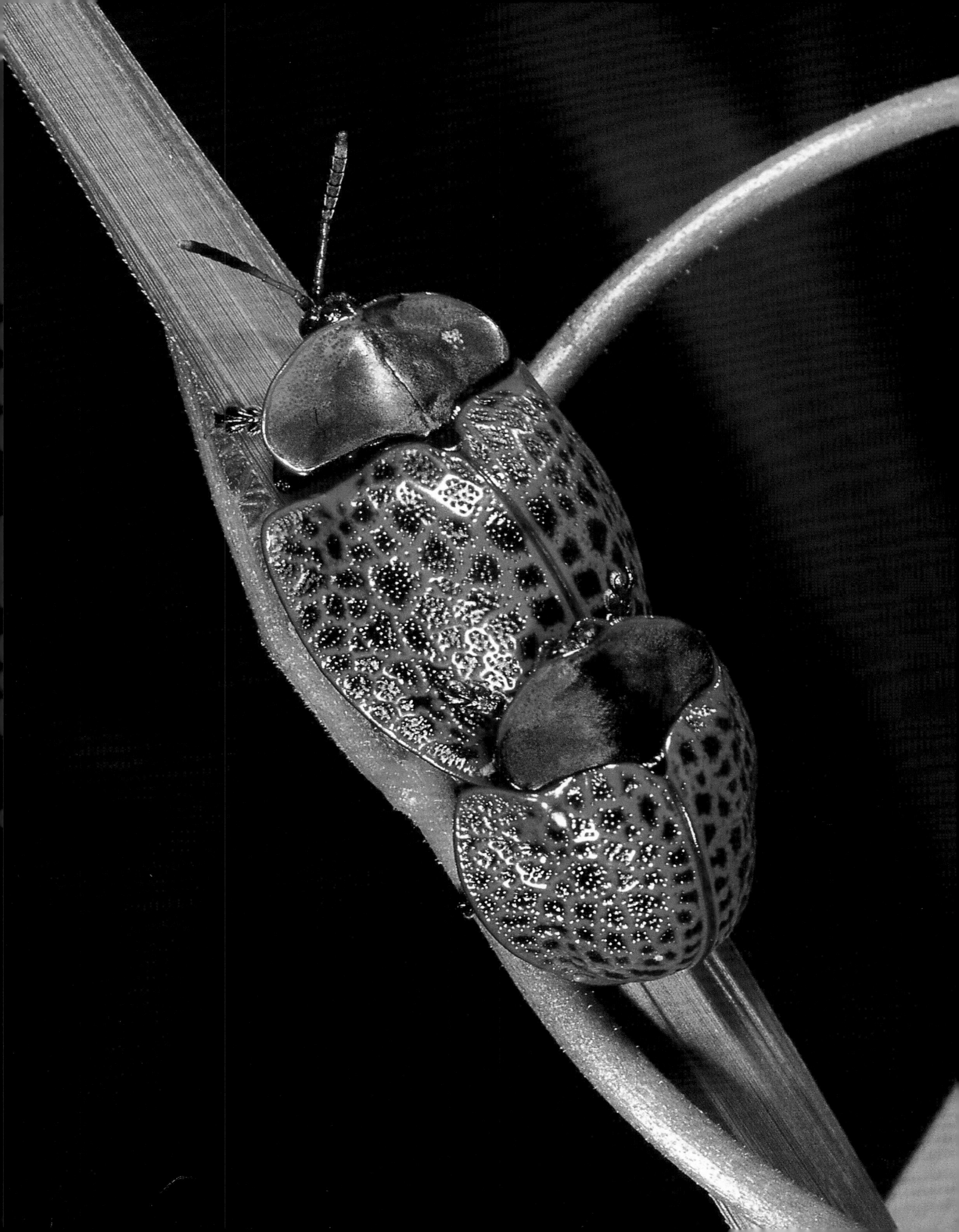

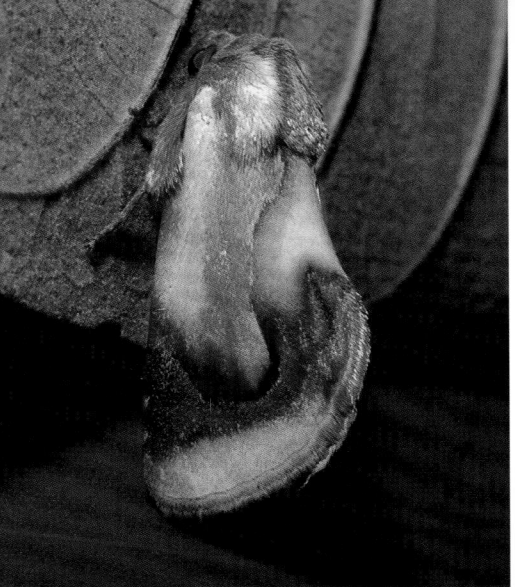

Because moths spend the daylight hours sitting quietly on vegetation, they require efficient camouflage. Although many resemble the vegetation, others do not, but lose their identity through a system of disruptive coloration (Photo 47).

PROTECTIVE TRANSPARENCY

Insects have a considerable repertoire of methods that enable them to pass undetected. Although not camouflage in the normal sense, protective transparency is yet another method of blending with the immediate surroundings. The transparent butterflies that flit through the dense forests of tropical America are excellent examples, for they are almost impossible to see when flying through dark shadows close to the forest floor.

When they settle to drink from damp river sands, certain insects with transparent wings are fairly visible, although sometimes they resemble wasps or bees to discourage attack. However, when they fly, often quite rapidly, they are very difficult to follow because their behavior closely resembles that of flies. This form of protection is not truely passive, but passes into the domain of active camouflage.

SUMMARY

Camouflage is the art of loosing one's identity. It takes many forms, most of which the insects have managed to exploit with considerable success. The simplest form of camouflage is crypsis, which involves the insect blending passively with its immediate surroundings. A somewhat more advanced strategy is protective resemblance, where the insect closely resembles the color and shape of natural objects, often leaves or sticks. However, this does not seem to require any special effort on behalf of the

Photo 47 This beautiful moth (Noctuidae) was photographed at midnight in the Ranomafana Forest in central Madagascar. It has an unusual color pattern that tends to modify the overall shape of the insect. Length 1¼ in/3 cm.

Photos 45, 46 (left and right, previous 2 pages) Non-camouflage! Not all insects seek to camouflage themselves, having other means of protection. For example, the chrysomelid beetles, (Photo 46), mating on a vine near the edge of the Orinoco River in Venezuela, are protected by toxic body fluids. And the pentatomid bug (Photo 45), clearly visible on the edge of a track in the Tikal Forest, Guatemala, similarly has no real need for camouflage. Its nauseating odors, when touched, render it unattractive. In these cases, when the insect is poisonous or otherwise unpalatable, predators are warned by its relatively bright, often red, aposematic coloration.

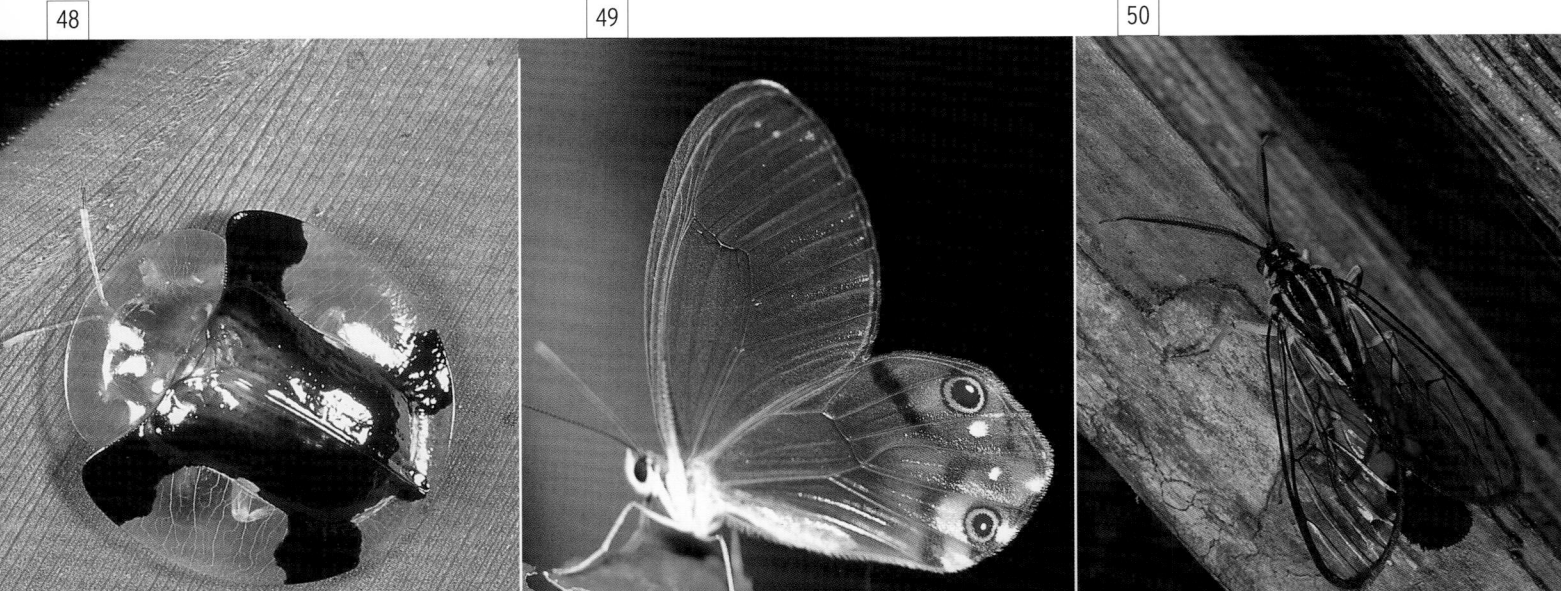

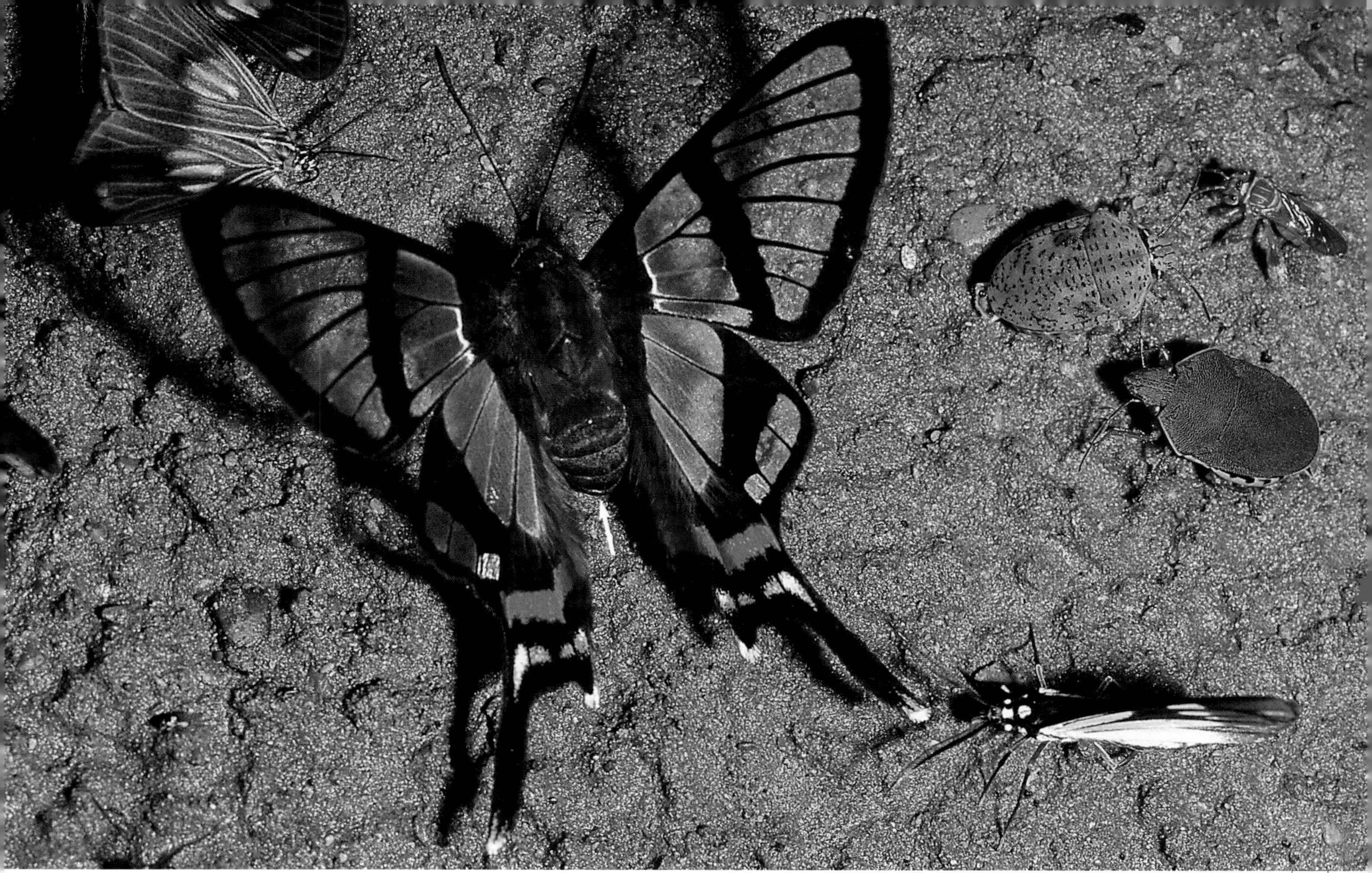

insects, and although their similarity to particular objects (including bird-droppings!) is fairly convincing, it must be admitted that these resemblances, at least in part, may be coincidental.

In the following chapter we will illustrate more sophisticated forms of active camouflage, where success results from a deliberate effort on behalf of the insect.

Photo 51 This small riodinid butterfly, *Chorinea*, drinking from damp river sands in the Peruvian Amazon, escapes notice partly because of the transparent nature of its wings. This individual has curved its abdomen (arrow) to urinate on dry sand. The urine dissolves salts in the sand, facilitating the access that its tube-like proboscis has to nutrients. Wingspan 1¼ in/3 cm.

Photo 48 The shape of an insect may appear to be modified when it is transparent, thus complicating its identity. This small chrysomelid beetle, with its partly transparent carapace, has an unusual shape that may perplex a predator. Lomie, Cameroon; length ¼ in/6 mm.

Photo 49 This curious butterfly, *Haetera* (Satyridae), which flies within the shadows of the forest floor, is very difficult to see mainly because of its transparent wings. Saül, French Guyana; wingspan 2½ in/6 cm.

Photos 50, 52 Although both insects are moths, their transparent wings tend to mask their identity. The moth in Photo 50 (Sesiidae) was photographed in Tambopata Reserve in the Peruvian Amazon, the one in Photo 52 in central Malaysia. Lengths about ¾ in/2 cm.

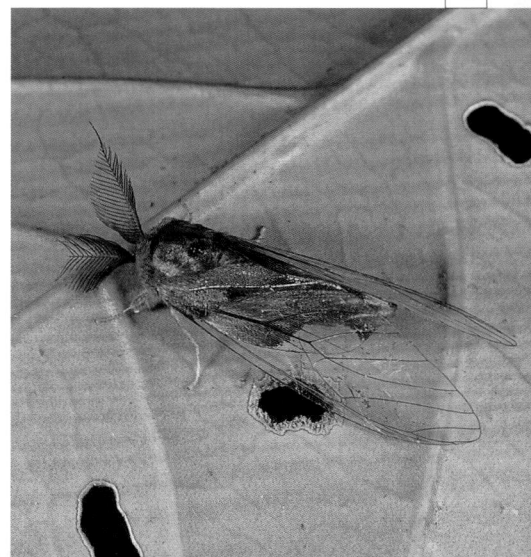
52

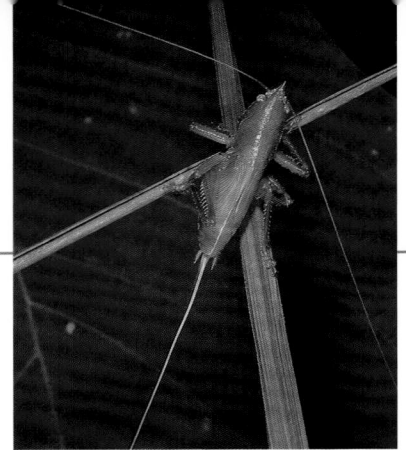

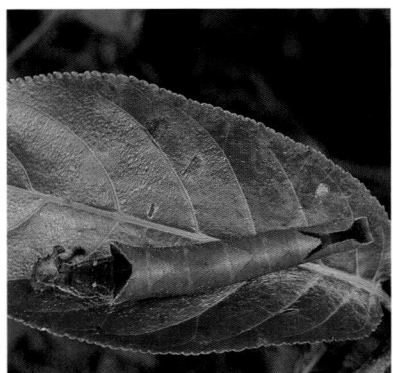

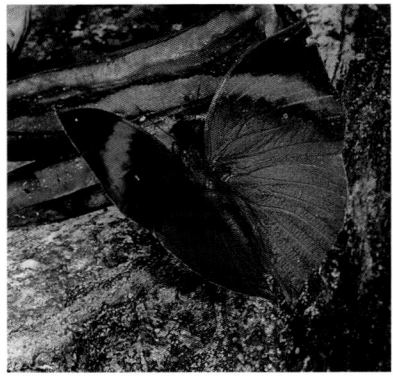

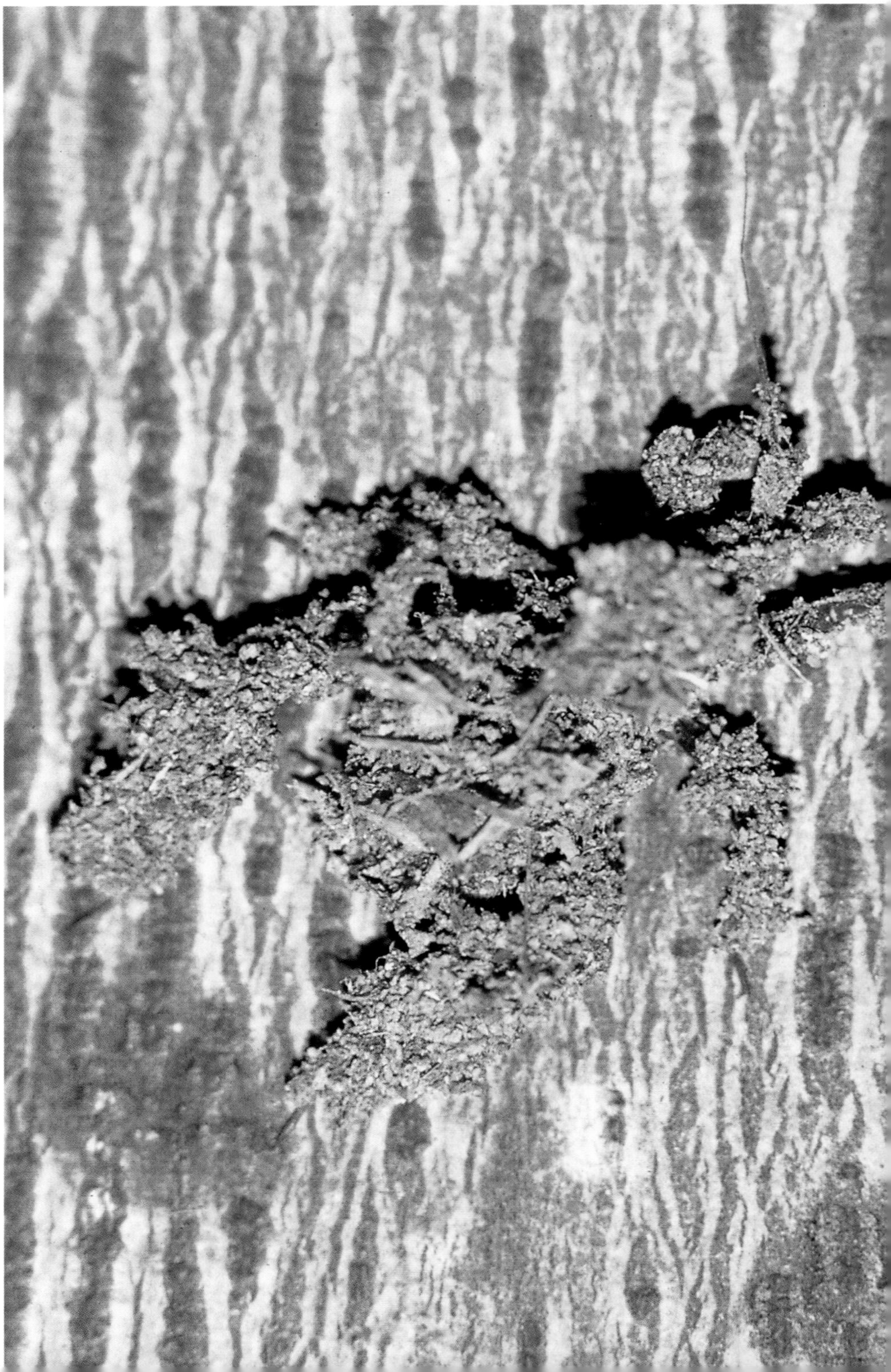

CHAPTER THREE

Active Camouflage

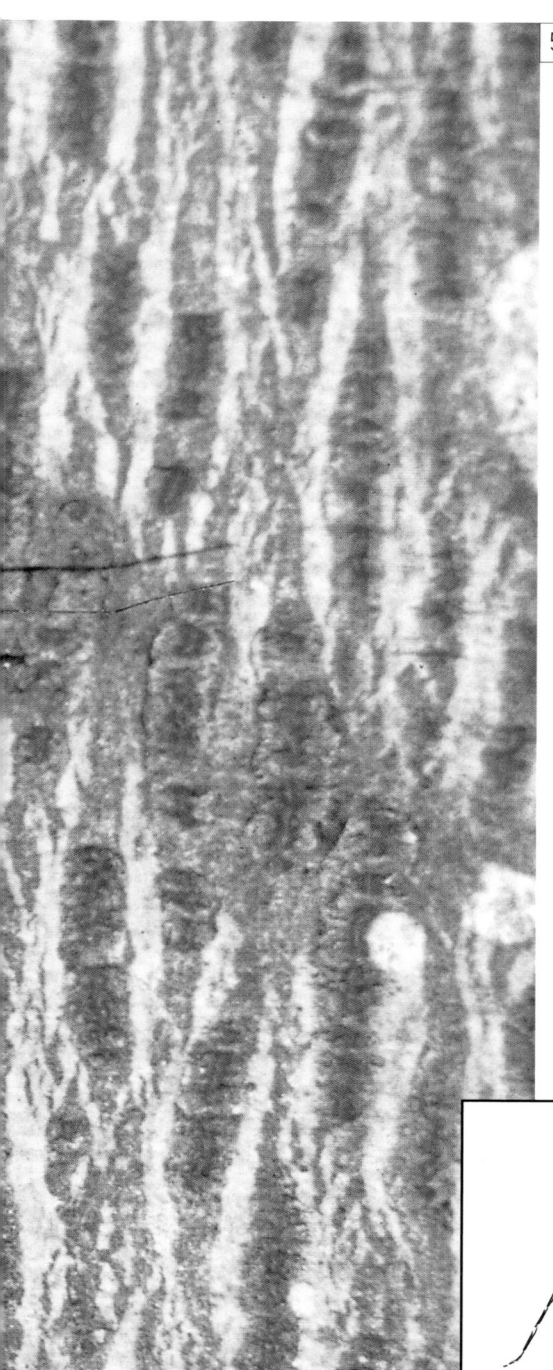

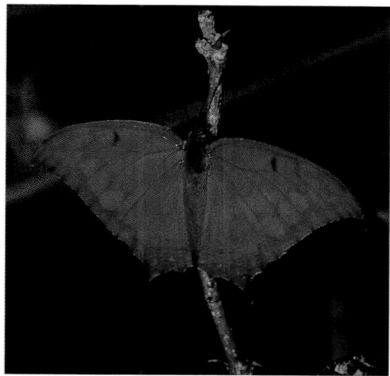

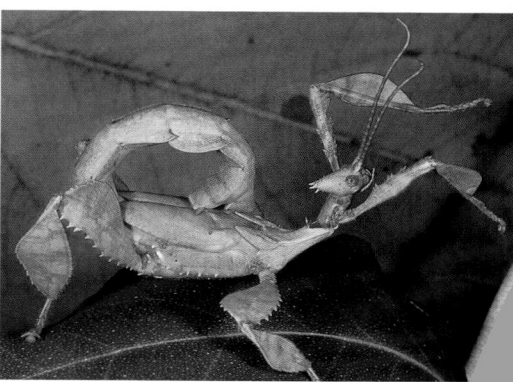

An insect may blend with the colors and shapes of its immediate surroundings, its loss of identity requiring no apparent effort. It thus gains a certain degree of protection from predators. In other cases camouflage may be perfected when the insect makes a special effort to improve its disguise. This active camouflage represents a more sophisticated form of protection, when the insect makes a clearly motivated gesture to better adapt to its surroundings.

The distinction between passive and active camouflage is rather arbitrary and possibly even subjective. It is not always possible to tell the difference. For example, when one observes a moth or a mantid camouflaged on a tree trunk one cannot be sure whether this loss of identity is

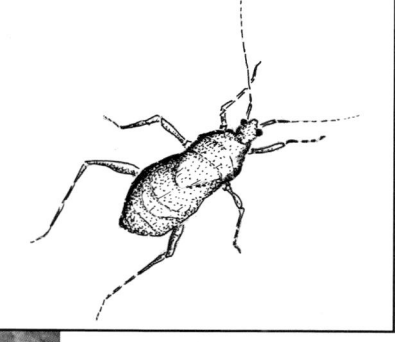

Photo 53 Almost impossible to recognize, the irregular object in the center of this photo is an insect. This reduviid bug covers itself with fine dust, which it glues to its body. Then the insect virtually disappears and can be detected only when it moves. Because it usually lives in very dusty places, often under the bark of dead trees, it is very well camouflaged. The sketch shows the insect without its dust cover. Blanquillo, Madre de Dios, Peruvian Amazon; length ¾ in/2 cm.

calculated or fortuitous. In this case we can only observe and, in the absence of direct evidence, describe it, simply, as "camouflage." If, on the contrary, we can prove by observation that the insect made a deliberate effort to camouflage itself, then we can interpret this as active camouflage and not merely coincidence.

As we shall see, there are a number of distinct ways in which insects adjust themselves to better merge with their surroundings. Probably the most frequent is that adopted by many katydids, close relatives of grasshoppers, which generally live on green vegetation. They are not easy to see and their presence may often be deduced only from specific "calls," which carry for considerable distances through the forest, especially at night. In tropical forests, the larger tettigoniid grasshoppers often frequent the higher vegetation and canopy, from which they may descend only when attracted by a strong lamp. Then they settle on nearby shrubs and, in most cases, actively orient themselves parallel to the hanging vegetation (Photo 54), assuming a fairly convincing camouflage. Other insects seem to go to unbelievable extremes in order to achieve effective camouflage. This is particularly true of many moths, which are generally fairly somber in color and therefore readily disappear among the dead vegetation. Not satisfied with what seems to be effective camouflage, these moths may adopt very unusual positions. Some even stand on their heads, hanging upside down to closely match a particular fragment of vegetation such as a dead leaf or stick.

One of the most sophisticated examples of active camouflage is that of certain reduviids or assassin bugs (see Photo 181). These creatures cover themselves with small fragments of plants and other fine debris, which they conscientiously stick to their bodies. While rendering them virtually invisible, this detritus does not seem to hamper their mobility.

A quite extraordinary use of active camouflage is achieved by certain weevils that live in the highlands of New Guinea. These beetles carry a garden on their backs made up of living vegetation, most notably moss. When immobile, they are completely invisible. However, it is not entirely clear whether these little ambulatory gardens are actually the work of the the weevil, or whether the plants grow by accident. This represents one of the most intriguing examples of camouflage.

Active camouflage is more frequent among certain insects, including particular families of moths, grasshoppers, phasmids and mantids. These same groups also adopt simpler forms of cryptic camouflage, as seen in the previous chapter. Whether it be passive or active, camouflage characterizes insects whose survival requires protection. As we have already noted, moths and grasshoppers often spend their daylight hours exposed

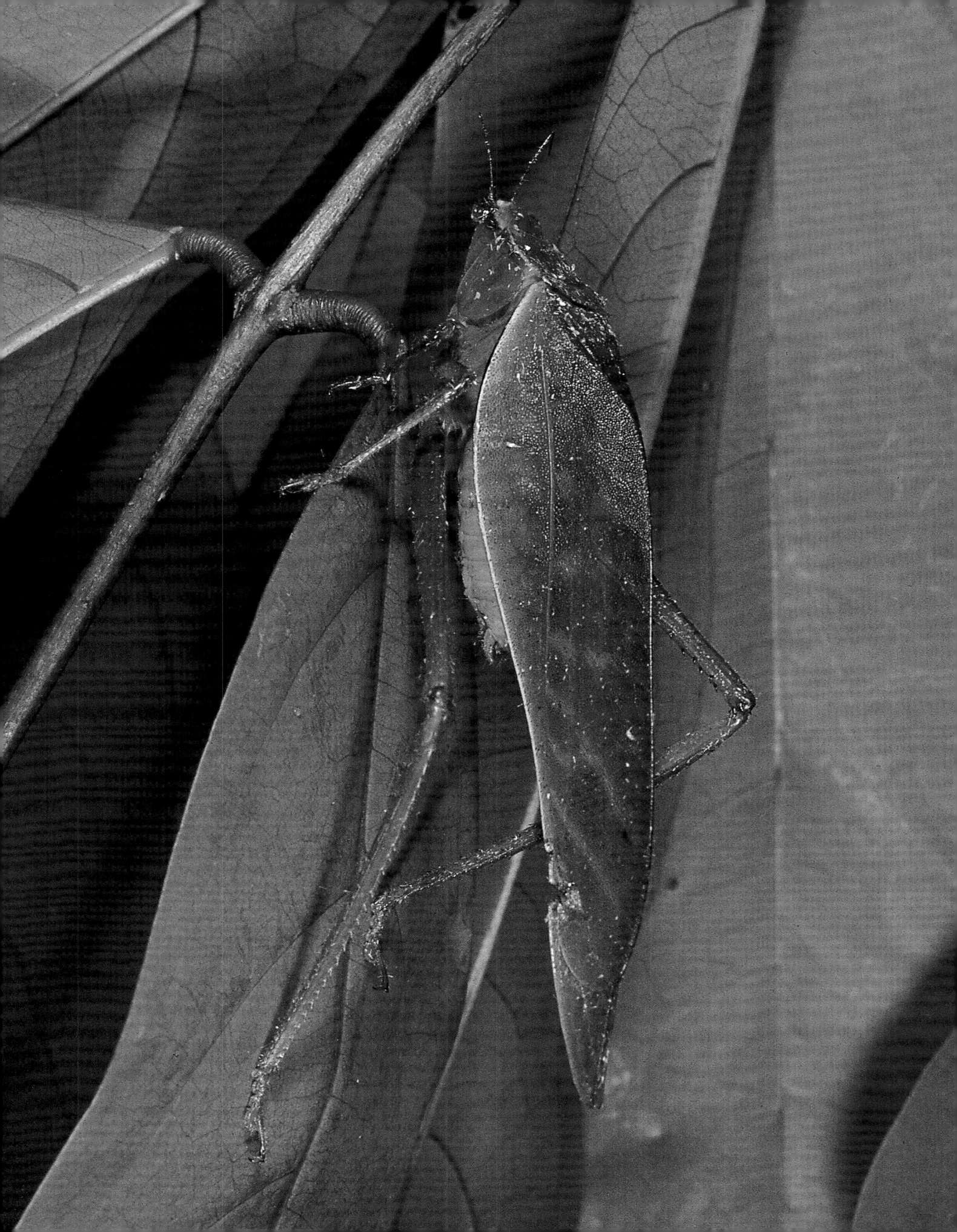

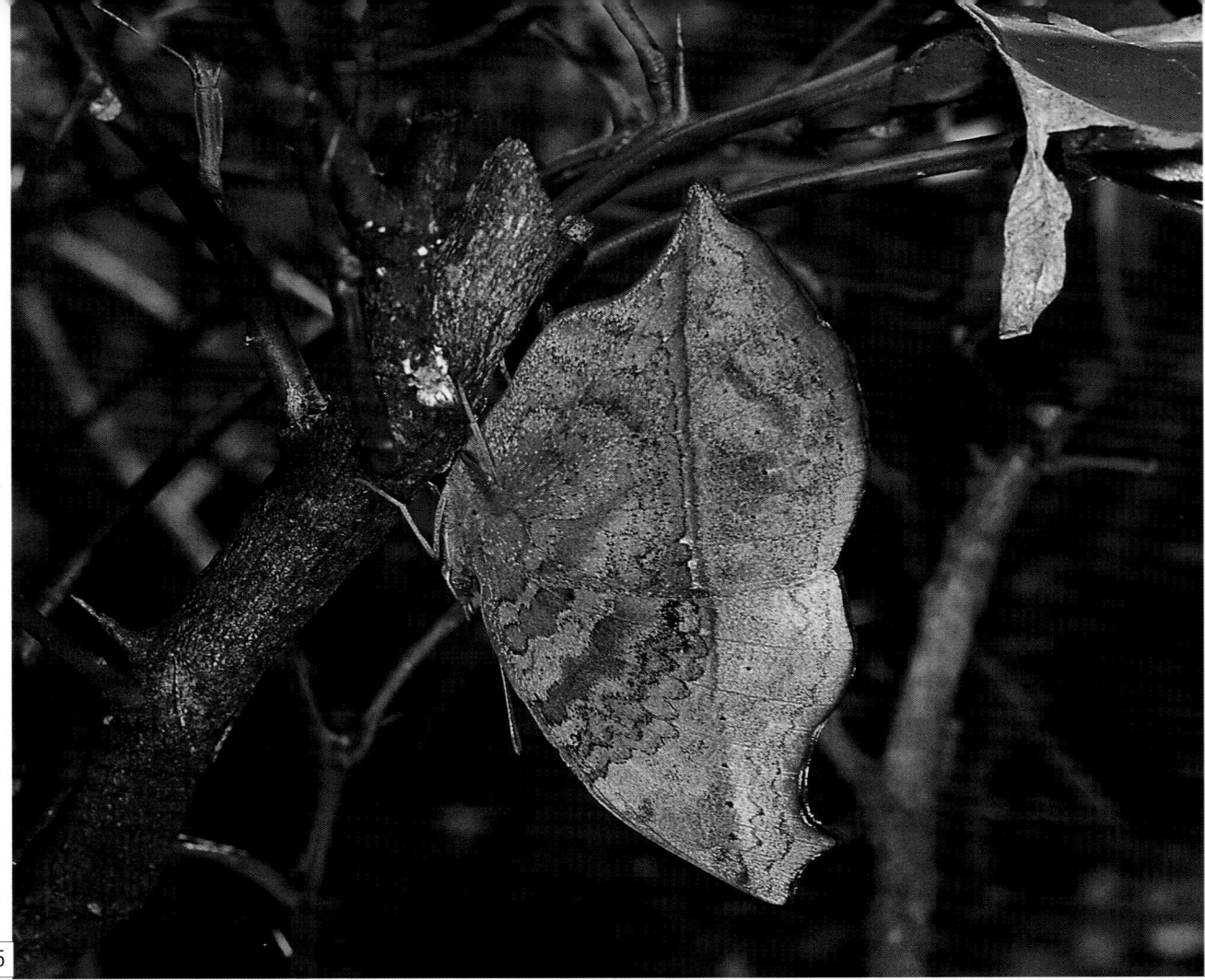

Photo 55 A leaf-like butterfly, *Salamis anteva*, suspended below a branch in secondary forest near Mandraka, Madagascar. The butterfly, clearly visible because of the flash from the camera, is well camouflaged in natural light. Wingspan 2½ in/ 6 cm.

Photo 56 (opposite) This young female katydid (Tettigoniidae), when disturbed, jumped repeatedly before assuming this rather photogenic position. Whether deliberate or coincidental, its attitude resulted in a fairly convincing camouflage, since its long antennae and ovipositor (arrow) match the long leaves on which it sits. The oviposter is a knife-like organ used for depositing eggs. Photographed near Puerto Ayacucho, Venezuela. Length 2 in/5 cm.

on vegetation where they are prone to attack. They lose their identity through camouflage. Beetles, on the other hand, tend to dig and hide and thus do not require camouflage, while butterflies are often on the move (at least during daylight hours) and therefore are less likely to be successfully camouflaged.

BUTTERFLIES

Butterflies, however, even during daylight hours, do spend considerable periods of time settled on vegetation, where many are susceptible to attack. Most seem to have overcome this threat by developing a marked color asymmetry: while the upper surfaces may be brightly colored, the lower (under) surfaces are somber, and are often decorated with subtle patterns that facilitate camouflage. In that most butterflies fold their wings vertically when resting, only the somber lower surfaces are exposed, and these tend to blend with the immediate surroundings. Thus, a butterfly, on landing, may virtually disappear.

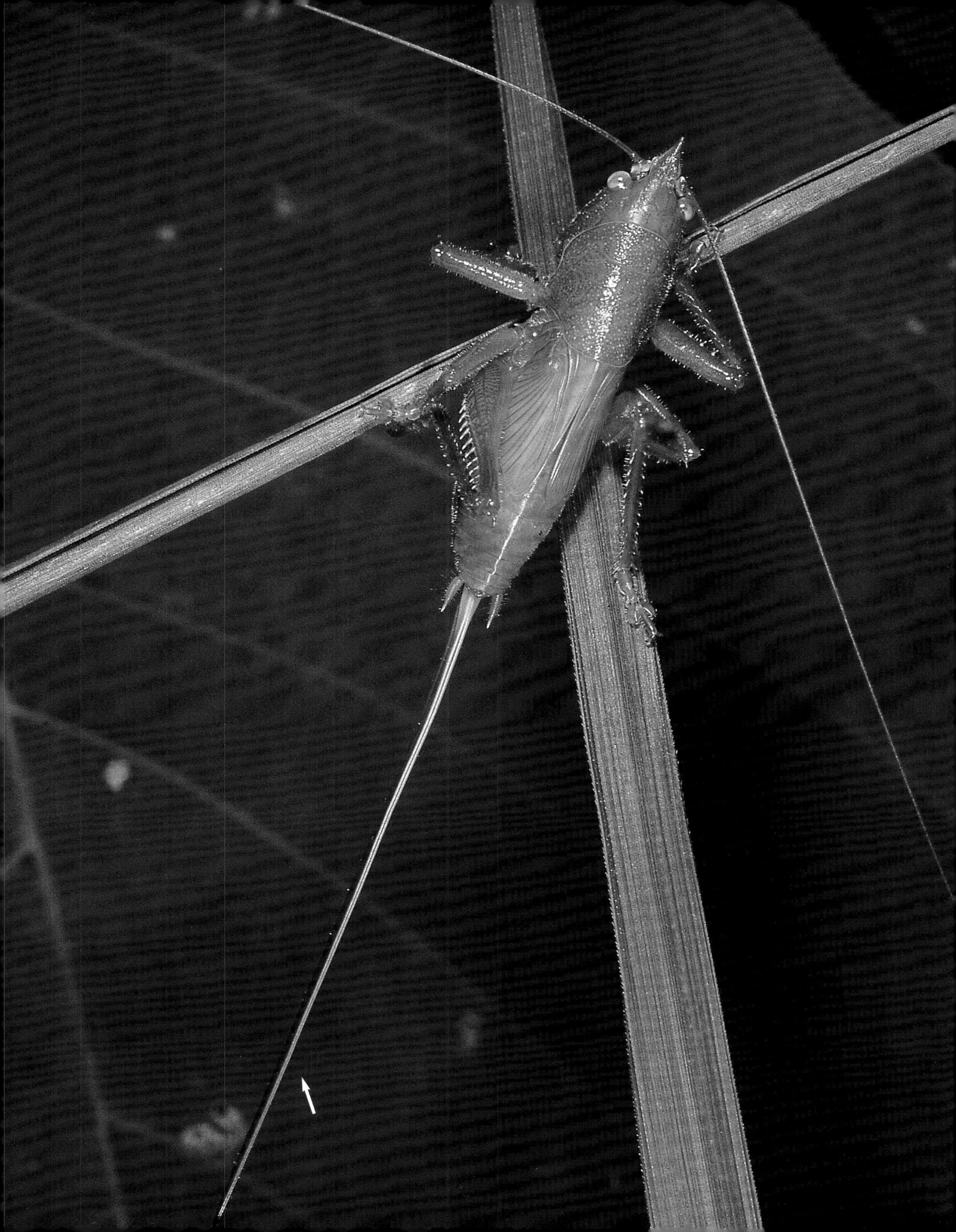

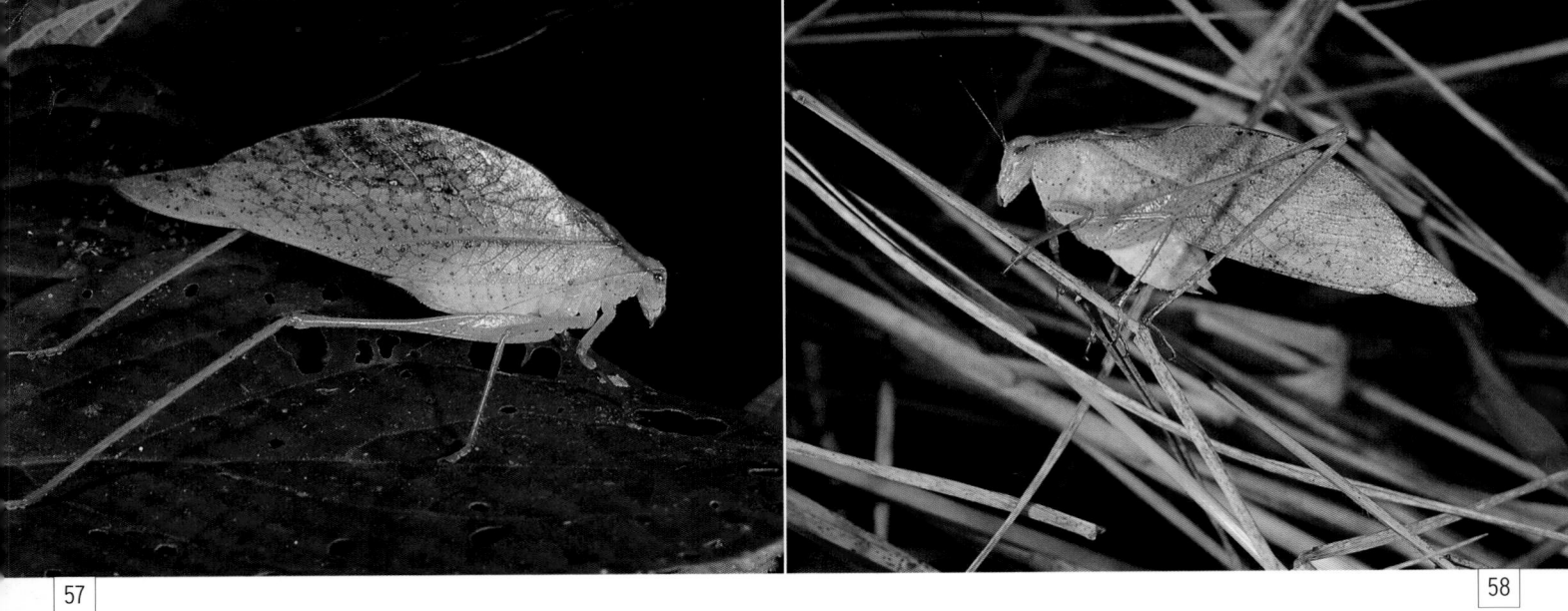

Photos 57, 58 These two photographs, taken near Turrialba in Costa Rica, show how certain insects tend to "choose" their surroundings. Although closely related, the beige variety in Photo 57 lives mainly on dead, beige-colored grass, while the light green form in Photo 58 frequents living (green) plants. Length of katydids 2½ in/6 cm.

Photo 59 The well-known leaf butterfly, *Kallima* (Nymphalidae). Leaf butterflies generally settle with their heads oriented downwards (arrow) and their wing pattern thus conforms better with adjacent vegetation.

Photo 60 *Kallima* feeding on fermented banana, showing the colorful upper surfaces of its wings. When closed (Photo 59) these bright colors disappear. This live butterfly was photographed in Malaysia; wingspan 3¼ in/8 cm.

Some butterflies make a very deliberate effort to camouflage themselves when at rest, as shown in Photos 59 and 60. They are nearly all brightly colored insects, but when they settle on low vegetation they virtually disappear. This vanishing trick is due to several related factors: when the butterfly lands it closes its wings so that only the somber lower surfaces are visible. These are decorated with lines resembling veins of a leaf. The butterflies invariably land with their heads oriented downwards. This has the effect of prolonging the main vein as a short tail, which often touches a branch and thus resembles a short stem. Leaf butterflies are extremely confident when camouflaged and, once located, may be photographed with ease. They occur on most continents; *Kallima* in Asia, *Salamis* in Africa and Madagascar, and *Anaea* in tropical America.

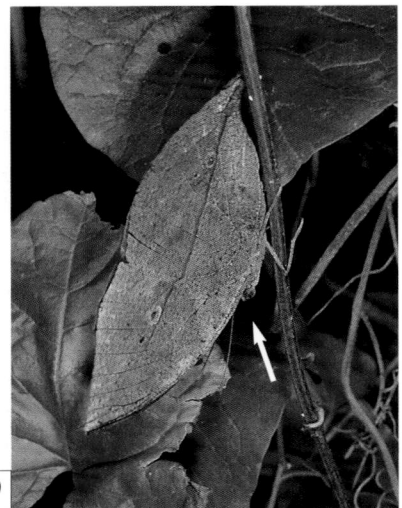

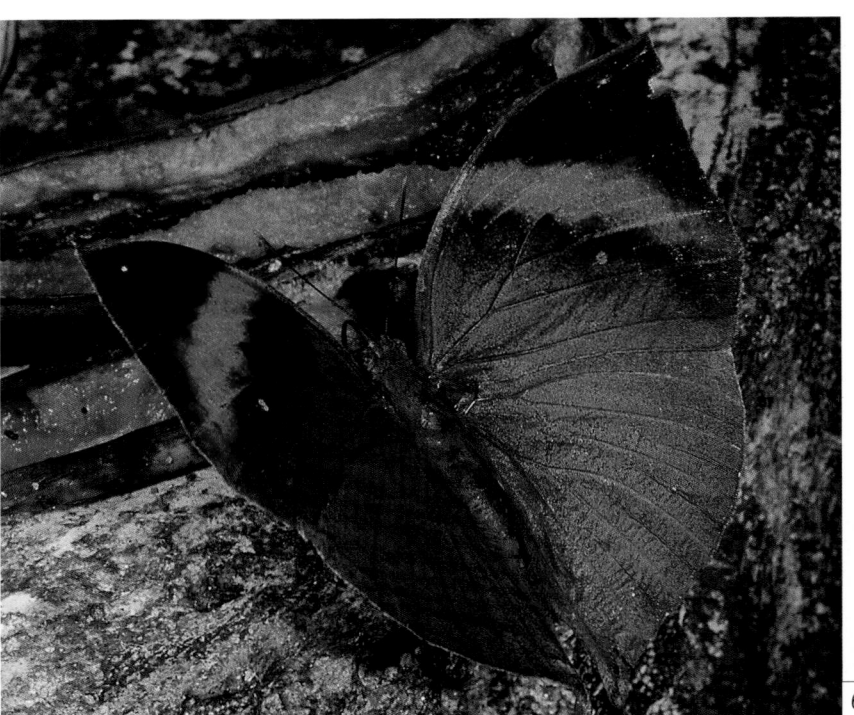

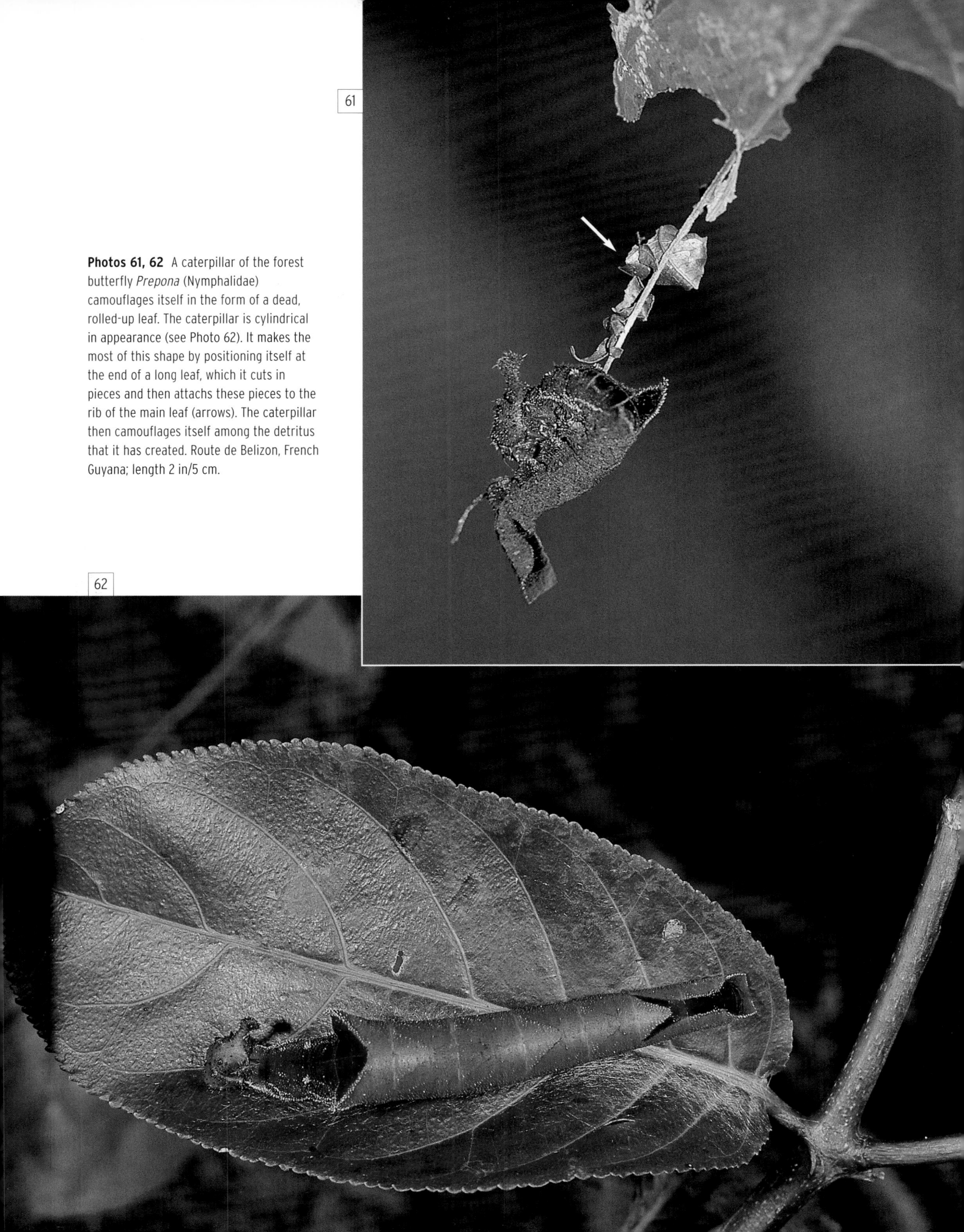

Photos 61, 62 A caterpillar of the forest butterfly *Prepona* (Nymphalidae) camouflages itself in the form of a dead, rolled-up leaf. The caterpillar is cylindrical in appearance (see Photo 62). It makes the most of this shape by positioning itself at the end of a long leaf, which it cuts in pieces and then attachs these pieces to the rib of the main leaf (arrows). The caterpillar then camouflages itself among the detritus that it has created. Route de Belizon, French Guyana; length 2 in/5 cm.

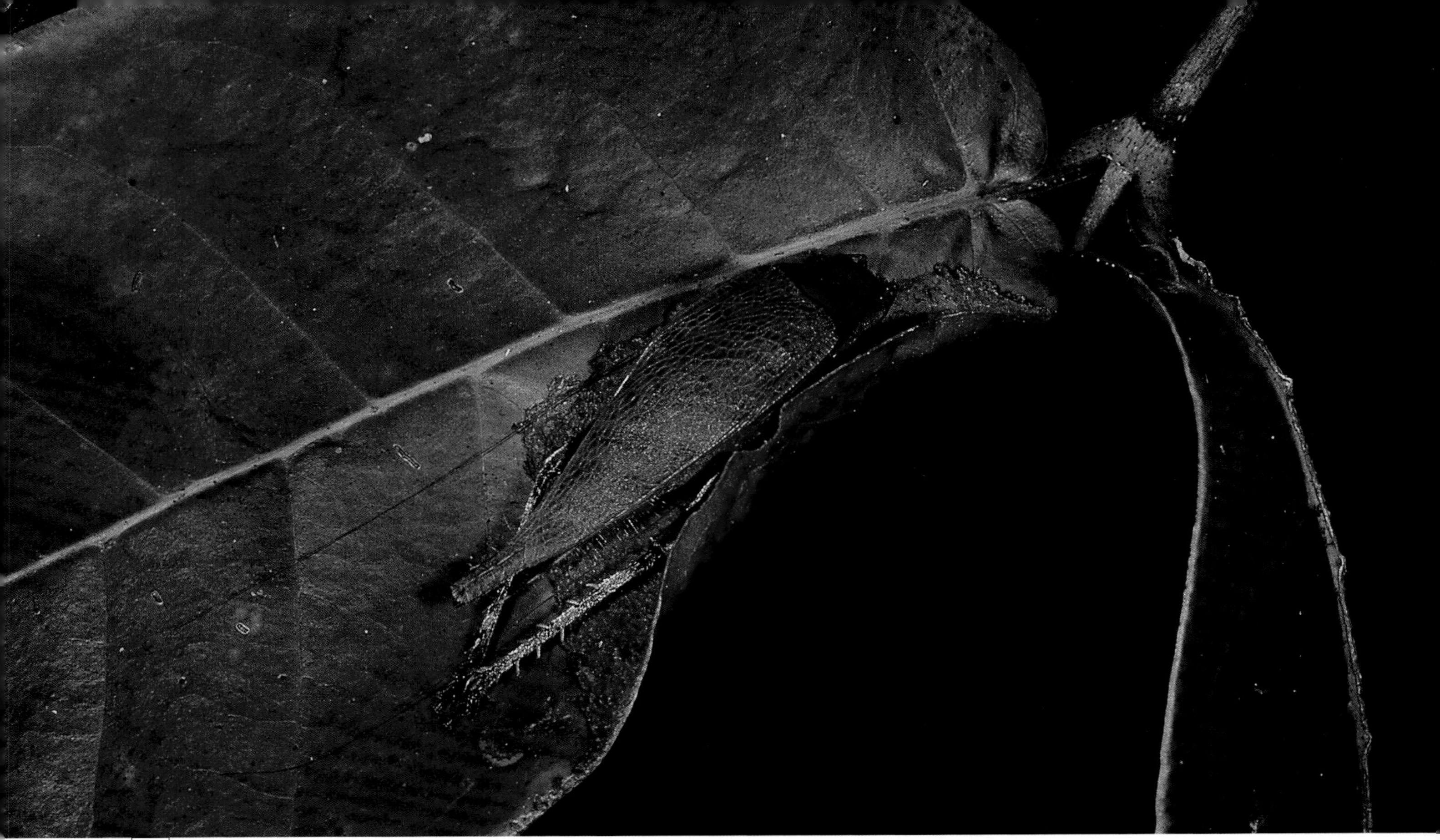

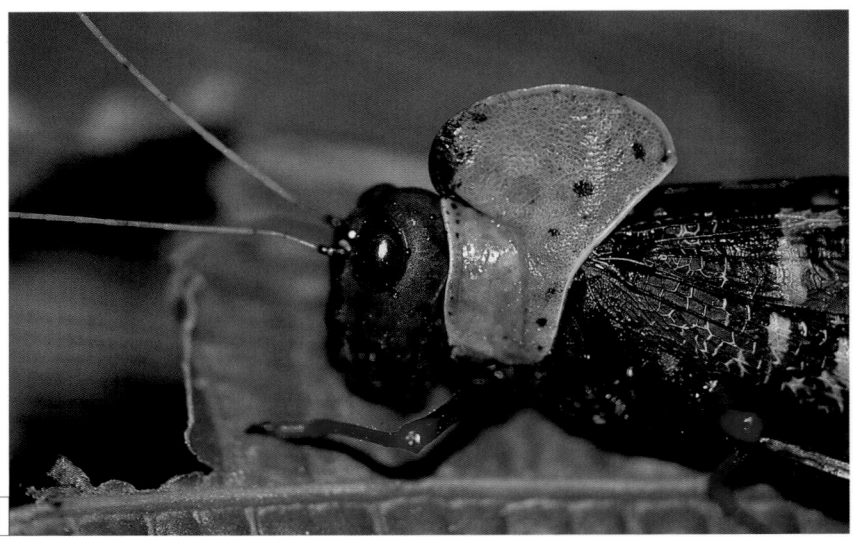

Photo 63 This brown cricket (Grylliidae), which appears to be sleeping, has chosen the only brown patch on the green leaf. Whether by accident or by design, the result is a fairly effective camouflage. Sinamary, French Guyana; length 2 in/5 cm.

GRASSHOPPERS AND CRICKETS

Grasshoppers and crickets are masters of camouflage, as illustrated. However, this same order of insects (Orthoptera) also includes many species that make no attempt to camouflage themselves; on the contrary, their flamboyant colors render them highly visible. This paradox is best explained in terms of necessity. The majority of grasshoppers are edible and therefore are hunted by birds and reptiles. To escape they have evolved effective camouflage, which they seek *actively*. They have

Photo 64 Many grasshoppers do not need to seek camouflage because they are protected by noxious body fluids. Often they are brightly colored as a warning to predators, like this individual (Acrididae). Photographed near Saül, French Guyana; length 2¾ in/7cm.

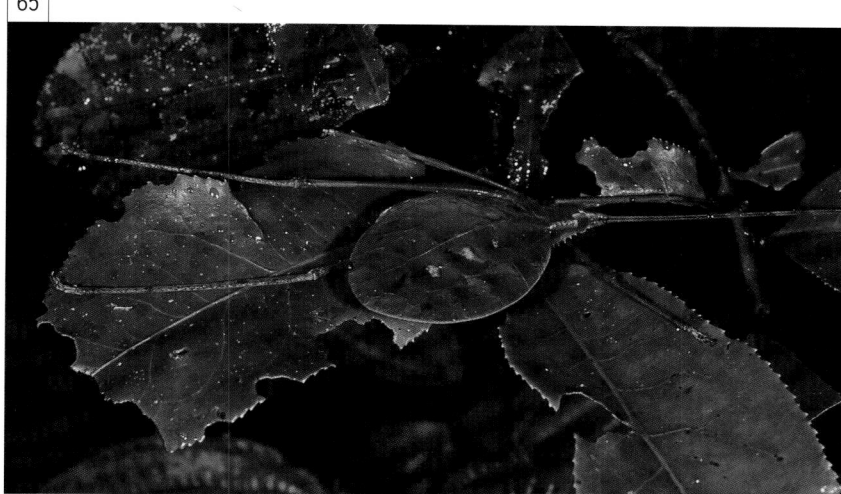

65

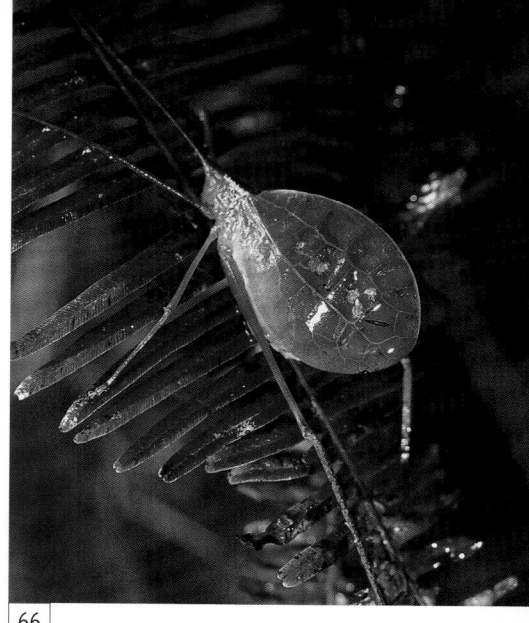

66

developed brown or green colors that blend well with the surrounding vegetation. There are grasshoppers that have noxious body fluids, with some African forms being extremely poisonous. These species generally are brightly colored (Photo 64), the antithesis of camouflage. These colors may be a warning to predators, the message being quite clear, "Don't eat me! I am poisonous!"

KATYDIDS

Katydids offer the best examples of active camouflage, as shown in Photos 65 and 66. In this particular case I was very lucky, for its deliberate effort to camouflage itself, which involved lying on its side, was played before my eyes. Its green, leaf-like wings matched perfectly with the leaves of the shrub it chose to land on. As I watched this performance I could not escape the impression that the insect really knew and understood what it was doing. However, when working systematically along forest trails one often disturbs a katydid or grasshopper, which will jump or flutter a short distance before landing on nearby branch. Frequently it will walk a short

Photos 65, 66 This katydid (Tettigoniidae) was found sitting on a fern leaf (Photo 66), with which it did not blend. Realizing that it had been discovered, it moved about three feet (one meter) to more suitable surroundings, where it proceeded to lie on its side (Photo 65) in order to conform with the surrounding leaves. Photographed in primary forest near Andasibe, Madagascar; length 2 in/5 cm.

Photos 67, 68, 69 Another example of active camouflage is offered by this katydid (Tettigoniidae), photographed in roadside vegetation in the Peruvian Amazon. Because of its leaf-like shape and veined wing structure, the insect was very difficult to locate. Camouflage was improved by adopting a head-down position (Photo 67), which resulted in the oblique, leaf-like orientation of its wings. It also oriented its antennae (arrow) downward, where they resembled the stalk of a leaf. Only in shifting from its natural surroundings (Photo 68) was its true nature evident. Atalya, Madre de Dios, Peru; length 2½ in/6 cm.

67

68

69

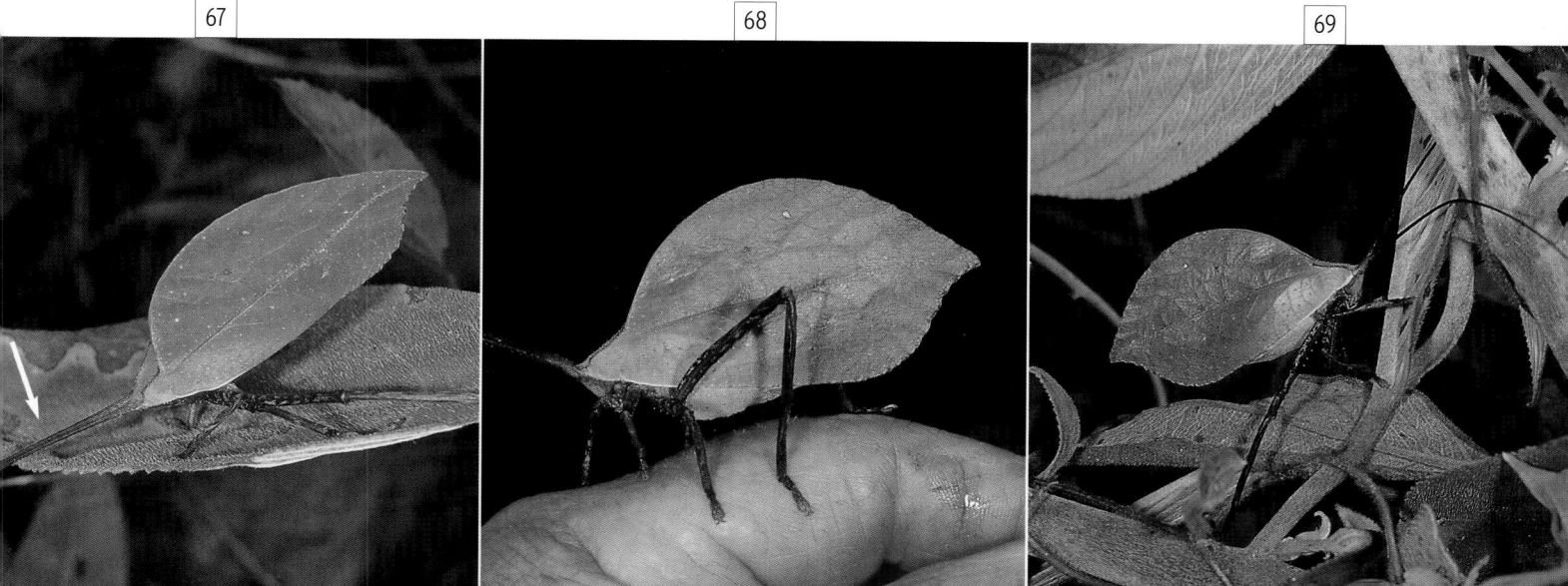

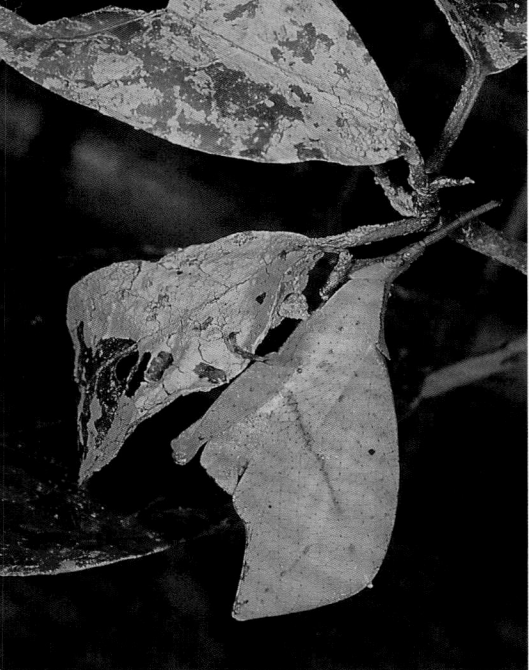

Photos 70, 71 Katydids deliberately assume positions that conform well with the adjacent vegetation. In Photo 71, taken near Wau, Papua New Guinea, a family of seven katydids (*Siliquofera*) are carefully camouflaged. Length 1 ¼ in/3cm. The grasshopper (Tettigoniidae) shown in Photo 70 flew along a muddy track in Hutan Lipur Reserve, Central Malaysia, until it found a satisfactory branch from which it refused to move. Length about 2 in/5 cm.

distance to nearby vegetation, where it will hesitate before aligning its elongate wings to conform with the disposition of the hanging leaves.

These very convincing efforts to camouflage may be observed among the forest katydids and grasshoppers on most continents.

PHASMIDS

Phasmids are nearly always well camouflaged, as shown in these photos. They appear to make a distinct effort to blend with their immediate surroundings and one may observe them adjusting their body and legs to better match the orientation of leaves and twigs on which they sit. When disturbed, some will fly to another tree or shrub, while others, usually those lacking wings, will fall to the ground, where they remain immobile among forest detritus.

The Phasmidae are an interesting group of insects, found in warm temperate and tropical climates throughout the world. Related to the grasshoppers and mantids, with whom they share the tendency to camouflage, phasmids differ nevertheless from their cousins, notably in their style of reproduction. While usually sexual, there are many examples of parthenogenesis (asexual reproduction), in which only the female phasmid is known.

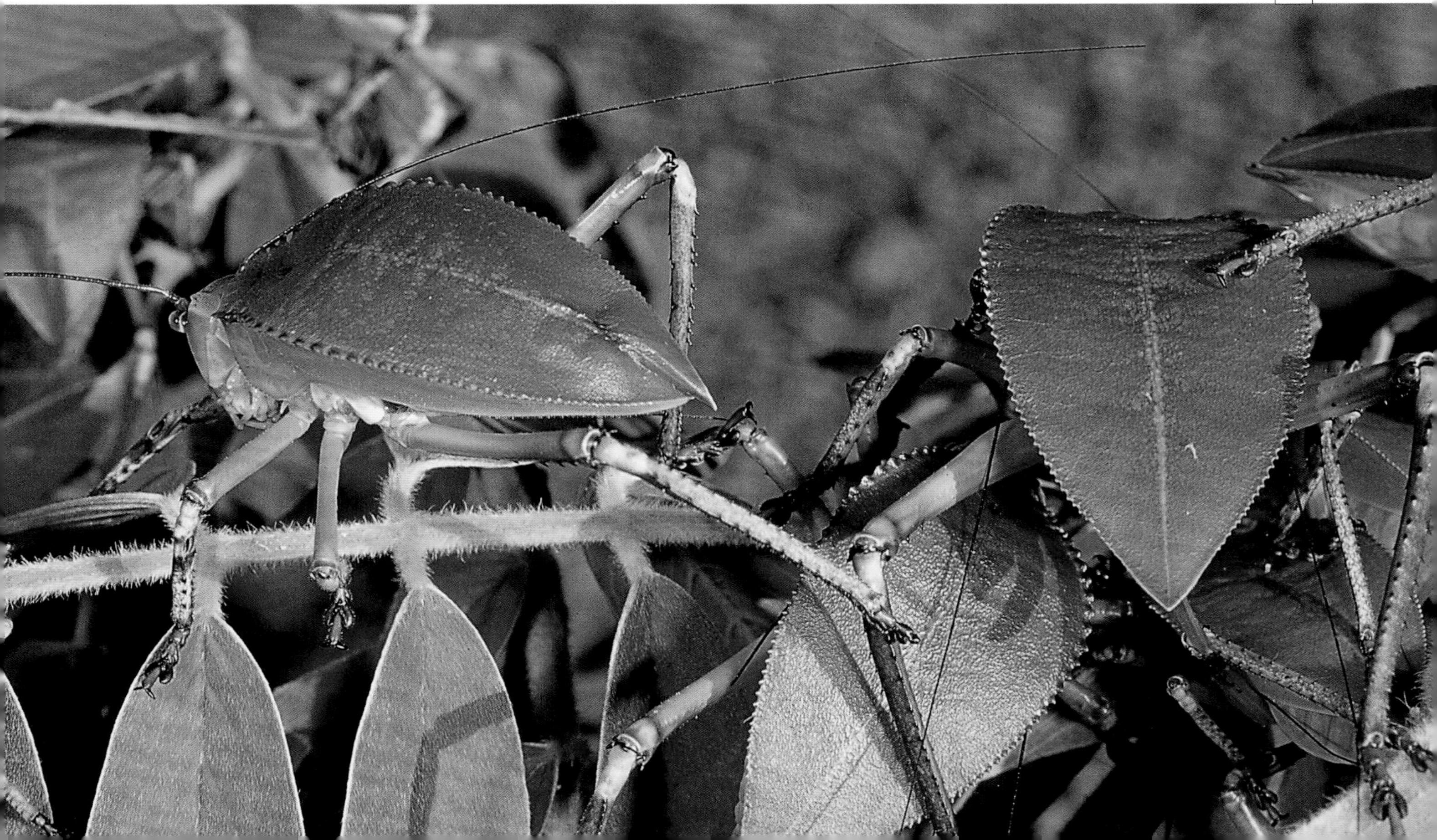

72

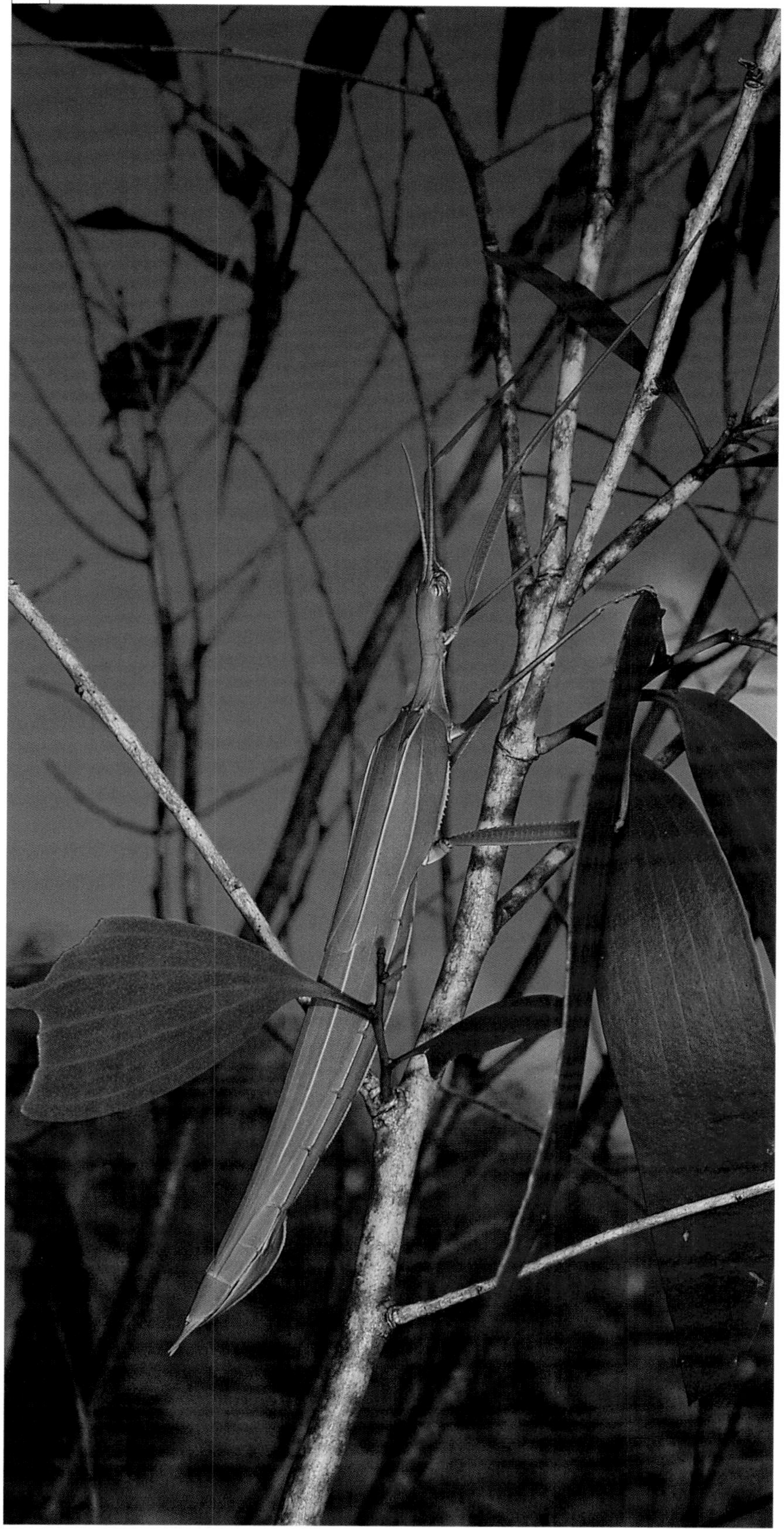

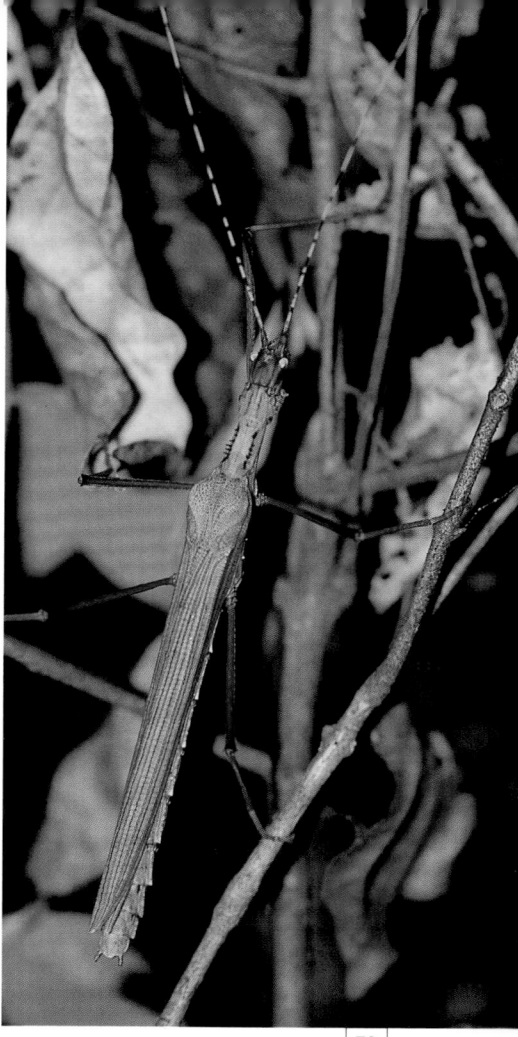

73

Photo 73 This phasmid was seen to fly some 55 yards (50 meters) before landing on dead vegetation suspended in a tree. It seemed to choose this particular spot deliberately. Upper Orinoco, Venezuela, length 3¼ in/8 cm.

Photo 72 Another phasmid, whose color and shape are quite different from those of the phasmid in Photo 73. This example from Australia illustrates the close similarity between the shape, parallel-veined wing structure and vertical orientation of this phasmid, all of which match the adjacent eucalyptus leaves. Davies Creek Reserve, Kuranda, Queensland, length 4 in/10 cm.

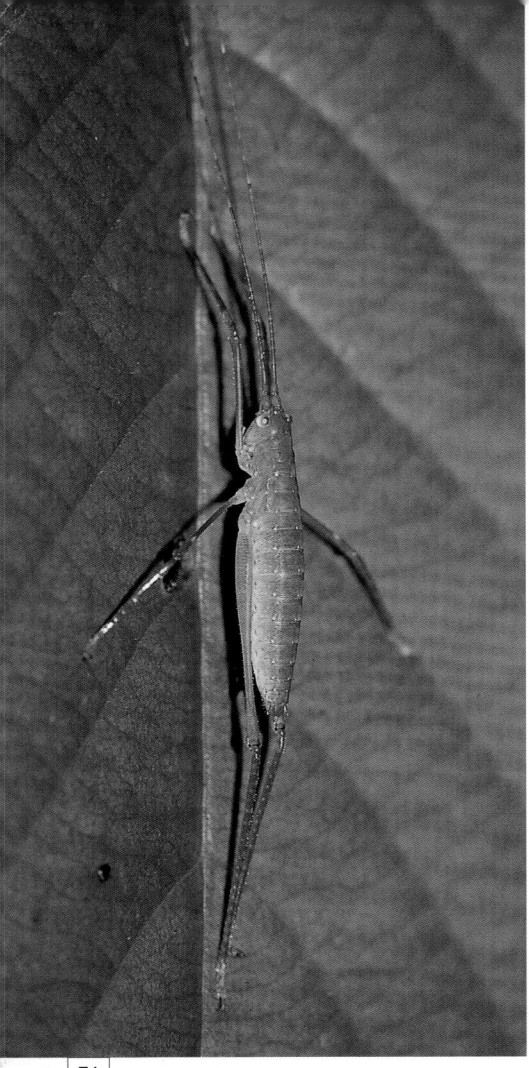

74

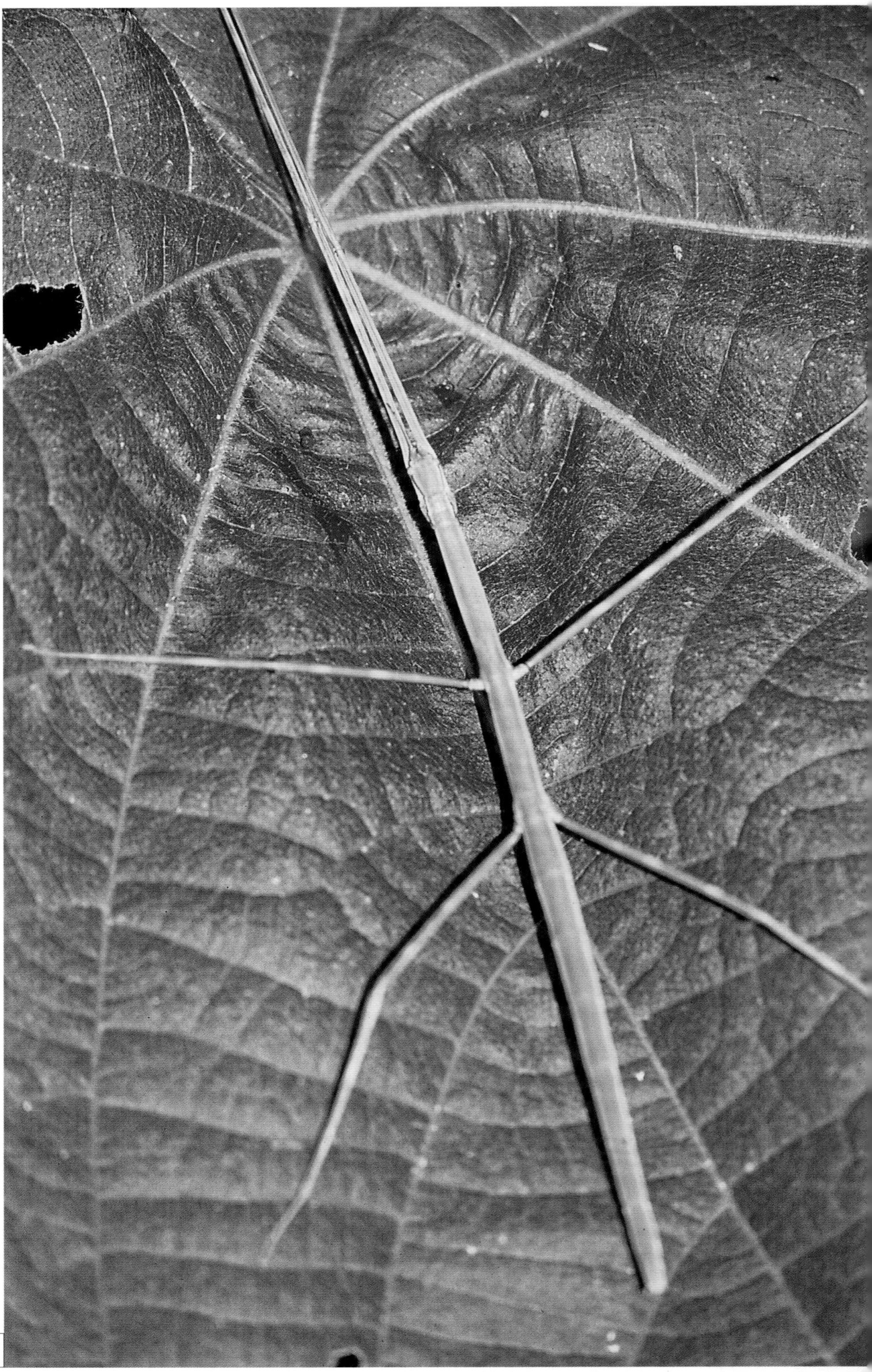

Photo 74 Katydids and grasshoppers may adopt unusual positions in order to best conform with their surroundings. This individual has placed the main axis of its body parallel to the rib of the leaf, its legs disposed obliquely to conform with the veins of the leaf. This active camouflage is very effective. Canaima, Venezuela; length 2½ in/6 cm.

Photo 75 A phasmid sitting quietly in the center of a broad leaf has spread its legs seemingly to better conform with the radiating vein structure of its substrate. Mai Hongson, Thailand; length 2¾ in/7 cm.

75

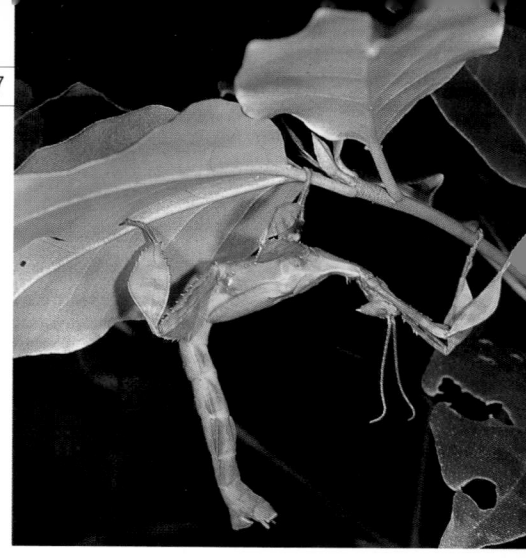

Phasmids and grasshoppers frequently make considerable efforts to orient their legs and bodies in order to match the structure of leaves on which they rest. In that their efforts appear to be deliberate, they clearly offer good examples of active camouflage. These photos illustrate the very meticulous manner in which these insects dispose themselves. In both instances (Photos 74, 75) the antennae and forelegs are stretched out towards the front as a direct prolongation of the body. Because the body is lying close to the main rib of the leaf, the fore-legs, antennae, body and leaf form an entity. Camouflage is perfected by the disposition of the remaining legs for, in both cases, these are disposed in an oblique manner, seemingly to conform with the radiating vein structure of their support.

There are several distinct groups of phasmid, and nearly all of them imitate a particular type of vegetation. The thin, wingless phasmids tend to resemble twigs — and hence are termed "stick insects." Others have brown or green wings, which they fold along their elongate bodies (shown in Photos 72 and 73). These phasmids tend to imitate long, thin leaves. In Australia and New Guinea, some phasmids, including *Extatosoma*

Photos 76, 77 Queensland is particularly rich in phasmids, one of the largest being *Extatosoma*, shown in these photos. Like most phasmids, it spends the daylight hours suspended below branches, where its irregularly shaped body and peculiar flattened legs tend to resemble dead vegetation. Photographed at night near Kuranda, Queensland; length 2 ¾ in/7 cm.

76

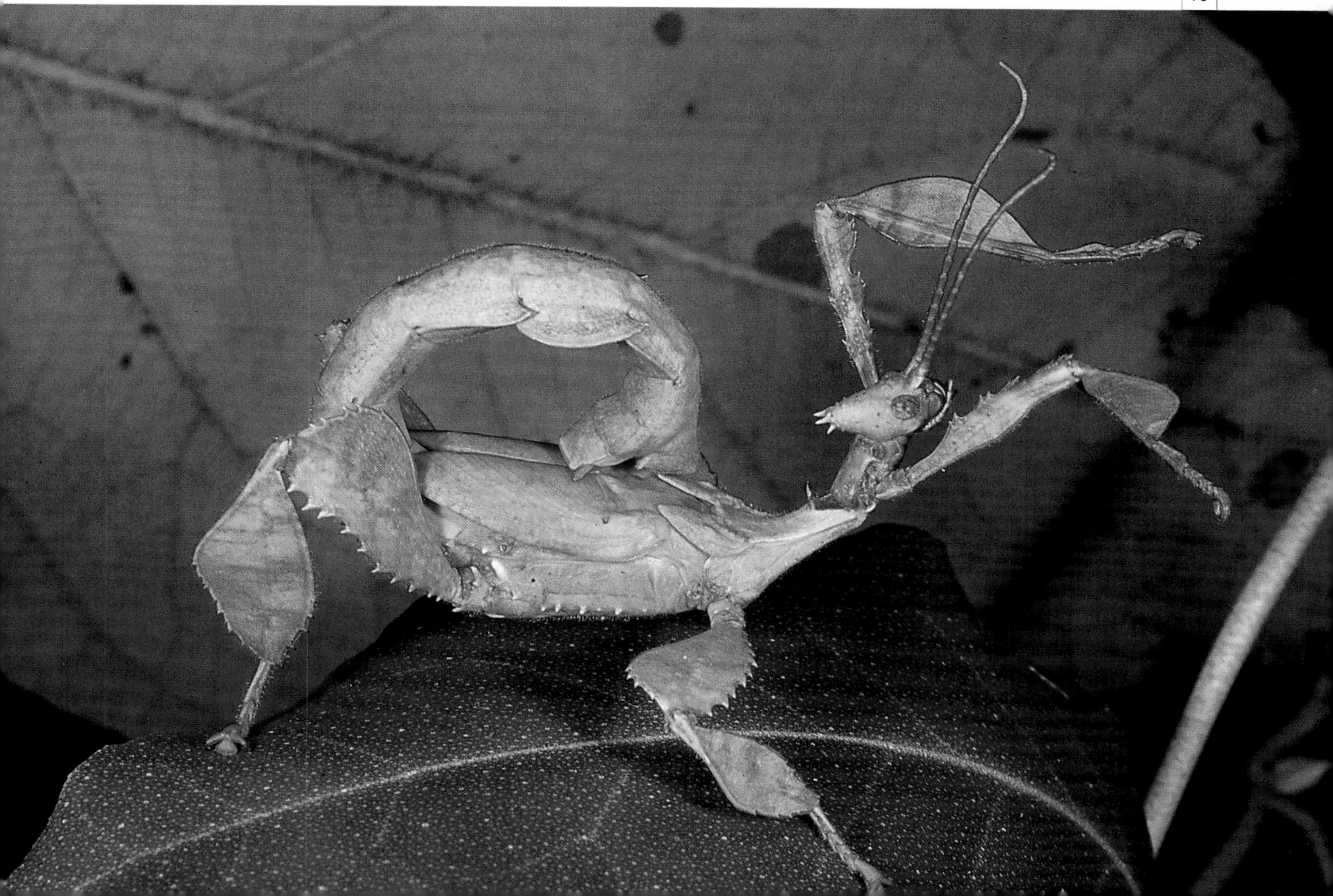

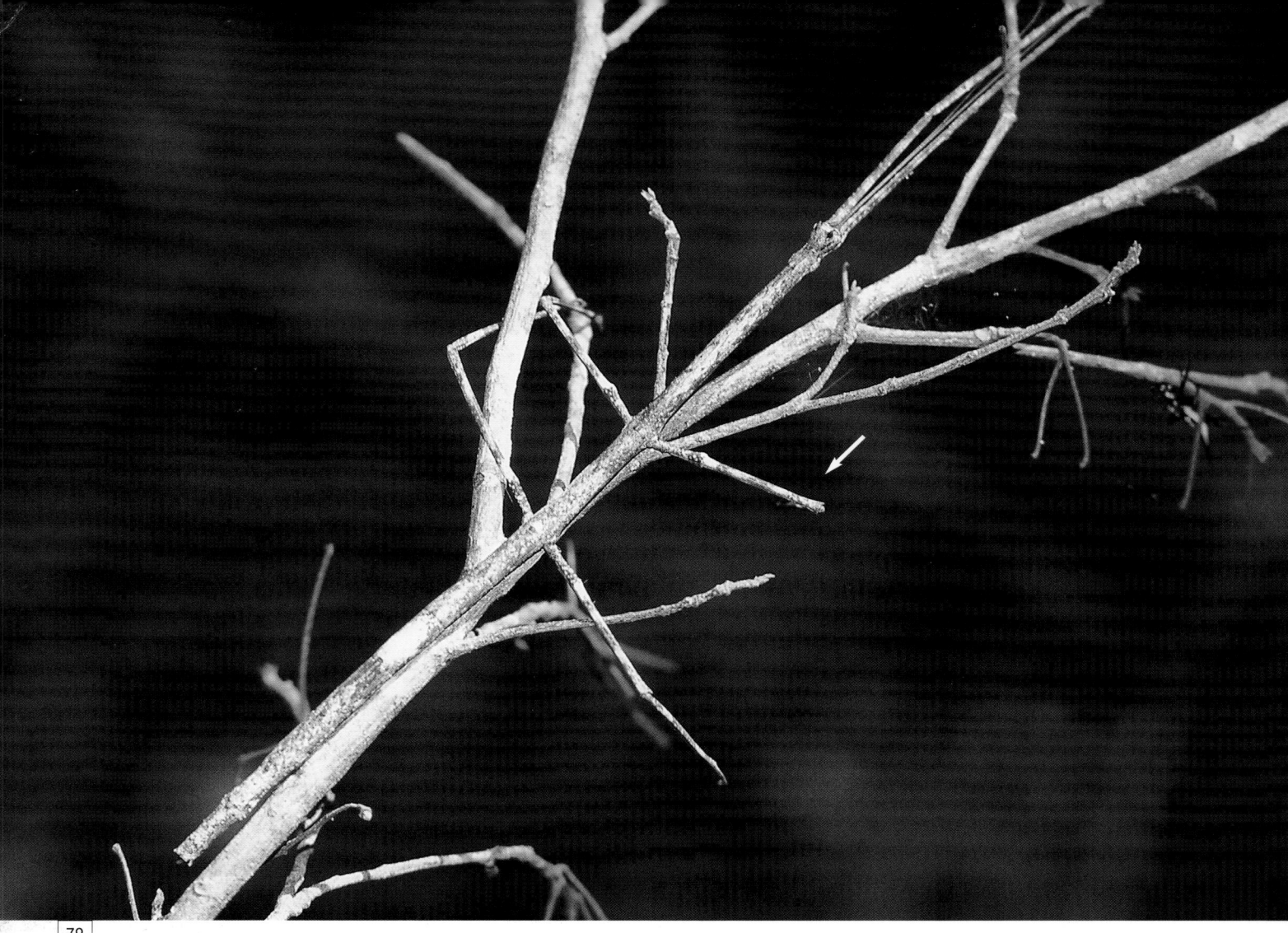

78

Photo 78 Phasmids may make a considerable effort to camouflage themselves. This individual, when disturbed, walked about 11 yards (10 meters) across the dead leaves of the forest floor before climbing onto a dead branch. It then proceeded to orient its legs into seemingly unnatural positions (see arrow) to better conform with the surrounding branches. El Dorado, Venezuela; length 4 ¾ in/12 cm.

(Photos 76 and 77) have only rudimentary wings. However, their legs and bodies are unusually thick and very irregular in shape, and this appears to help them blend with adjacent vegetation. Their camouflage is improved by deliberate body contortions that modify their shapes, rendering identification by predators more difficult, as seen in these photos.

Phasmids may have well-developed wings and be able to fly several hundred yards. Others, perhaps the majority, lack wings. Both groups actively seek effective camouflage on the living vegetation on which they feed, and occasionally on dead branches and other dry vegetation, as in Photo 78. When forcibly removed from these respective substrates, the phasmids often make a distinct effort to relocate vegetation which suits their color and shape. The wingless forms may walk considerable distances across the forest floor before climbing onto a fallen branch, where they will remain immobile. In observing the behavior of these remarkable stick insects one can not escape the conclusion that they are conscious of their particular requirements, for their choice of substrate can be very selective.

STRANGE GRASSHOPPERS

Certain grasshoppers, like their cousins the phasmids, are long and thin and blend readily with sticks and grass. Most pass unnoticed but, when disturbed, may fly to nearby vegetation where, providing one is careful, their behavior may be observed. The very thin acridid grasshoppers (Photos 79, 80) will select a straight branch or stem against which they will flatten themselves, almost becoming part of the support. Their thin shape is accentuated both by their bodies, their antennae and even their eyes, all of which are elongate parallel to the branch. In other words, the insect, seemingly conscious of its unusual shape, appears to make the most of this by positioning itself deliberately in order to obtain effective camouflage.

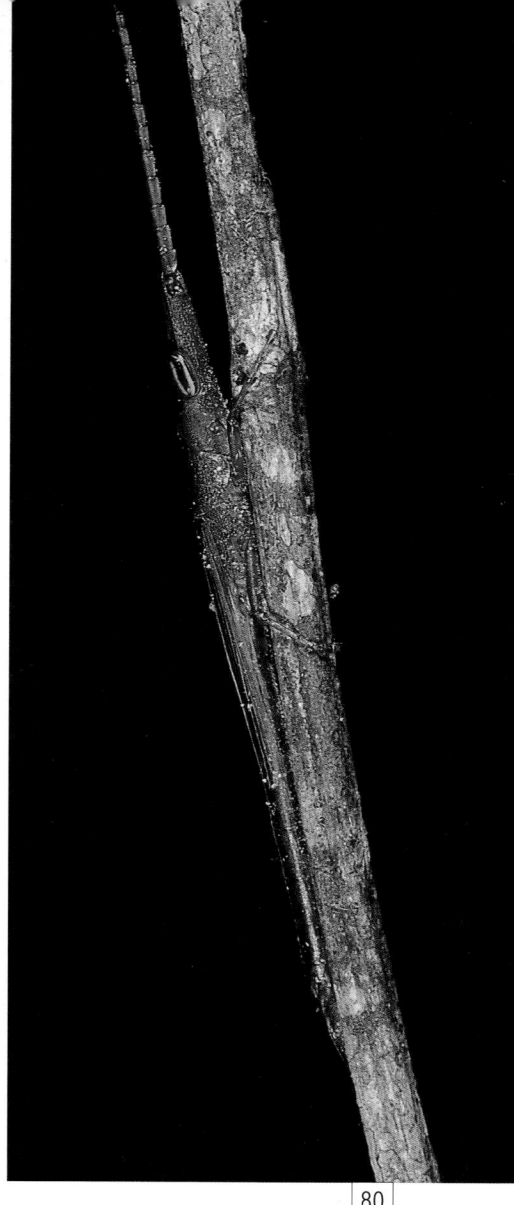

80

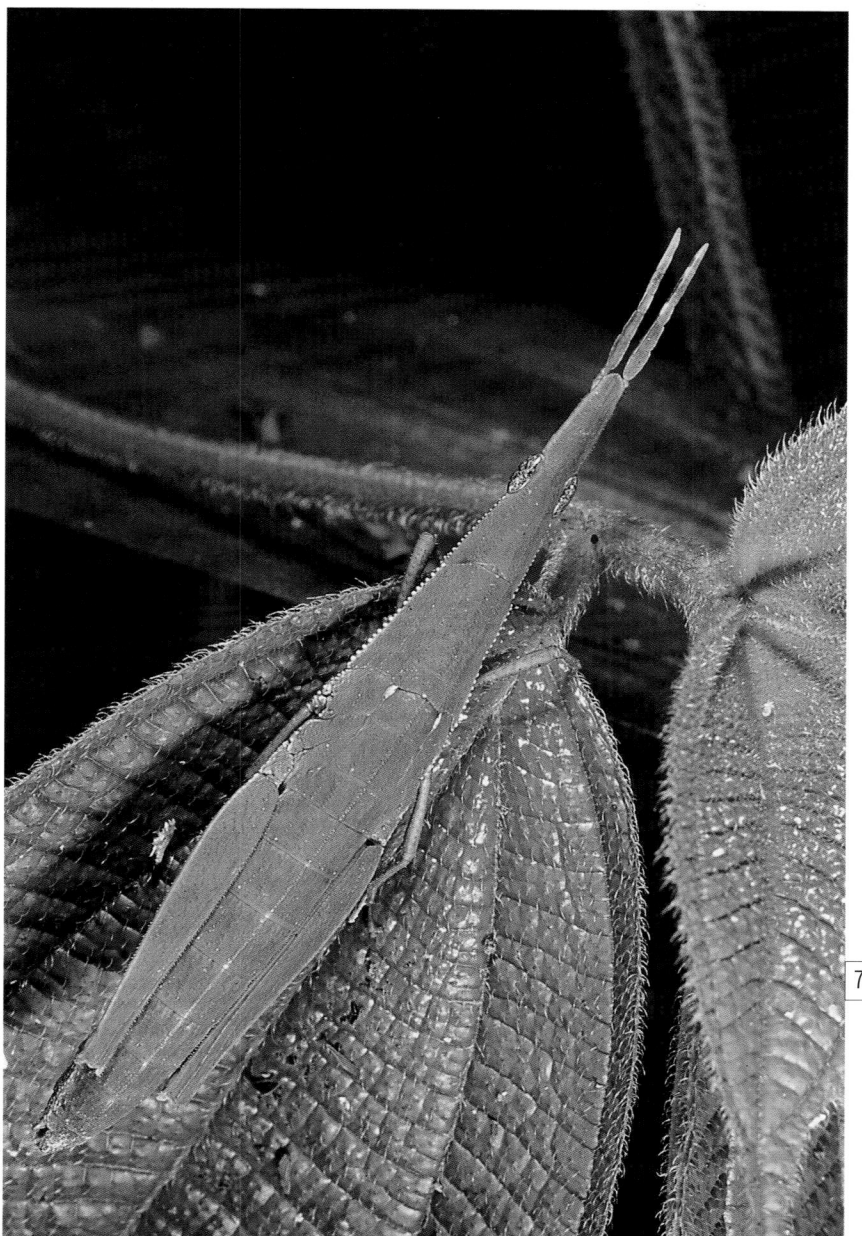

79

Photos 79, 80 Acridid grasshoppers are very long and thin. Their stream-lined appearance enables them to blend perfectly with certain types of vegetation, as shown in these photos. The grasshopper seems to be conscious of its shape, for it deliberately selects suitable vegetation in order to gain maximum benefit from this. Photo 79 was taken in the Peruvian Amazon; length 2 in/5 cm. Photo 80 was taken in Kelantan, Malaysia; length 1½ in/4cm.

MOTHS

Photo 84 A katydid (Tettigoniidae) flattens itself against the branch of an acacia shrub. Its deliberate positioning combined with a mottled color pattern provide a very effective camouflage. Sierre de Chuacus, Guatemala; length 2 3/4 in/7 cm.

Photos 81, 83 What appear to be twigs are in fact caterpillars (arrows). In adopting rigid, immobile positions, they readily escape notice. Photo 83 taken near Puerto Ayacucho, Venezuela; length 1 in/3 cm. Photo 81 was taken near Gopeng, central Malaysia; length 2 in/5 cm.

Photo 82 Caterpillars are not always camouflaged, as shown here. Bright colors and poisonous spines are warnings to predators that the owner is poisonous and better left alone. Photographed in the lower Urubamba Valley, Peru; length 2 1/2 in/6 cm.

Photo 87 Moths may resemble broken sticks. This little fellow, attracted by the mercury-vapor lamp, finally landed on a stick. It then positioned itself in such a manner that its unusually-shaped head and thorax closely resembled the end of the stick. Peruvian Amazon; length 1 1/4 in/3 cm.

I have noted already that virtually all insects have evolved a protective strategy. This is pushed to extremes among insects such as grasshoppers and moths, which spend the daylight hours motionless on forest vegetation where they are prone to predatorial attack. Because most moths have no other form of protection, they are dependant on camouflage, which they have refined to a remarkable degree. When walking through the forest during daylight hours one may disturb an occasional moth. Their great numbers are not apparent for their camouflage is nearly always effective and only systematic examination of tree trunks will reveal the occasional moth. However, when I light a lamp in a forest, within moments I am surrounded by a multitude of fluttering insects, and by nine p.m. a white sheet and the surrounding vegetation may be covered by up to 50,000 individuals. While most of these will make no effort to camouflage themselves, others will settle on adjacent vegetation where most will be camouflaged in a rather haphazard manner.

A minority of moths will make a considerable effort to camouflage themselves by adopting very unusual positions. Typically moth-like when examined superficially, they change shape drastically when they settle. Wings can be distorted and may even be partly folded around a twig to conform with the shape of the substrate. The moth in Photo 87 appears capable of erecting tufts of fine hair around its head and thorax, accentuating the resemblance to ragged ends of a broken stick.

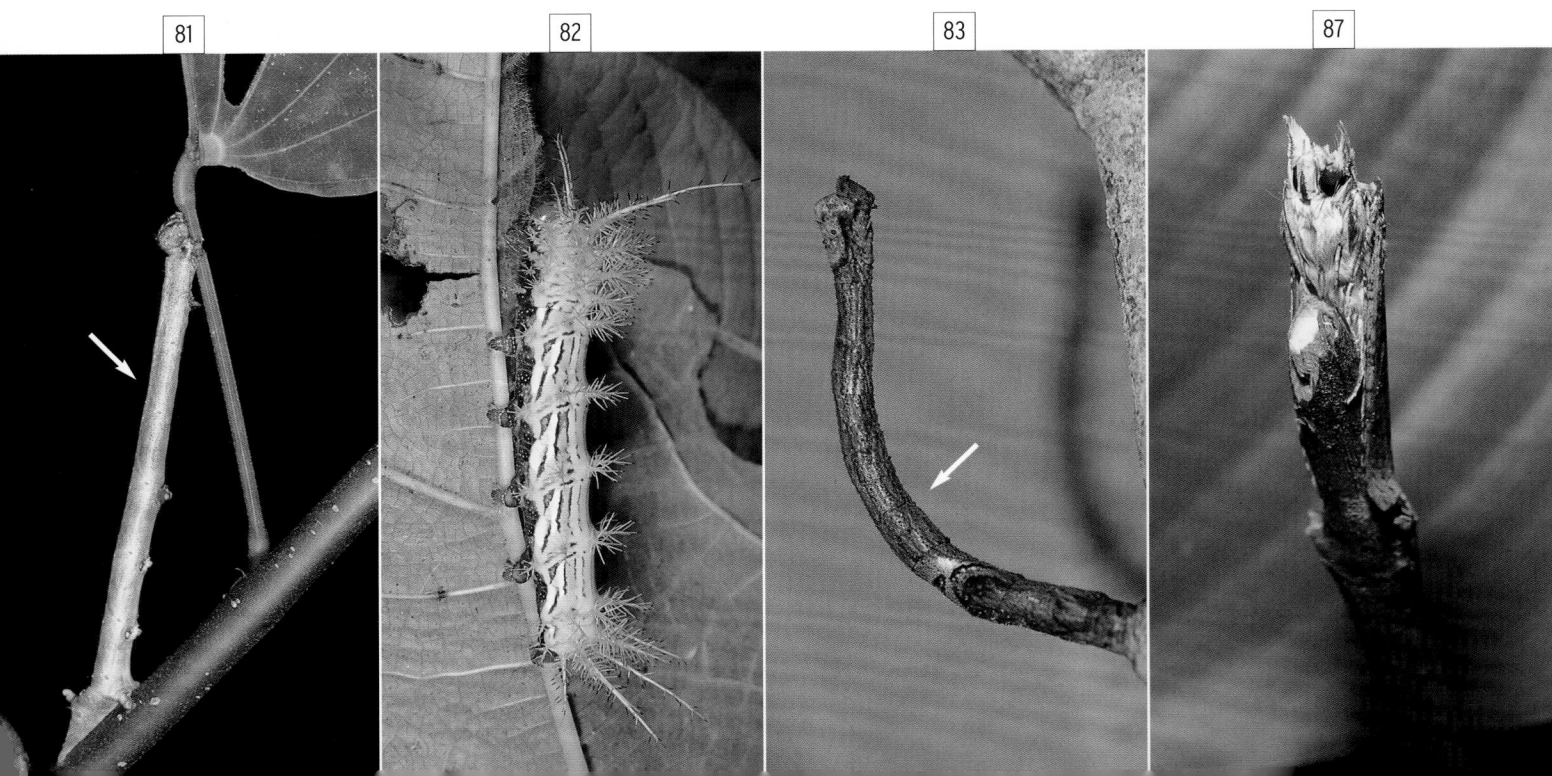

81 82 83 87

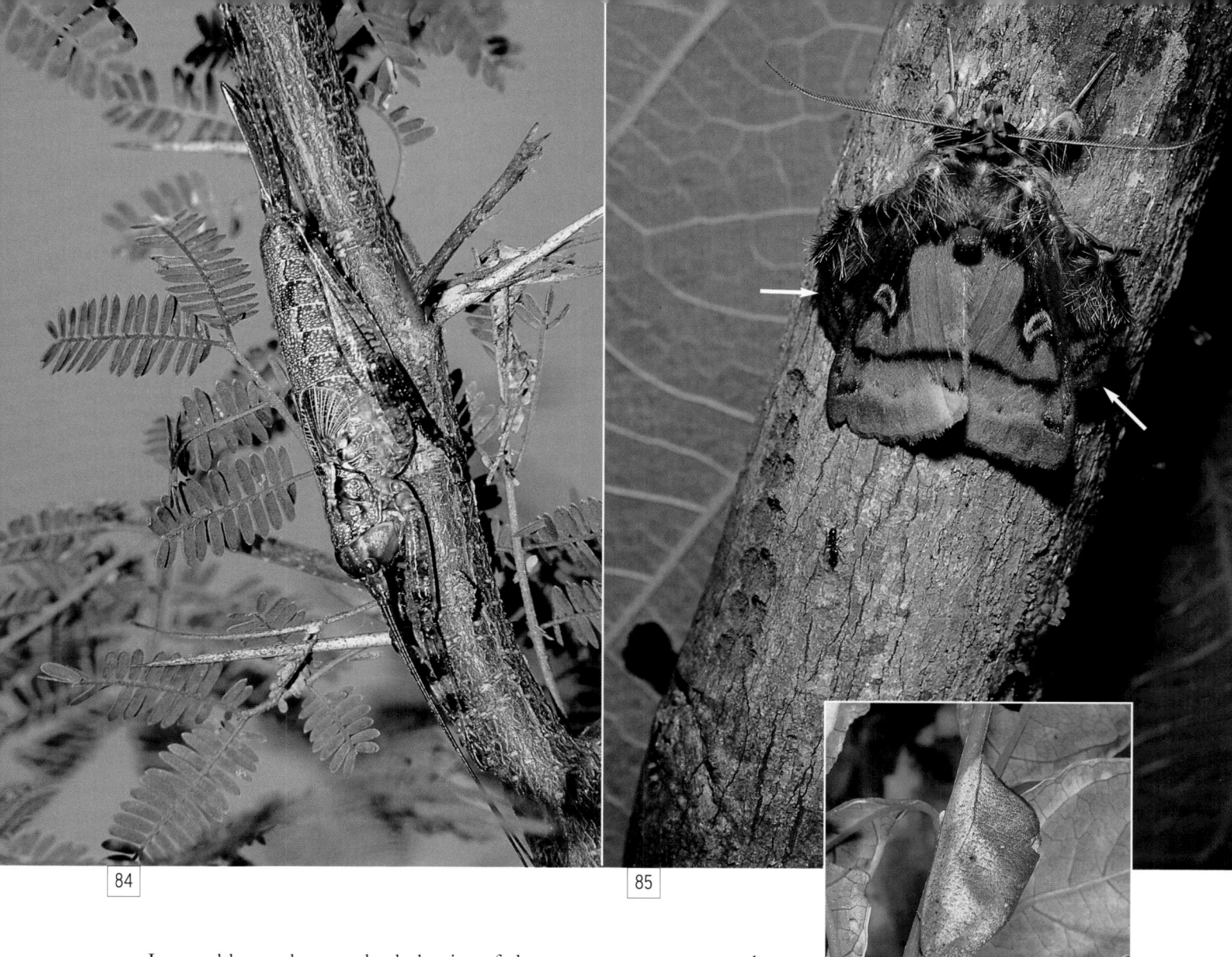

84

85

86

I was able to observe the behavior of these strange creatures only because of the rather unnatural conditions; attracted by the lamp, I saw them land. But under natural circumstances within the forest, unless disturbed, these strange insects would surely pass unnoticed.

Certain moths may change shape in order to better resemble particular elements of the vegetation. Others will simply move along a branch until they find an irregularity to which they can adapt, mainly by tucking their legs beneath their body and by arranging their antennae so that they seem to become part of the natural support.

Moths, notably the tropical Lymantriidae (Photo 85) are often dark green in color. They are frequently found resting on green bark or leaves. This association possibly indicates a deliberate choice of substrate. The camouflage is improved by the positioning of the wings; the hindwing is pushed forward so that its leading edge protrudes beyond the forewing, giving the moth a very irregular outline, as seen in Photo 85.

Photo 85 A lymantriid moth has carefully chosen a green stick on which it is fairly well camouflaged. The hindwings protrude beyond the leading edge of the forewings (arrows), giving it an unusual appearance. Photographed in Manu National Park, Peruvian Amazon; length 1½ in/4 cm.

Photo 86 Moths may modify their shapes in order to best conform with the color and shape of their substrates. This moth has folded its wings and arranged its antennae to resemble a dead leaf that has fallen among living vegetation. Photographed at Frasers Hill, Malaysia; length 2 in/5 cm.

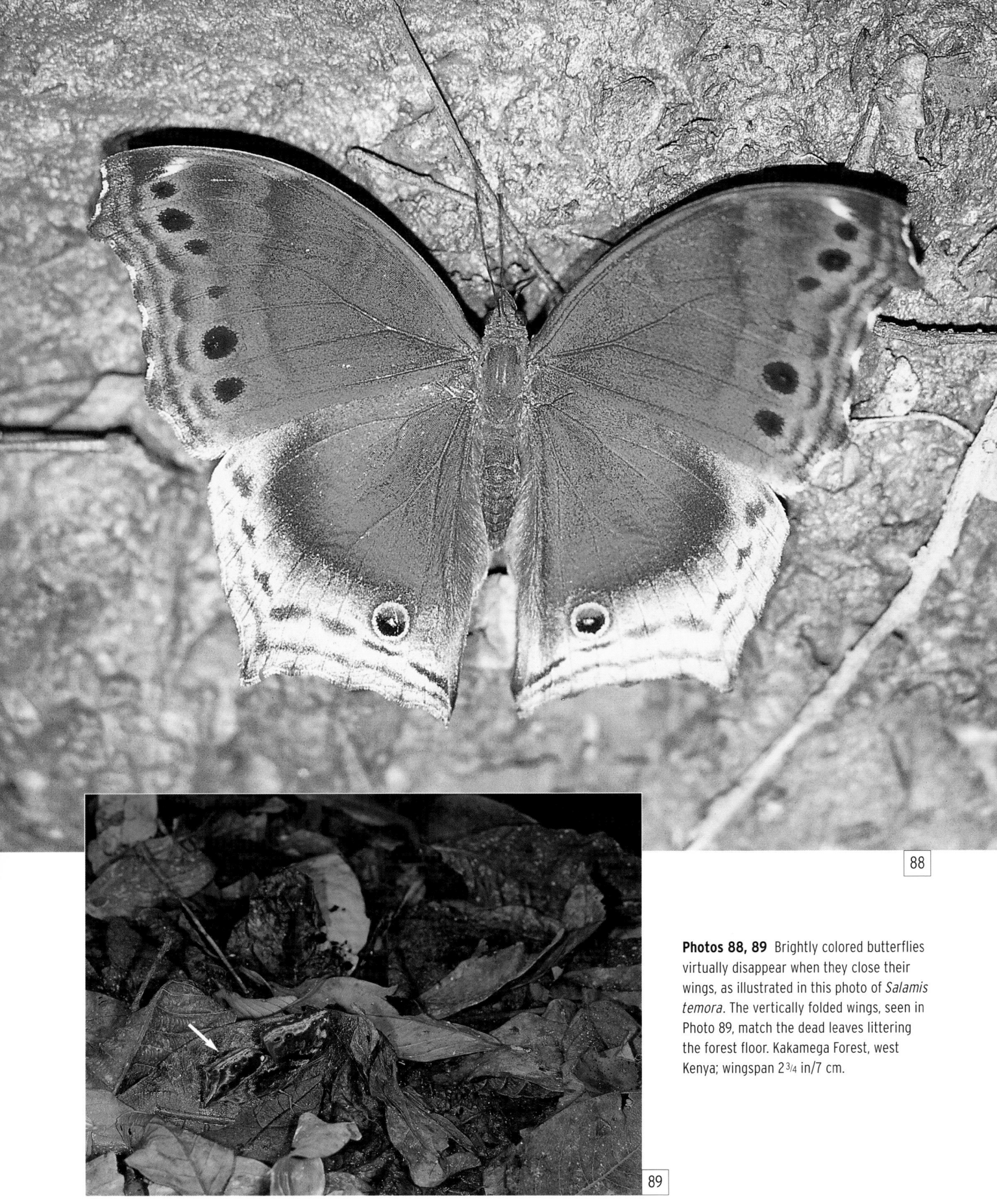

Photos 88, 89 Brightly colored butterflies virtually disappear when they close their wings, as illustrated in this photo of *Salamis temora*. The vertically folded wings, seen in Photo 89, match the dead leaves littering the forest floor. Kakamega Forest, west Kenya; wingspan 2 3/4 in/7 cm.

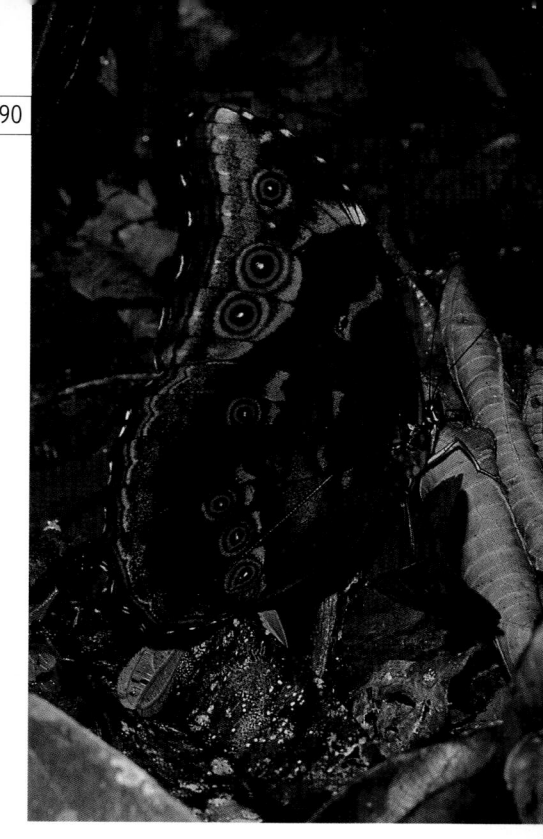

VANISHING BUTTERFLIES

The upper surfaces of butterflies' wings often are brightly colored, which is the antithesis of camouflage. However, even butterflies require protection from predators. Those that inhabit forested regions often are remarkably well camouflaged, thanks to the lower surfaces of their wings, which normally are grey or brown in color. These surfaces match the dead vegetation of the forest floor on which the insect seeks fallen fruit. These insects rarely reveal their bright colors while feeding and, on several occasions, I have walked on them quite unintentionally.

Photos 90, 91 *Morpho* butterflies are a characteristic element of the American tropics, where their bright metallic-blue wings (Photo 91) flash through the dimly lit forests. However, when they settle on the forest floor to feed on rotting fruit, they virtually disappear, as clearly shown in Photo 90 of *Morpho didius*. The brown color and subtle shading blend well with the jungle litter of the Peruvian Amazon. By contrast, Photo 91 shows the metallic-blue colors of the upper surfaces of the wings of *Morpho achilles*. Upper Palcazu Valley, central Peru; wingspan 6 ¼ in/16 cm.

91

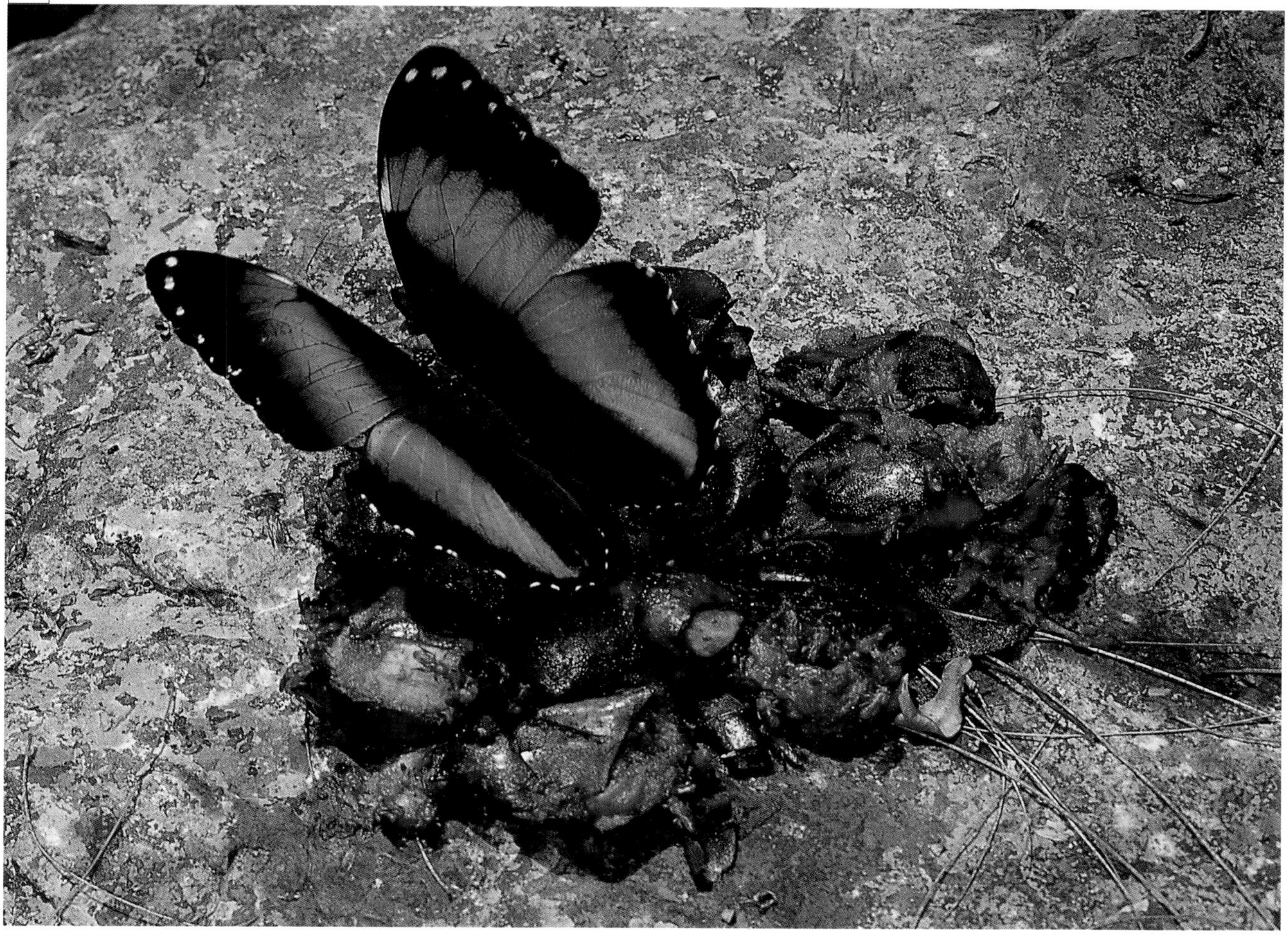

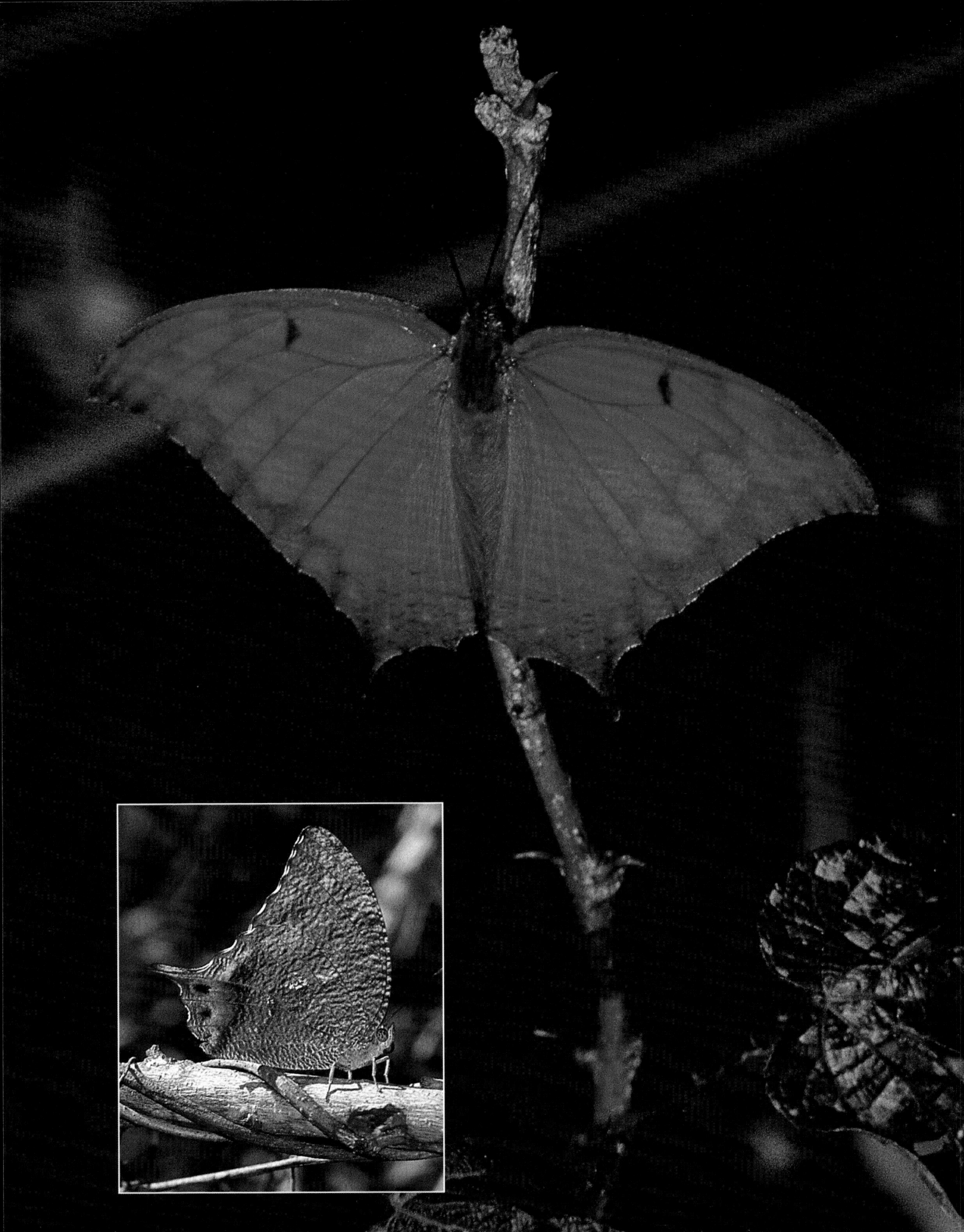

Butterflies may or may not be camouflaged depending on their habits. There are three major groups. The first consists of brightly colored butterflies that fly much of the day, pierids being good examples. Because they are constantly on the move they have little need for camouflage. This group also includes butterflies that are protected by other means, notably their noxious body fluids. The second group comprises brightly colored butterflies that spend part of the day settled, either on vegetation or on the ground, where they may feed on fermented fruit or mineral-rich soil waters. When settled they require protection and therefore their wings, when closed, often merge with their immediate surroundings. This group includes many of the forest-dwelling morphos (Photo 90, 91).

The third group of butterflies spend nearly all their time sitting on the forest floor or on low vegetation, from which they occasionally flit a very short distance. Because they are usually immobile insects, they have much in common with moths; their wings are generally brown or transparent and thus blend very effectively with dead leaves and other forest detritus. This group is composed of forest satyrids, nymphalids and ithomiids.

Hunting these butterflies in dense forest is very hard work, for not only are they very difficult to see but they are very timid creatures; on the slightest pretex they flit away through the forest shadows.

GYMNASTIC MOTHS

Moths are masters of disguise. In order to escape detection they may adopt various ruses including simple cryptic camouflage, modifications of their shapes to better conform with that of their substrate, or even unmoth-like positions such as those seen in Photos 94, 95, 97 and 98. Instead of flat-

Photos 92, 93 (opposite page) The small remnants of dry forest located near the northwest coast of Haiti contain a moderately rich butterfly fauna. A brightly colored *Anaea* butterfly (Nymphalidae, large photo) has settled on dry vegetation (inset) where its folded wings blend effectively with adjacent detritus; Bombardopolis, Haiti; wingspan 2½ in/6 cm.

Photos 94, 95 Many moths seem to change shape when they settle. These moths (Hepialidae) are suspended by their front legs, adopting an unmoth-like position, in which they resemble dead leaves. Both were photographed during the day: Photo 94 in the lower Urubamba Valley, Peru; length 1¼ in/3 cm; Photo 95 near Turrialba, Costa Rica; length 2½ in/6 cm.

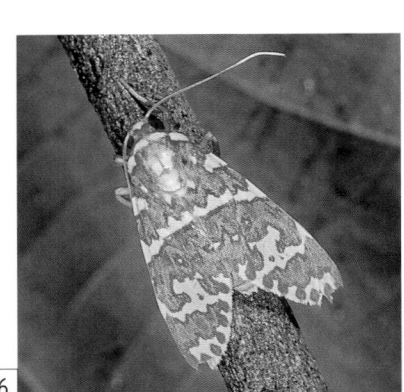

96

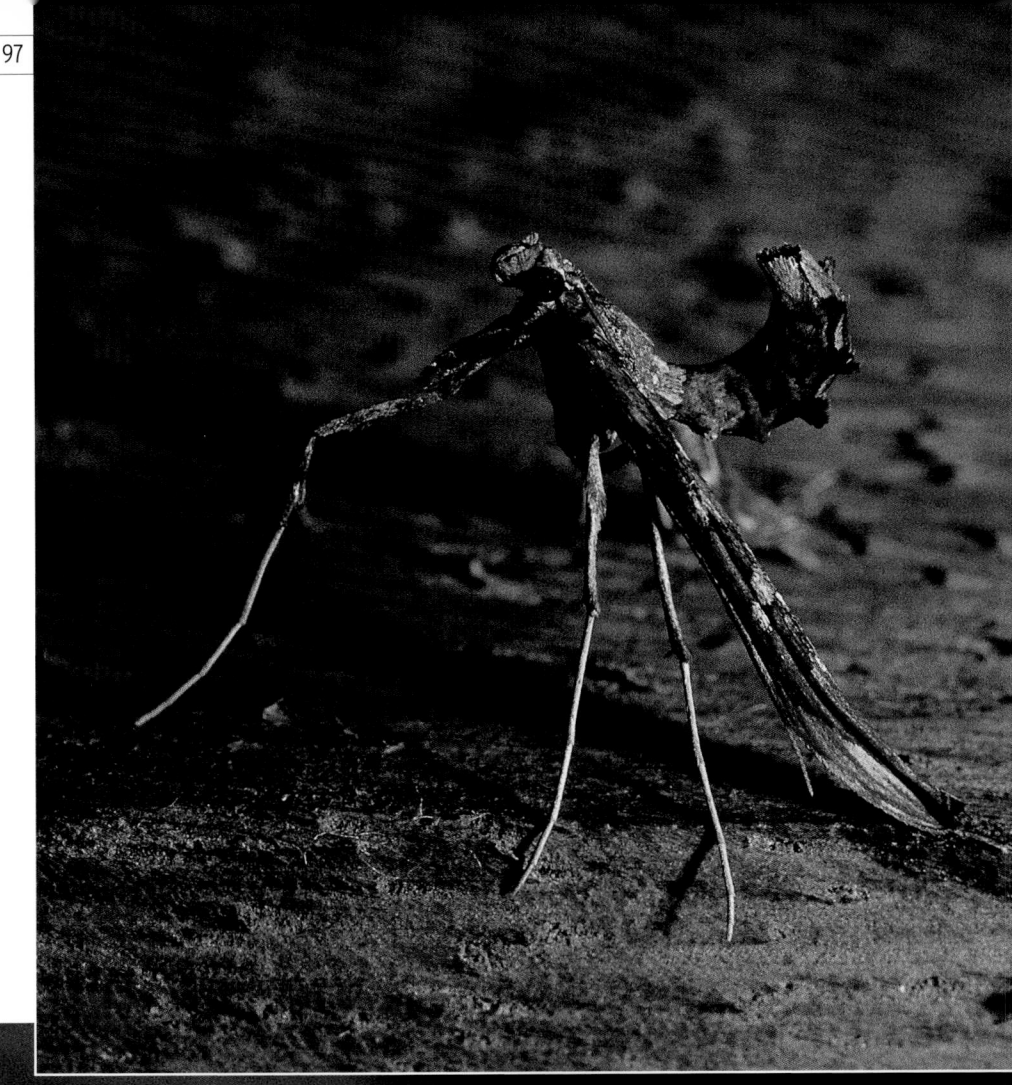

Photos 96, 97, 98 By adopting an unusual stance, these small moths may confuse their predators. In each photo the moth has lifted its abdomen and depressed its elongate wings, thus achieving a very irregular shape. Although quite visible in these photos, when settled among forest detritus both these insects would be very difficult to locate. Photo 97, Dja Valley, Cameroon; Photo 98, Peruvian Amazon; both moths about 5/8 in/1.5 cm. Photo 96: A small arctid moth photographed in the Kaw Hills, French Guyana. Length 3/4 in/2 cm.

98

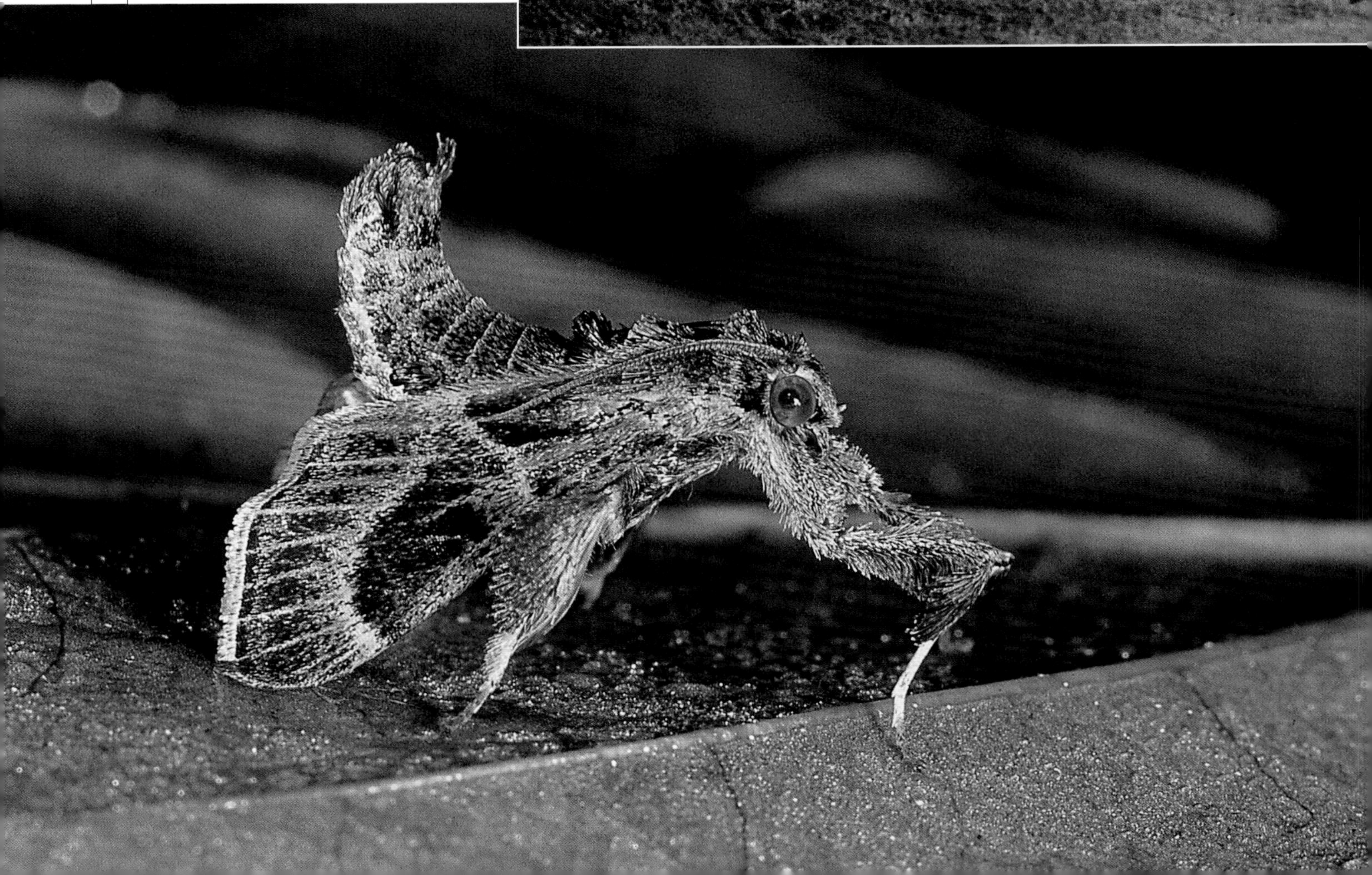

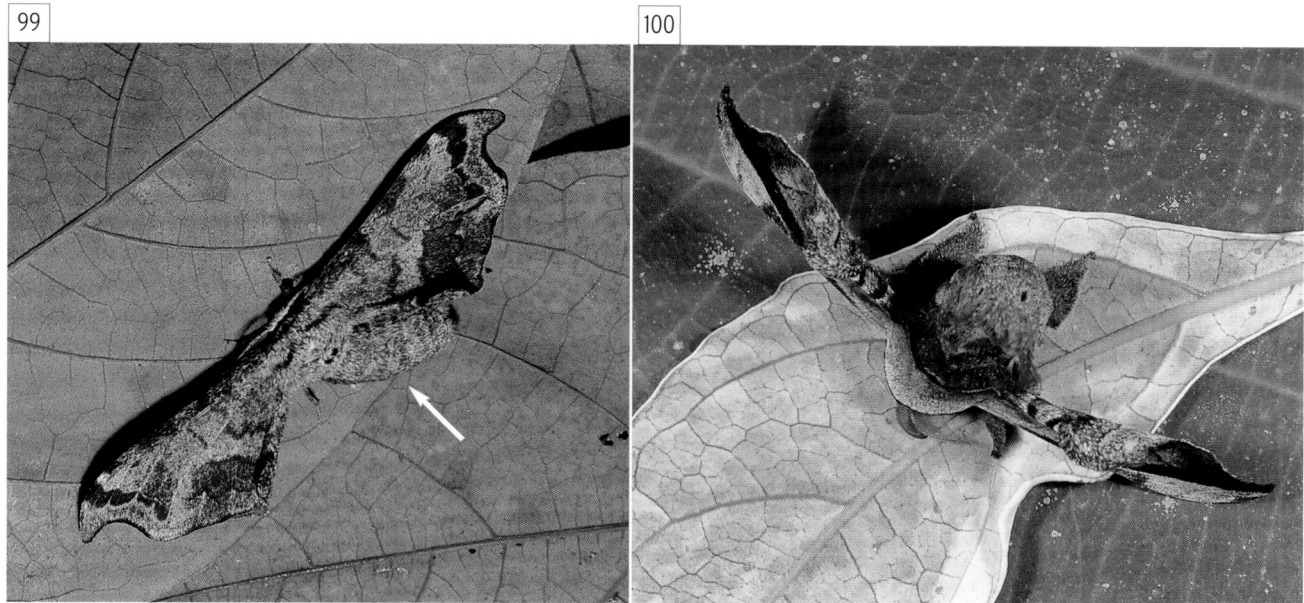

tening itself against its support, the moth may hang from its legs, elevate itself on its legs, or arrange its body at an unusual angle. The result of these unusual gymnastics is that the moth tends to loose its normal identity and thus may confuse potential predators.

Moths in prepared collections have unnatural post-mortem attitudes that bear little resemblance to their living forms. While, indeed, many assume classical moth-like positions (Photo 96), others will adopt very unusual poses, which differ markedly from dead specimens, as seen in these photos. By adopting these unusual position, the moths are actively seeking efficient camouflage. To emphasize the originality of this form of camouflage I have called the phenomenon *gymnasty*.

These unusual postures are most easily observed at night using a strong (250 watt), mercury-vapor lamp, but under truly natural conditions, when these same moths are sitting quietly on tree trunks or forest litter, their presence is rarely noticed.

As already noted, moths may adopt seemingly unnatural positions when at rest. Although difficult to interpret, these gymnastic attitudes seem to be a response to predatorial menace by escaping attention. These positions comprise two distinct styles.

The first, as illustrated in Photos 97 through 100, involves unusual body or wing positions that modify the insect's identiy quite considerably but do not resemble any specific element of its immediate environment (such as a dead leaf or twig). These gymnastic contortions change the identity of the owner and may confuse an aggressor. The positions seem unnatural, such as the erection of the abdomen into a vertical position,

Photos 99, 100 By orienting their wings or bodies in an unexpected direction, moths tend to lose their identity when settled. In Photo 99, taken in the Peruvian Amazon, the body of the moth (Cossidae) (arrow) is skewed to the right and as a result the insect loses its natural symmetry. Wingspans, both moths, 2 in/5 cm.

In Photo 100, photographed in central Malaysia, the entire body of this moth (Cossidae) is oriented upwards. In other words, the insect is standing on its head! It has thus assumed a very unmoth-like position that could blend well with dry vegetation.

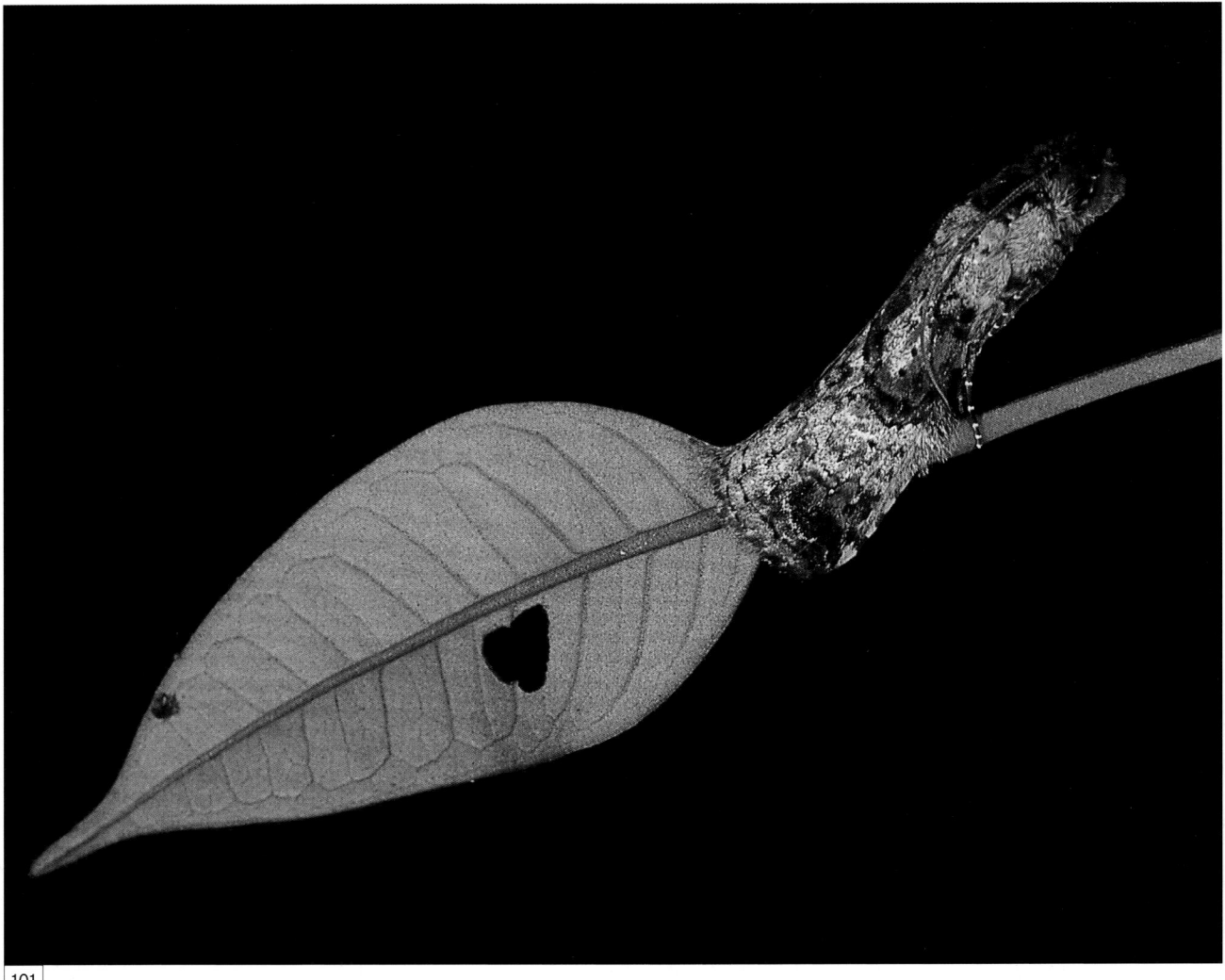

101

Photos 101, 102, 103 By orienting their wings or bodies in an unexpected direction, moths change their identities and resemble fragments of vegetation.

In Photo 101, taken in the Peruvian Amazon, the moth is oriented obliquely with respect to the branch on which it rests; it thus resembles a broken stick. Length 1¼ in/3 cm.

In Photo 102 (opposite), the moth is suspended head down by its hind legs. It may possibly resemble a dead leaf, but certainly not a living moth. French Guyana; length 1¼ in/3 cm.

In Photo 103 (opposite), the moth's entire body is oriented upwards. In effect, the insect is standing on its head! Central Malaysia; length 2 in/5 cm.

which makes the moth appear to stand on its head (Photo 100). The second style, illustrated in Photos 101, 102 and 103, also involves insect acrobatics. Certain moths will hang head-downwards and thus resemble a dead leaf, others will orient their wings and bodies obliquely to the twig on which they rest and thereby resemble a branch. These maneuvers are clearly an active form of camouflage.

As noted on the previous pages, moths exhibit many gymnastic tendencies in an attempt to camouflage themselves. When they position their wings and bodies at most unusual angles they no longer resemble insects but look like dead leaves and other forest detritus. Others simply hang from their hind-legs, rather like miniature monkeys. In natural surroundings they resemble hanging leaves, but certainly not moths. However, these very unusual antics are rarely observed under natural conditions within the forest. They have been discovered through repeated use of strong lamps suspended at different heights within the forest. These lamps attract great quantities of moths and other insects, which settle on adjacent vegetation.

The different positions adopted by certain moths tend to be characteristic of specific families. For example, the moth (Cossidae) that stands on its head (Photo 100) is seen to perform these same acrobatics in Malaysia and in tropical America.

Many insects have evolved complex systems of defense. One particular family of moth (Cossidae), (Photos 99, 100 and 106), common both in Asia and in South America, has colors that blend readily with dead leaves. But, in addition to this cryptic camouflage, these moths roll up their wings to attain an even closer resemblance to dry vegetation. Furthermore, they distort their bodies into strange positions thus completely modifying their original identity. However, this multiplicity of techniques does not seem to have generated an overwhelming success, for the moth, although widespread, never seems to occur in great numbers.

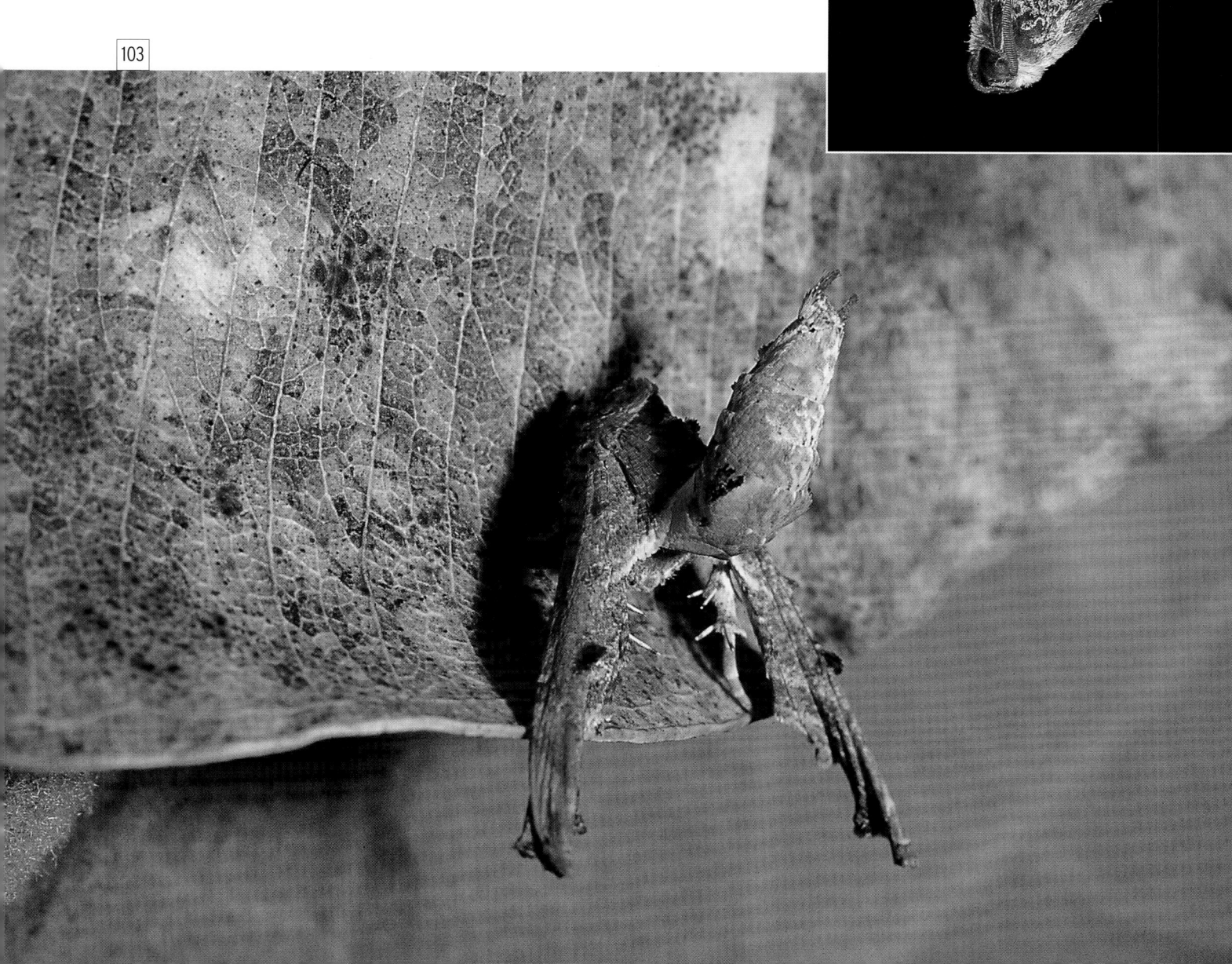

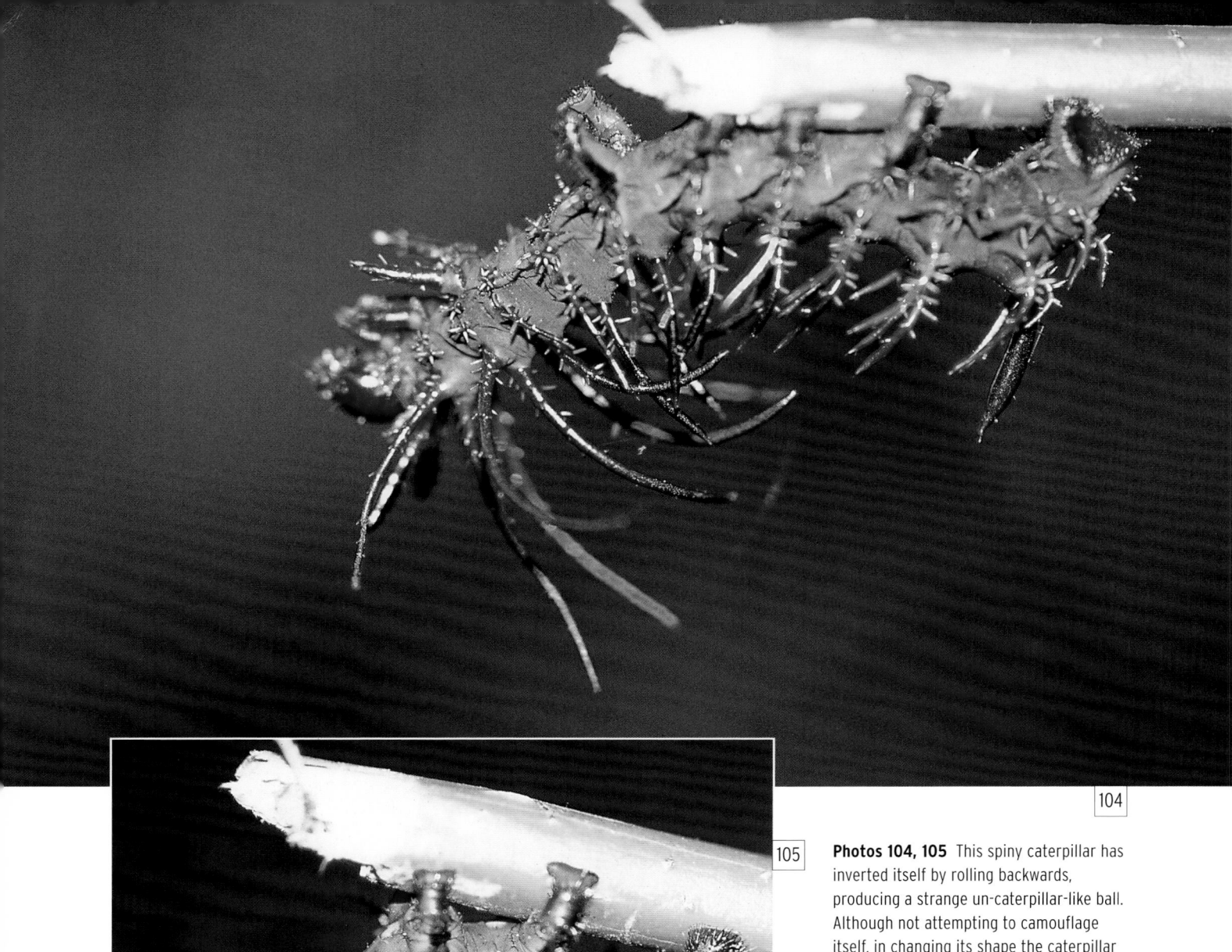

104

105

Photos 104, 105 This spiny caterpillar has inverted itself by rolling backwards, producing a strange un-caterpillar-like ball. Although not attempting to camouflage itself, in changing its shape the caterpillar may render identification by predators more difficult. Its red coloration suggests that it may be noxious — a second line of defense. Belizon, French Guyana; length 1½ in/4 cm.

CONTORTED CATERPILLARS

Caterpillars can be extremely complicated creatures. Their first line of defense may be camouflage, but failing this some have evolved an impressive system of barbed spines (Photos 104, 105). This same caterpillar, when disturbed, may change shape, rolling itself into a ball. Although the precise aims (if any) of these contortions are unknown, the change of shape does tend to modify the identity of the insect and thus may serve to confuse a predator.

SUMMARY

By examining the examples in this chapter, it is clear that camouflage is more than simple coincidence, for many insects appear to make a deliberate effort to improve their dissimulation, either by physically adapting to their immediate surroundings, or by severely modifying their identity. These adaptations take many forms. The grasshoppers and phasmids have opted for vegetation with which they tend to merge, while butterflies and moths seem to prefer dead leaves, which they may imitate to perfection. The leaf butterflies, found on many continents, invariably orient themselves so that the vein patterns on their wings conform with that of adjacent leaves. Other, often brightly colored butterflies such as morphos, disappear on landing simply by closing their wings, merging with the dead leaves of the forest floor.

Certain moths and caterpillars are masters of disguise, changing their identities by adopting acrobatic positions. Thus, a moth may change into a dead leaf or a broken twig.

These diverse strategies involve an active simulation of surrounding vegetation. As we will see, active deception is taken a step further when the insect tries to mimic the behavior of other insects, and in some cases, vertebrates.

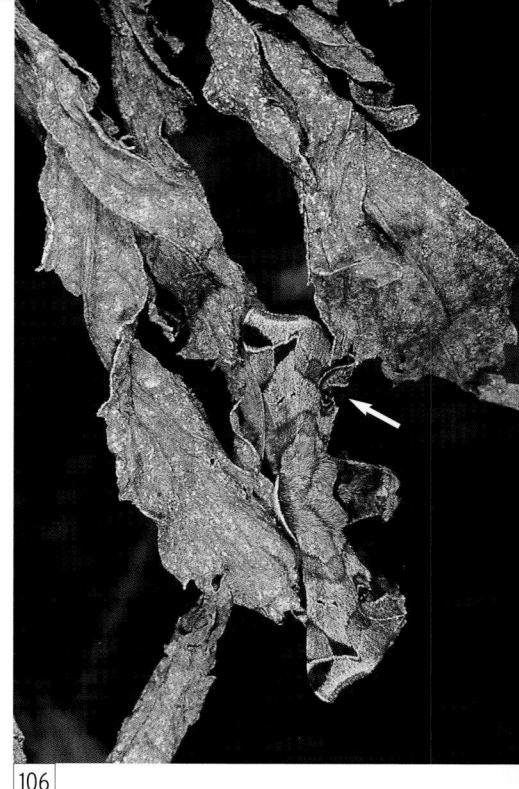

106

Photo 106 Certain moths, when at rest, roll up their wings to become less apparent. This moth (Cossidae) from Venezuela has only its hindwings rolled-up (arrow). With its disruptive coloration, the moth is effectively camouflaged among dead leaves. This particular moth, when I disturbed it, flew about 22 yards (20 meters) before adopting this position. Henri Pittier Reserve, Venezuela; wingspan 2½ in/6 cm.

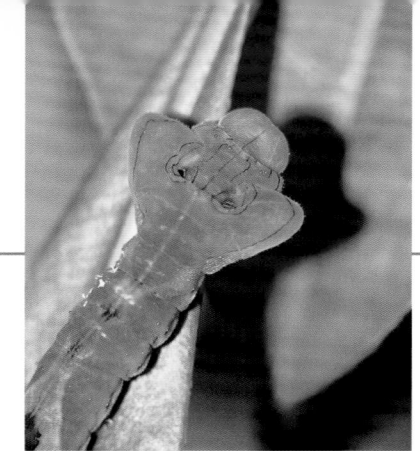

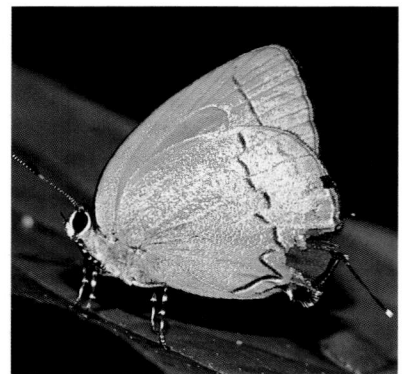

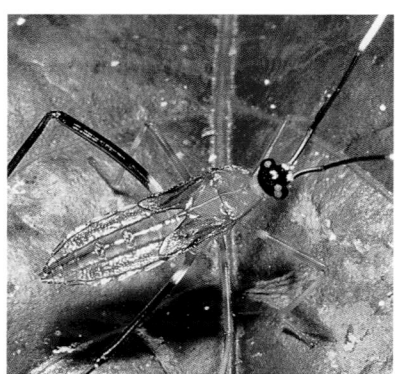

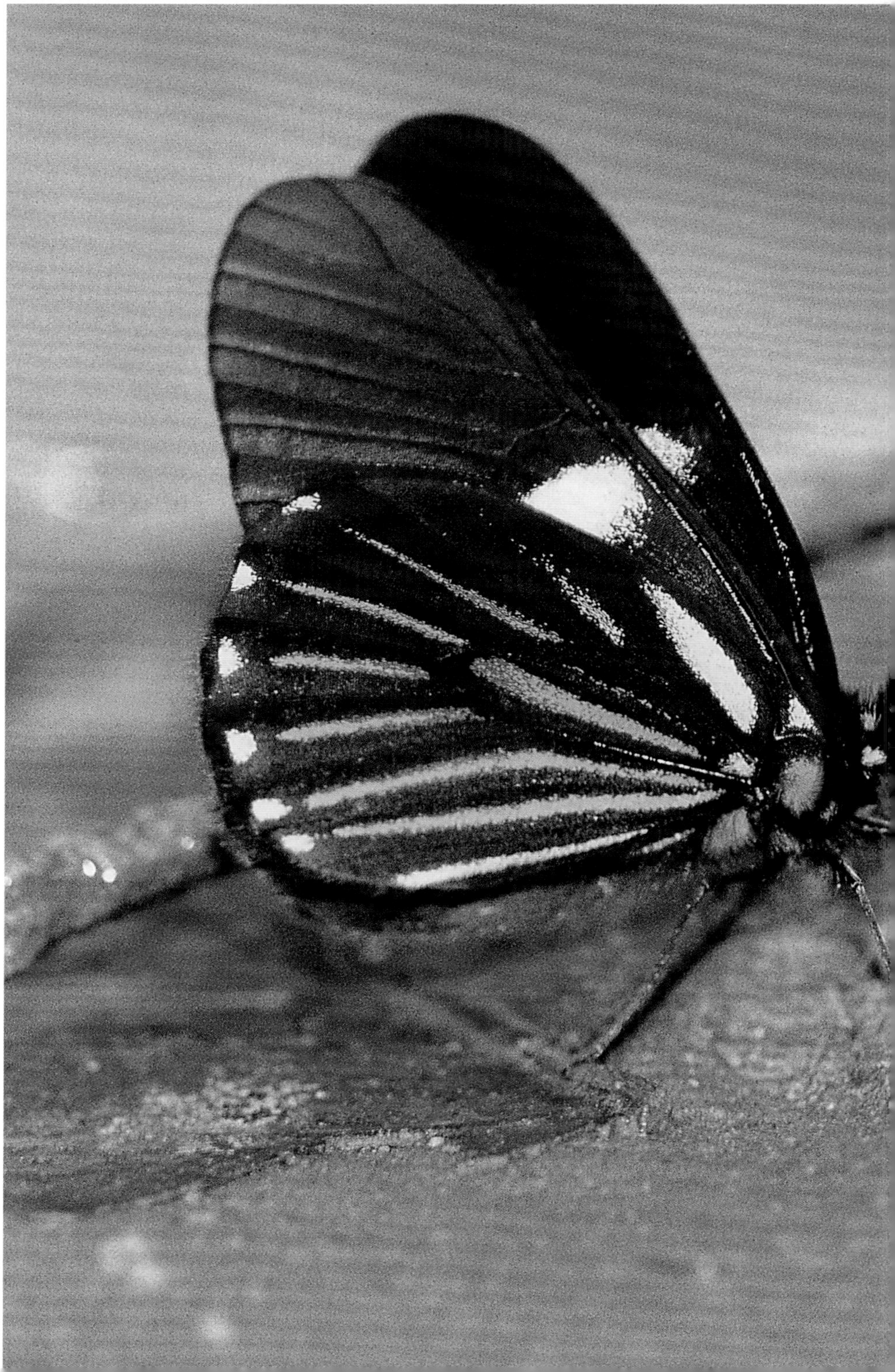

CHAPTER FOUR

Mimicry

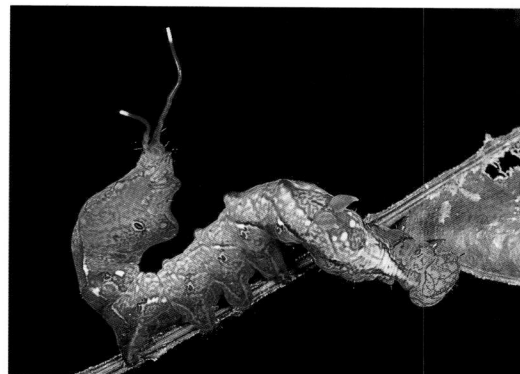

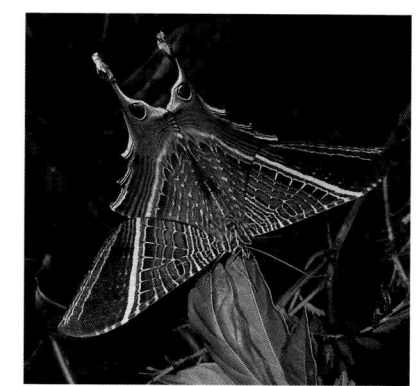

The overwhelming success and survival of the insects is the result of many favorable factors, both structural and behavioral. Their low density, rigid exoskeletons have assured their physical protection, while their great diversity has enabled them to live virtually anywhere and to eat almost anything and, sometimes, everything. Their ability to disappear, which is achieved not only by hiding but also by escaping notice because of their resemblance to natural objects is crucial. Camouflage, in its various forms, saves many insect lives.

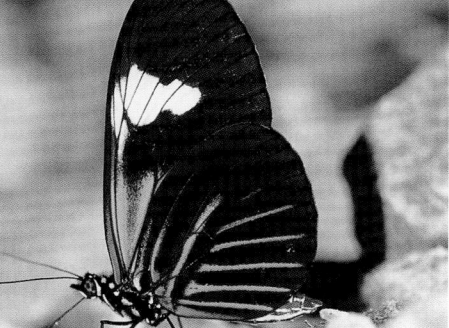

Photos 107, 108 *Heliconus melpomene* (Photo 108) is closely imitated by many unrelated butterflies and moths. This heliconiid is protected against predators by its unpalatable body fluids, while the pierid (Photo 107), which mimics it, is not. Both butterflies may occur together in the Peruvian Amazon; wingspan 2 3/4 in/7 cm, 2 in/5 cm, photos 107 and 108 respectively.

MIMICRY: A VISUAL SUMMARY

1
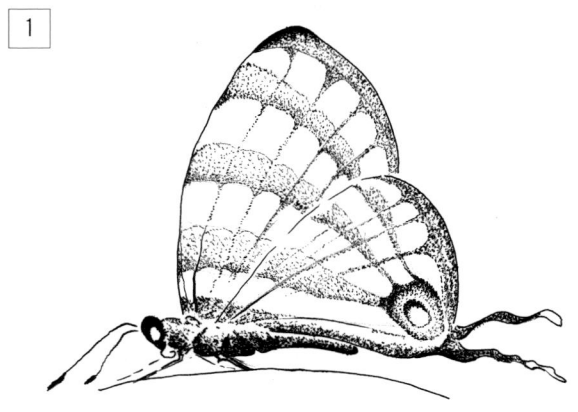

2
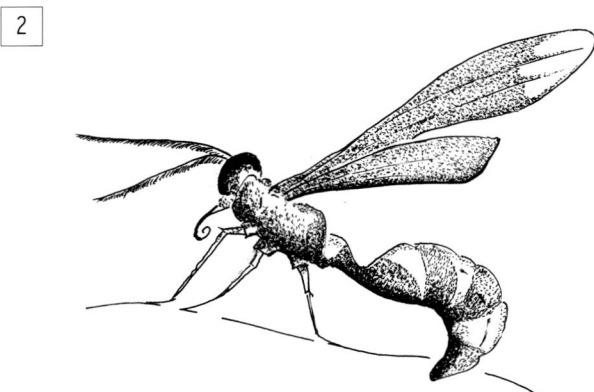

3
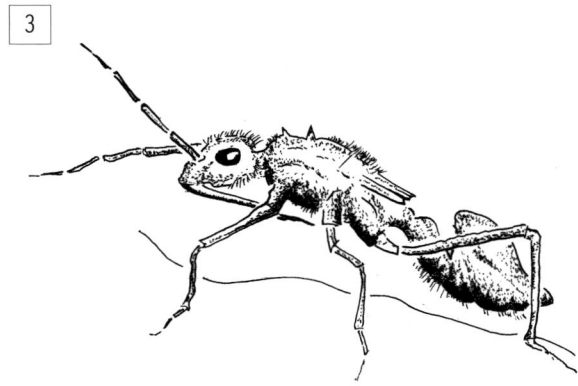

4
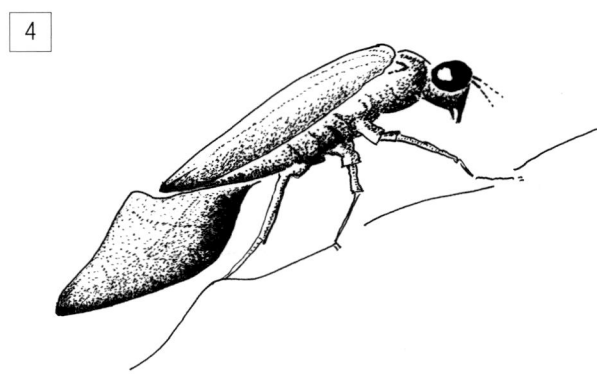

5
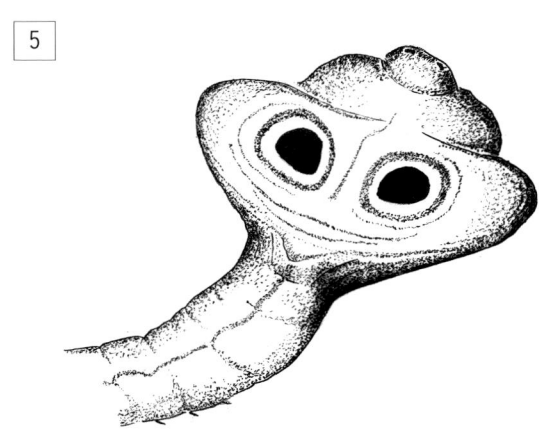

6
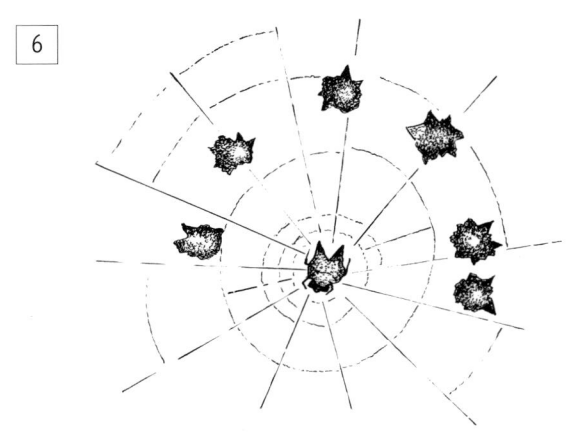

1. *partial mimicry:* a butterfly whose wing pattern includes a false head and antennae (right)
2. *Batesian mimicry:* an unprotected moth resembles a dangerous wasp
3. *Mullerian mimicry:* a dangerous (protected) bug resembles a noxious (protected) ant
4. *Wasmannian mimicry:* a beetle resembles an ant and is thus able to penetrate an ant colony
5. *vertebrate mimicry:* a caterpillar's head resembles the head of a snake
6. *automimicry:* a spider in the center of its web is surrounded by six dummies

Note that the level of complexity rises from relatively simple, #1, to relatively complicated, #6.

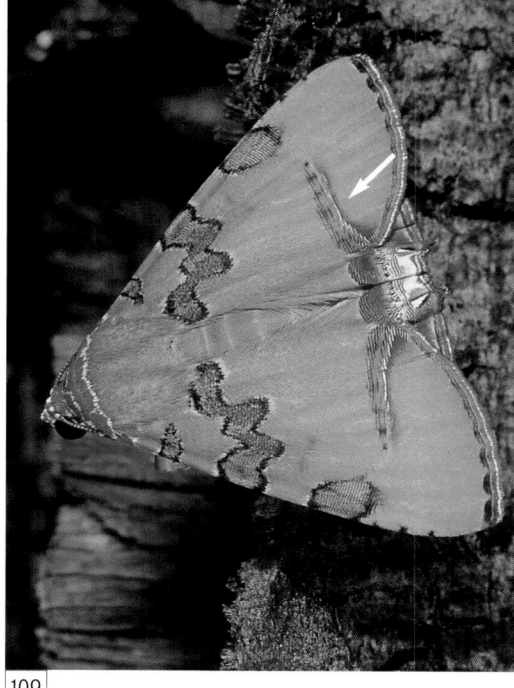

109

This masquerade is carried a step further when an insect, instead of resembling its surroundings through camouflage, actually mimics another insect. A moth may not only resemble a wasp but it will also behave like a wasp, and may even associate with wasps. In tropical forests certain butterflies sport color patterns that are almost identical to those of other, completely unrelated, butterflies (Photos 107 and 108). But the mimic goes even further, for it adopts the habits of its model, in this case the same style of flight. Furthermore, mimic and model are often seen flying together. In many instances the similarity between two quite different families of insect is so close that one can hardly escape the conclusion that the phenomenon is deliberate.

This close resemblance between basically different insects was recognised by the great naturalists of the nineteenth century: Henry Bates, Alfred Wallace, Charles Darwin, Fritz Müller and others and their term, "mimicry," was widely accepted.

The reasons why one insect should mimic another were proposed by Bates in 1862 during extensive studies in the Amazon. Bates noted that the model, in all cases, was protected by either a sting or by its noxious body fluids. Thus, the unprotected and edible mimic, by copying an inedible model, discourages potential predators with its disguise.

While camouflage concerns the imitation of leaves, sticks and other immobile objects, mimicry involves the simulation of moving objects such as other insects. Therefore, it is more dynamic than camouflage, where the basic requisite is immobility. Because mimicry involves movement, the mimic is generally very apparent; it does not blend with its immediate surroundings and in this respect is the antithesis of camouflage.

The stimulus for mimicry, as for camouflage, is protection from predators; insects being small, are hunted and eaten by birds, reptiles, frogs and, especially, by other insects. Insects must escape and to do this they have evolved an endless number of strategies.

Major differences emerge when a comparison is made of insects that have opted for camouflage (grasshoppers, phasmids and moths) with insects that have adopted mimicry as a form of protection (certain flies and butterflies). Camouflage has been evolved by certain insects that spend most of their time simply sitting. Therefore, to escape attention, they must imitate things which do not move, such as leaves or sticks. In contrast, insects that protect themselves with mimicry are nearly always on the move and to escape attention they must simulate things that move, such as other insects.

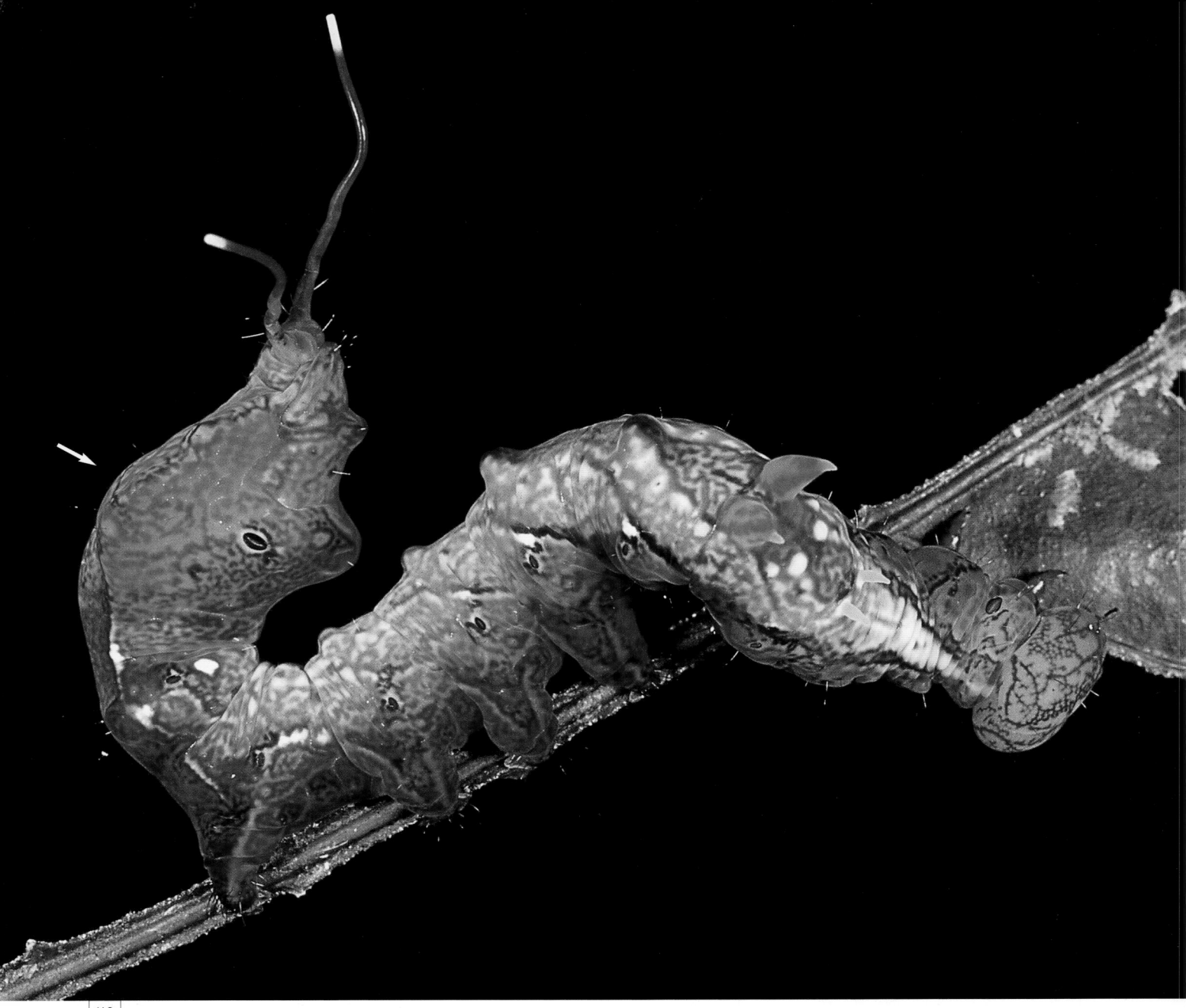

110

Photo 110 This caterpillar is clearly visible on the dark green forest vegetation, its bright colors probably a warning to potential predators of its unsavory taste. This first line of defense is backed up by the development of a false head (arrow), complete with false eyes and antennae. The true head, seen on the right, is less conspicuous. Photographed near Canaima, Venezuela; length 1¼ in/3 cm.

To be effective, mimicry involves the following constraints :

- the mimic must be less abundant than the model;
- mimics and models must have simple, easily identifiable, color patterns;
- mimics and models must inhabit the same region in order that their similarities be appreciated by the predator; and
- models and mimics should have similar behaviors.

It is interesting to note that the phenomenon of mimicry is most frequently developed by the female. This preference for feminine mimicry may favor the propagation of the species.

FALSE HEADS AND EYES

Partial imitation may involve only an extremity of the body, which may be modified to resemble a head. Thus, the caterpillar or butterfly appears to have two heads, one at each end of the body. The authenticity of the false head is often accentuated by its brighter coloration, by the presence of false eyes and antennae and, especially, by a specific behavior. This latter involves a more prominent positioning or erection of the false head and a corresponding lowering of the true head, seen in Photo 110.

The advantage of having two heads may not be immediately apparent and, indeed, the significance of the false head is subject to interpretation. One may suppose that having a second head must offer some advantage to the owner. For example, a predator will often seize its prey by the head. Therefore, having two heads implies that the prey has a 50 percent chance of deceiving the predator and, although perhaps suffering body damage, nevertheless may survive.

Almost without exception, butterflies that frequent the forest floor, have clearly defined circles on the lower surfaces of their wings (Photo 112). When sitting on forest litter with wings closed, the pattern resembles a glaring eye. Its authenticity is increased by the presence of a small central point that closely resembles the eye pupil. These eye-like patterns may help deviate the attention of reptiles and other forest-floor predators.

Photo 111 Which end of the caterpillar is the head? The true head (left) is darker and less apparent than the false (right), whose imitation is enhanced by the false eye and more prominent appearance. Sopong, Thailand; length 1¼ in/3 cm.

111

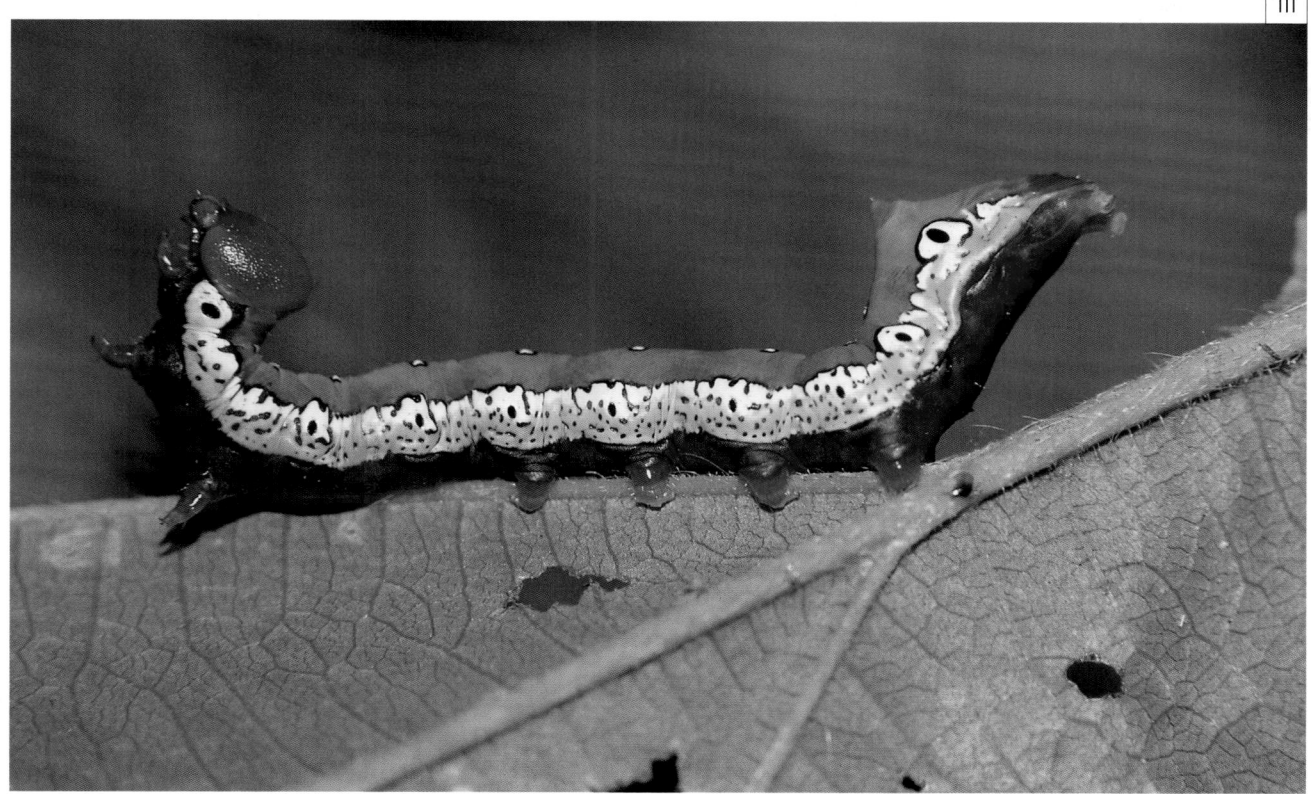

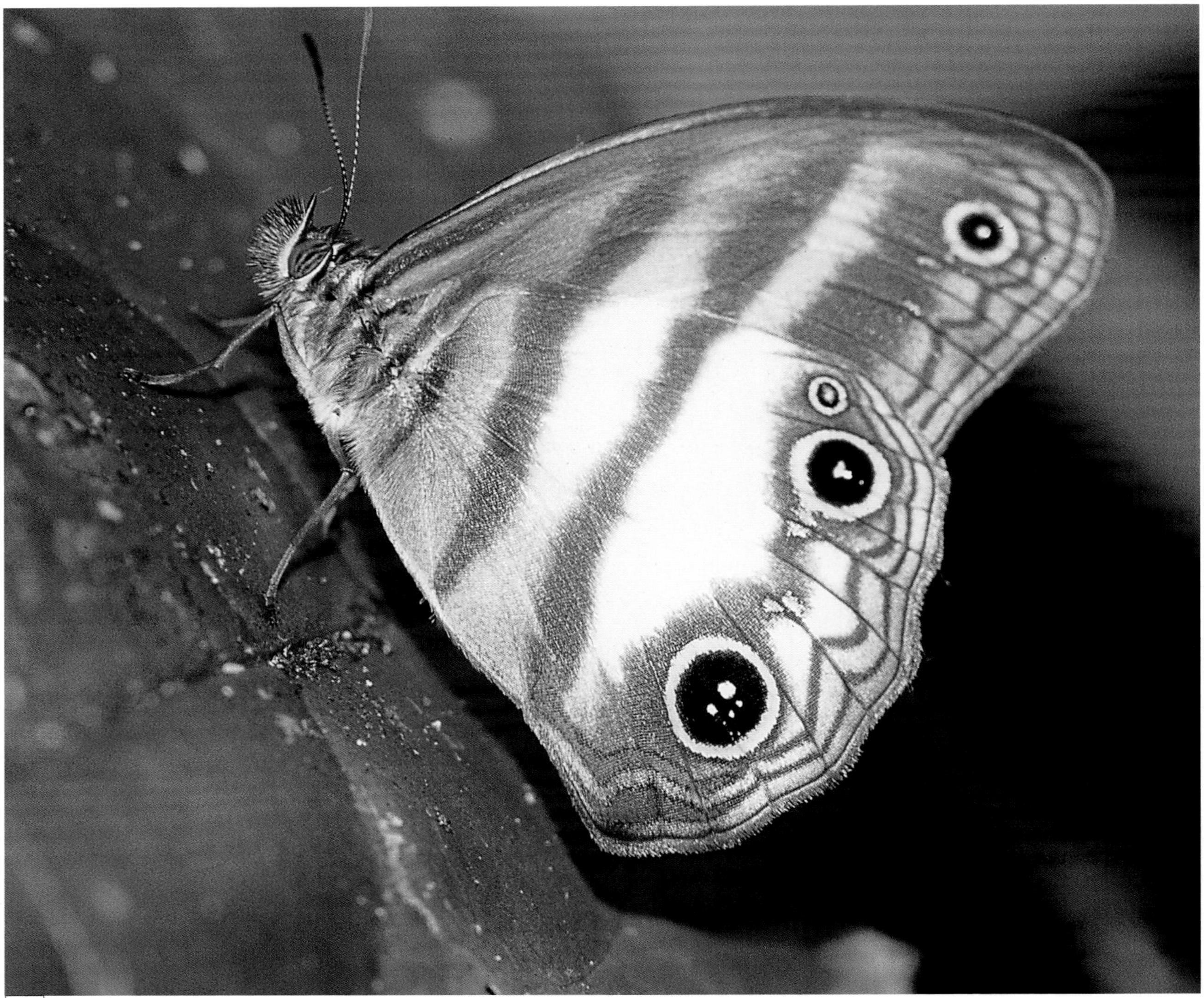

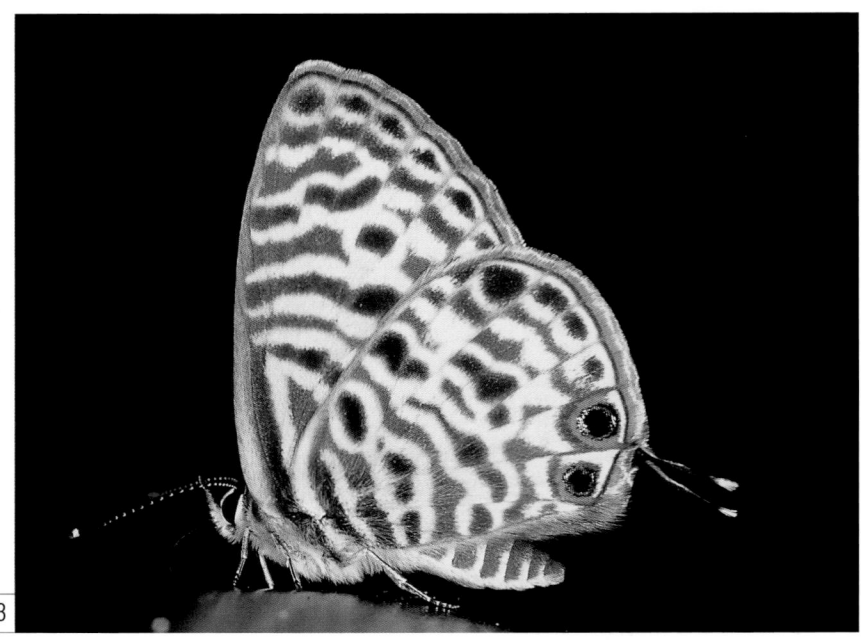

112

Photo 112 A small satyrid butterfly sitting among fallen leaves on the floor of a Guyana forest. The round, eye-like patterns may help to deviate the attention of predators from the more vital parts of its body. Photographed at Creek Voltaire, French Guyana; wing height 1 ¼ in/3 cm.

Photo 113 A small lycaenid butterfly sitting on my humid camera clearly demonstrates the double head effect. The false head (right), with a pair of false eyes and white-tipped antennae, is very convincing and could well mislead a predator. Photographed in the Dja Forest, Cameroon; length ³/₈ in/1 cm.

113

Partial mimicry is not haphazard. In fact, specific types of imitation tend to characterize specific families of insect. For example, a specific family of butterflies, the Lycaenidae, have developed what appear to be quite convincing false heads and eyes, as shown in Photos 113, 114 and 115. These little blue butterflies, whether they are in Europe, Africa or New Zealand, usually have these false heads.

Large saturniid moths (Photos 116, 117), both in Africa and in tropical America, have special patterns on the upper surfaces of their hindwings. These are set on a fairly brightly colored background and consist of a series of concentric rings with a transparent, pupil-like central zone. The pattern closely resembles a large, staring eye. These false eyes are normally covered by the forewings when the moth is at rest. However, when disturbed, the moth adjusts its forewings, suddenly exposing the expressive eye pattern. In other words, the moth makes a deliberate effort to frighten the predator. It may be human imagination that sees these patterns as menacing eyes, but whatever their significance, experiments have shown that they do frighten aggressors.

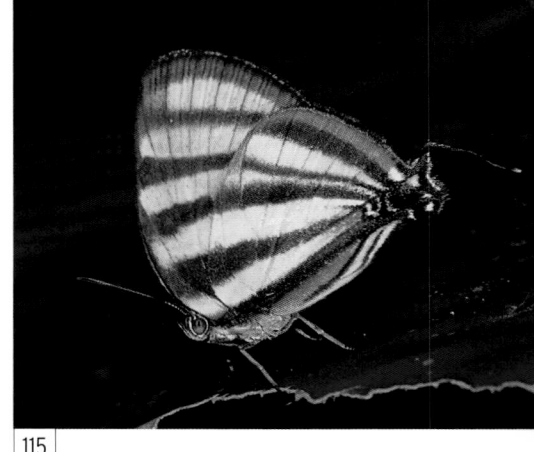

115

Photos 115, 114 Double-headed lycaenid butterflies: In Photo 115 of *Arawacus*, the radiating wing pattern tends to direct one's eyes towards the false head (right). In Photo 114 the false head has been broken, possibly during predatorial attack, which seems to confirm that this system of disguise helps to confuse predators. Photo 115 taken in the Peruvian Amazon, Photo 114 near Saül, in French Guyana; both about 5/8 in/15 mm in height.

114

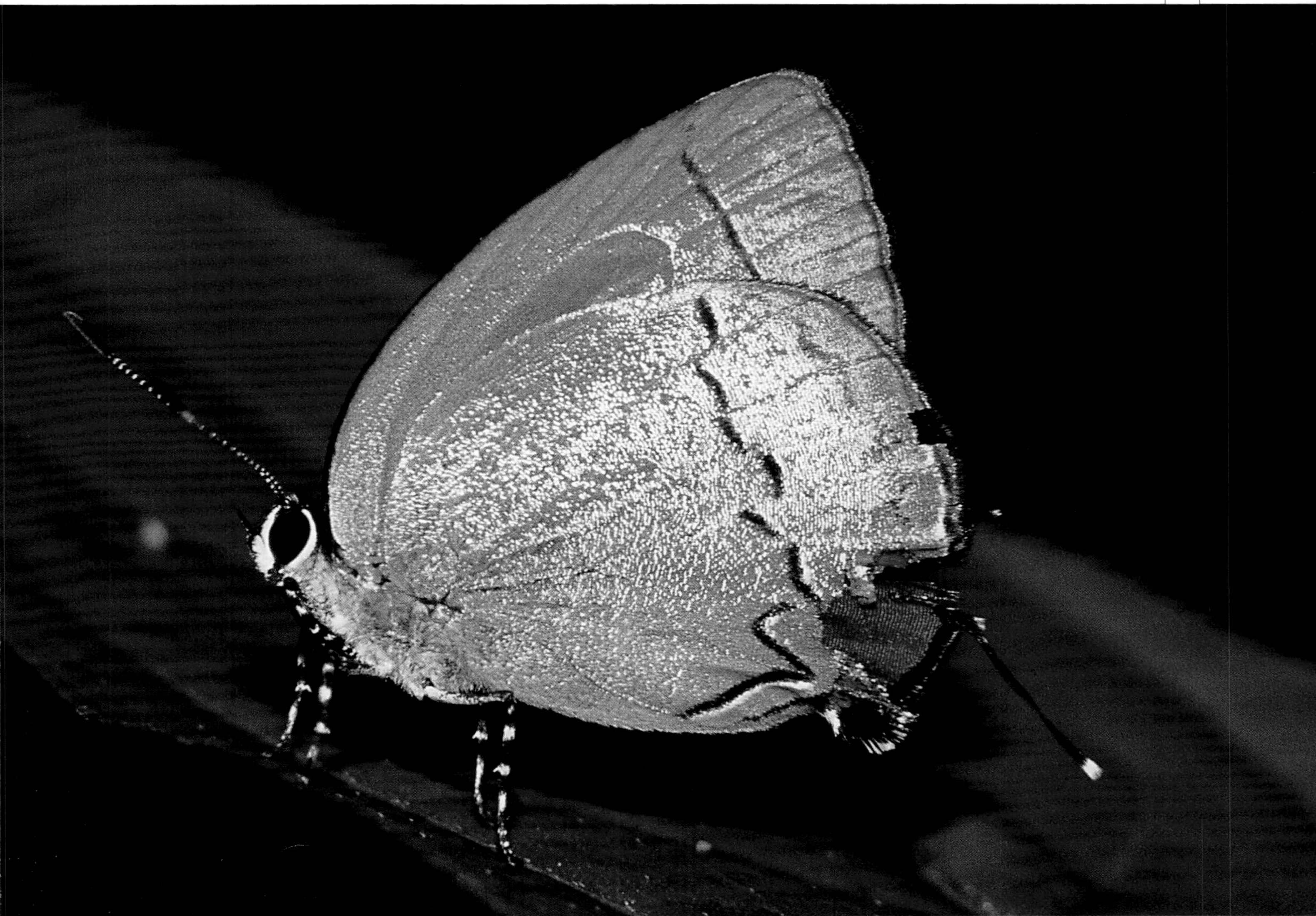

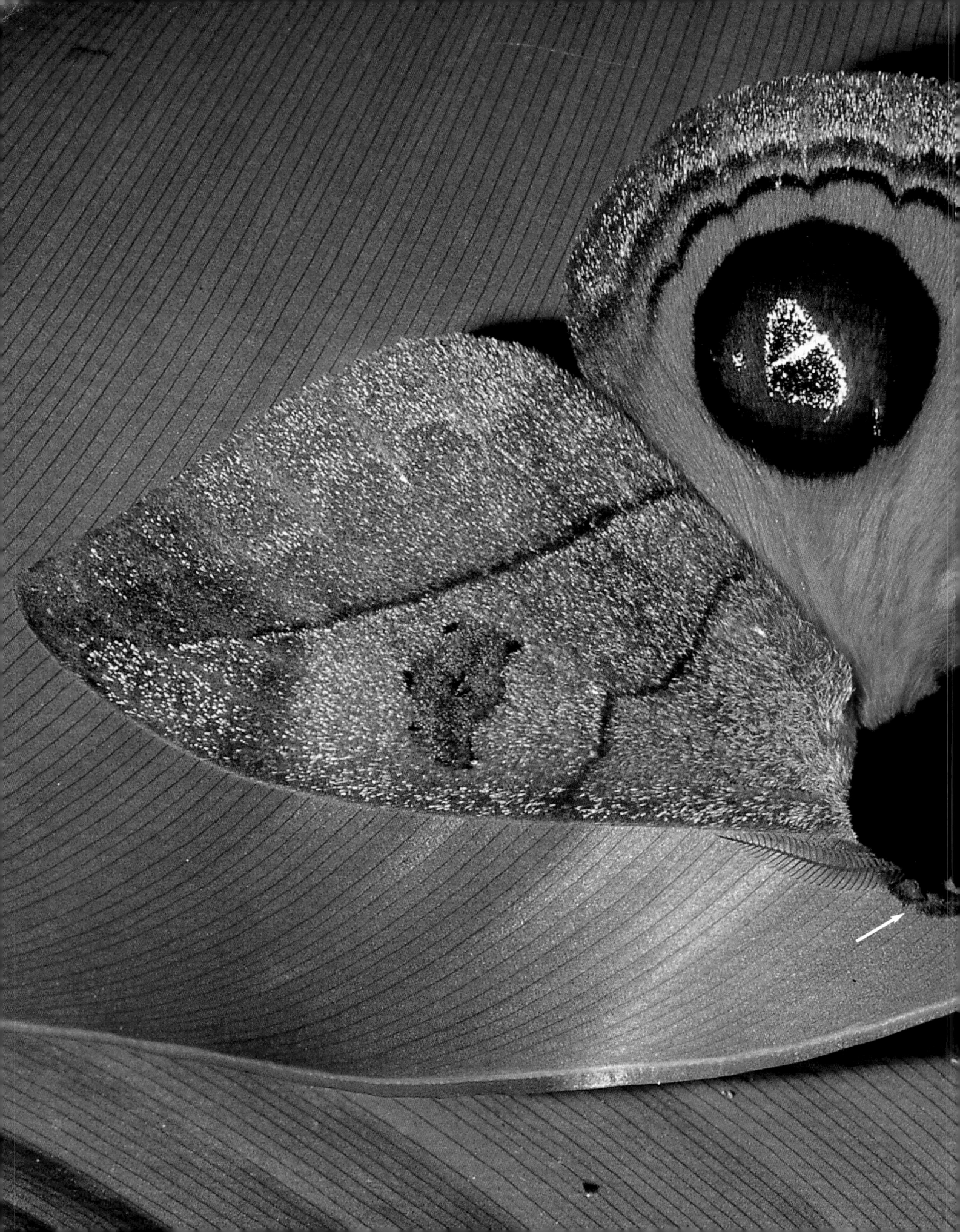

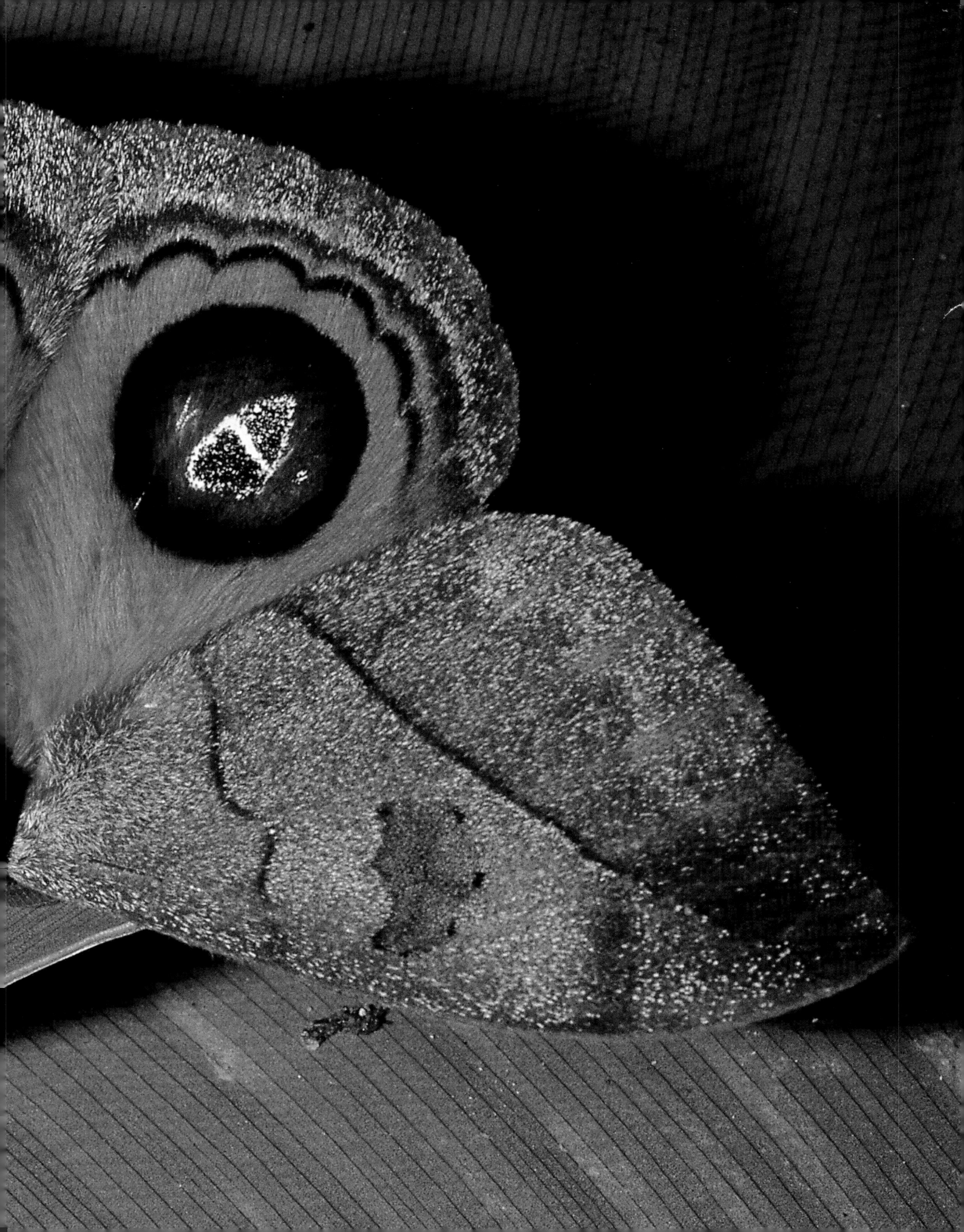

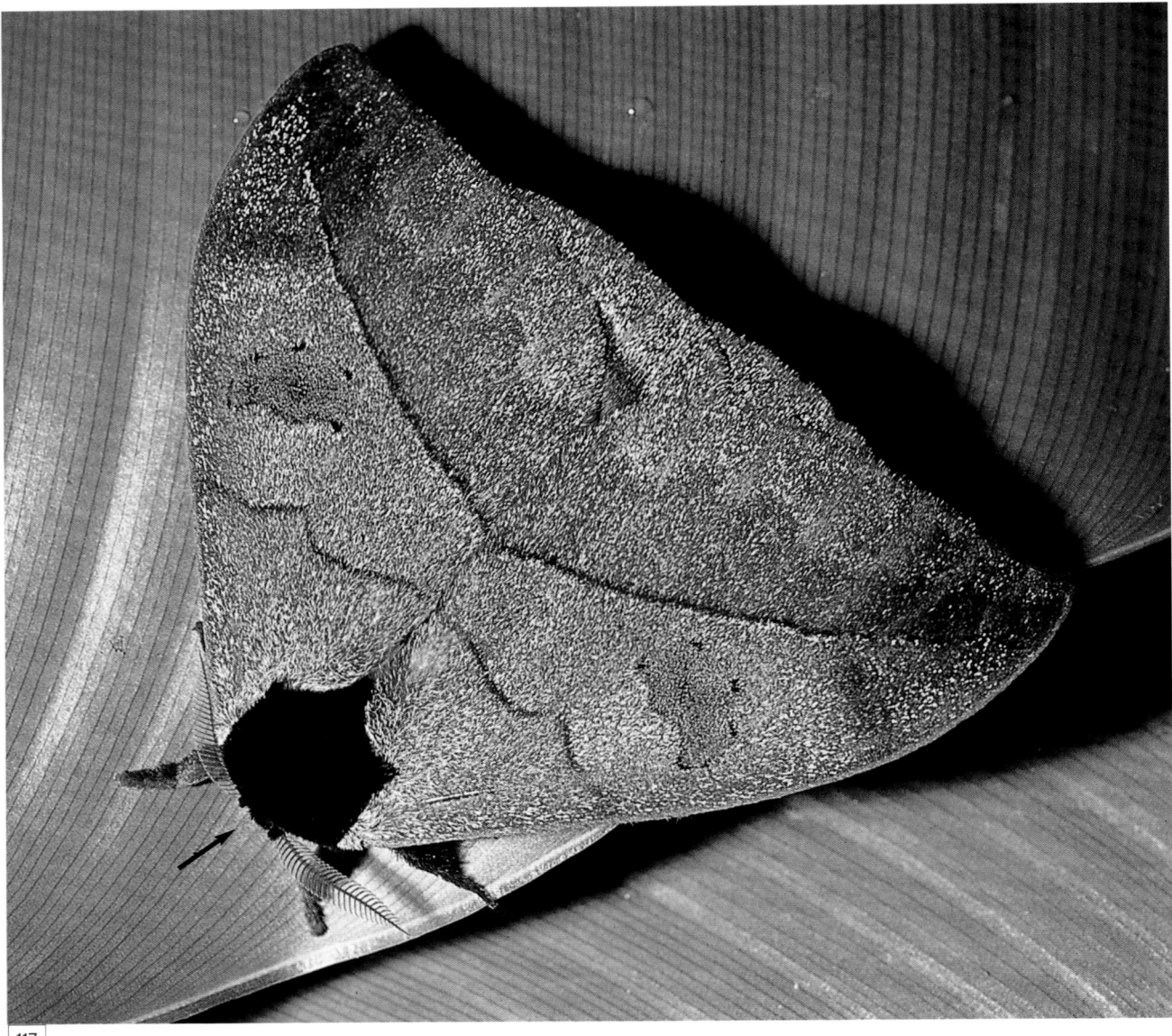

117

Photos 116, 117 The saturniid moth *Automeris*, frequent throughout most of tropical America, appears quite inoffensive when at rest (Photo 117). However, when disturbed (Photo 116, preceding page) *Automeris* advances its forewings, revealing an eye-like pattern on its hindwings. These impressive false eyes are set in a contrasting, orange-colored background. Note that the head and true eyes are situated on the lower edge of the moth (arrows). Peruvian Amazon; wingspan 2 ¾ in/7 cm.

The false eye patterns that decorate the hindwings of certain tropical moths (Photos 116, 117, 118 and 119) are quite remarkable for several reasons. Firstly, they tend to shine, giving a very realistic appearance to the "eye." Secondly, the moth seems to be conscious of these patterns, for it makes a calculated attempt to expose them by deliberately adjusting its forewings. And, finally, these patterns characterize a particular family of moths — the Saturniidae, found both in Africa and in tropical America.

Photos 118, 119 (opposite) The eye-like patterns characteristic of saturniid moths are rendered more realistic by their transparent "pupils" and also by the white circles surrounding the "eye." Photo 118 shows the entire moth, the arrow indicating the true head and eyes. This moth, attracted by a lamp, landed on the ground below it. During the day, however, they hide in trees. Photographed at night in the Dja Forest, Cameroon; wingspan 4 in/10 cm.

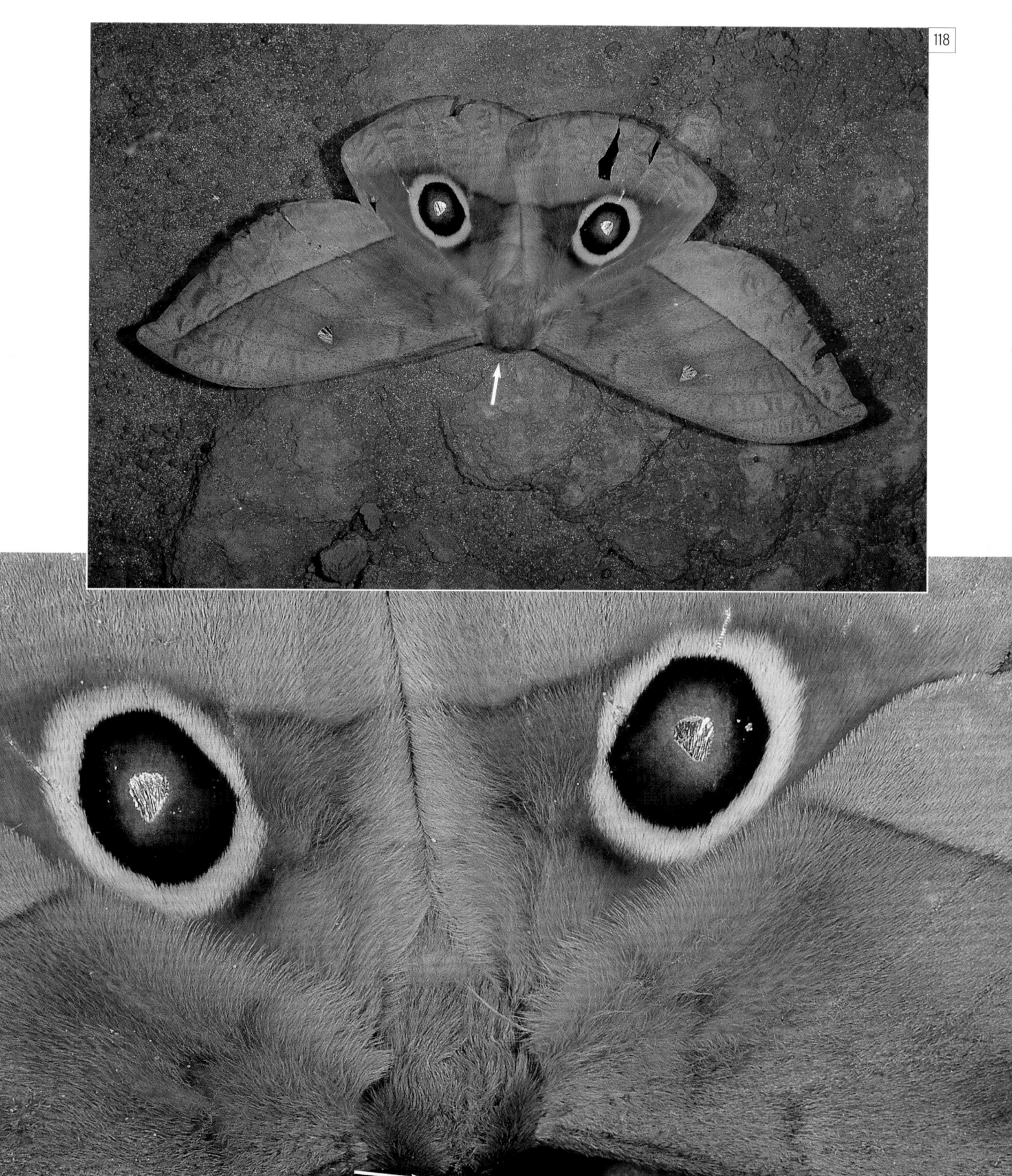

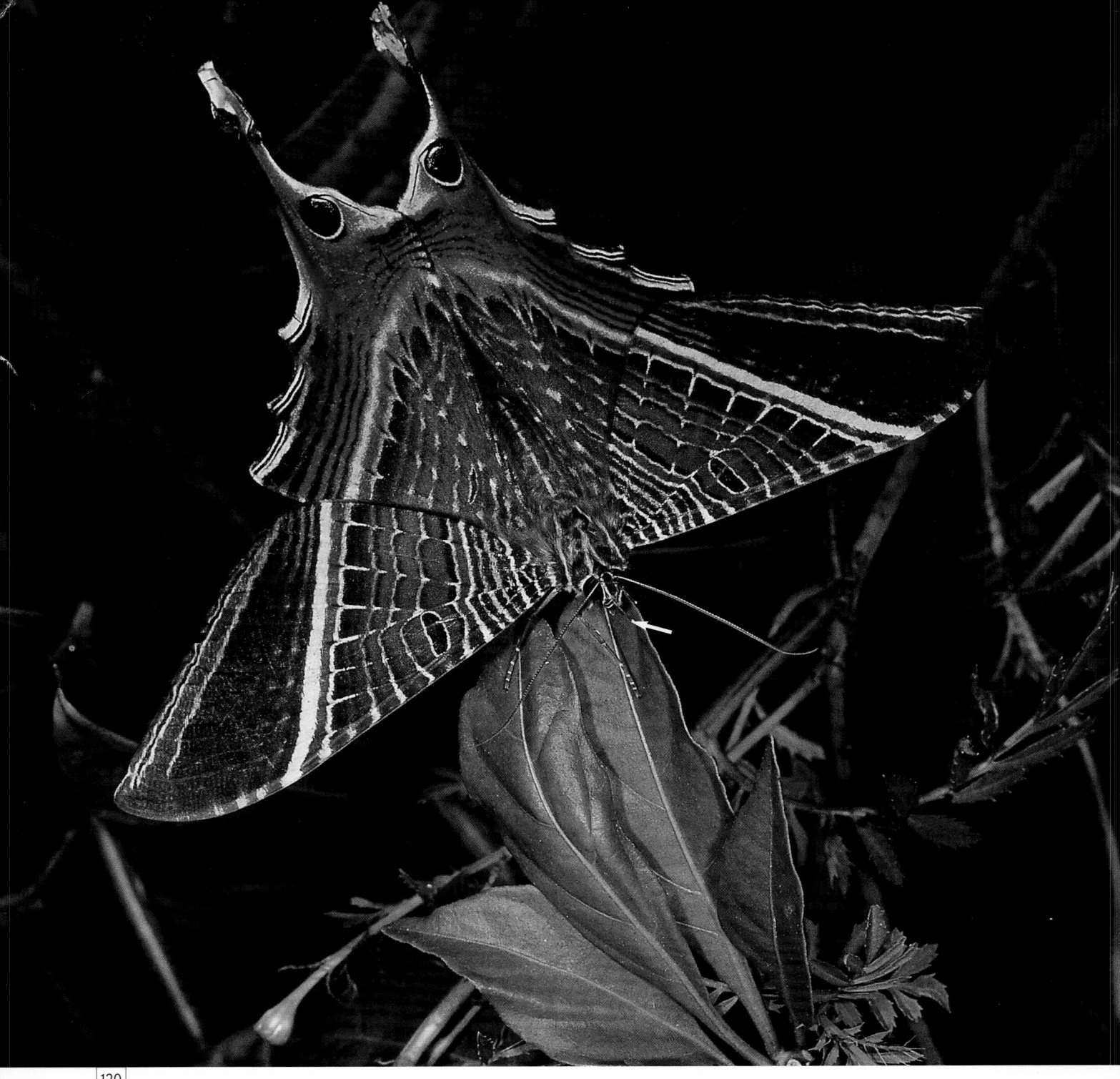

120

Photo 120 This uranid moth *Nothus* is distributed throughout tropical America, where it readily comes to lamps. The spectacular eye-like pattern and "horns" may frighten predators. The true head is situated at the bottom (arrow). French Guyana; wingspan 3¼ in/8 cm.

False eyes may have several purposes. They may frighten potential predators, as shown in the previous photos. Others, such as those carried by the uranid moths (Photo 120) are located at the extremity of the hindwing where, together with a pair of false antennae, they resemble a head. These eyes may deviate the attention of aggressors, preserving the more vital parts of the body.

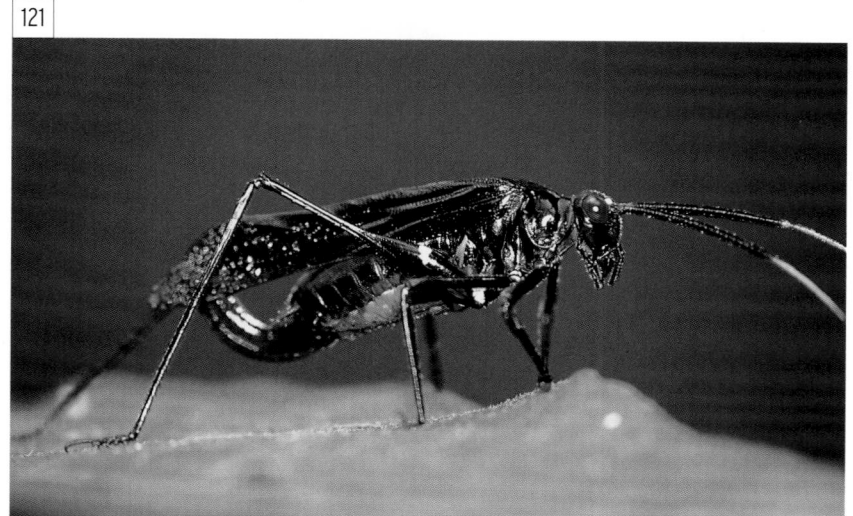

Photo 121 Because they are well protected by painful stings, wasps are mimicked by many forms of insect. In this photo what appears to be a large, metallic-blue wasp, is in fact a harmless katydid grasshoppper, *Scaphura*. This intriguing insect has acquired the habit of flying almost continuously, as does a wasp as well as twitching its antennae in a very wasp-like manner. When I photographed it, I actually mistook it for a wasp! Saül, French Guyana; length 2 in/5 cm.

Photos 122, 123, 124 Probably the most convincing false eyes are those developed by caterpillars of certain sphinx moths (Sphingidae). This photograph, taken on the upper Orinoco in Venezuela, demonstrates the amazing bluff attempted by this green caterpillar. When resting (Photo 122), the caterpillar is pale green in color and there is barely a trace of its false eyes. However, when irritated (Photo 123), its body darkens and a pair of black, eye-like structures appear on the caterpillar's back. This snake-like appearance is further enhanced by the erection of the body and the swelling of its lateral appendages, comparable to those of a cobra. The whole performance is most convincing and would almost certainly intimidate an aggressor. The true head and eyes are indicated by the arrow. Length 2 in/5 cm.

This form of mimicry is not limited to the South American continent. Certain sphinx moth caterpillars both in Madagascar (Photo 124) and Malaysia have developed similar strategies. Again, it would seem that protective mimicry is closely related to family affinity.

BATESIAN MIMICRY

Like camouflage, the manner in which mimicry has been acquired by certain species is usually explained in terms of Darwinian natural selection: certain natural variations (mutations), by pure chance, tend to resemble other *protected* species. These mutants, rather by luck than by design, thus suffer less persecution than the non-mutant stock. Following the wear and tear of many generations, the favored mutant (the mimic) survives in greater numbers than the normal stock, which disappears progressively.

Thus edible insects gain protection by imitating distasteful or poisonous insects. In honor of Henry Bates, who first described the phenomenon, this has been termed *Batesian mimicry*. It may be a relatively simple one-to-one resemblance, such as that between an edible katydid seeking protection, and its model, a dangerous stinging wasp. Not only does the katydid (Photo 121) look like a wasp, but its behavior resembles that of the wasp. For example, a katydid spends most of its

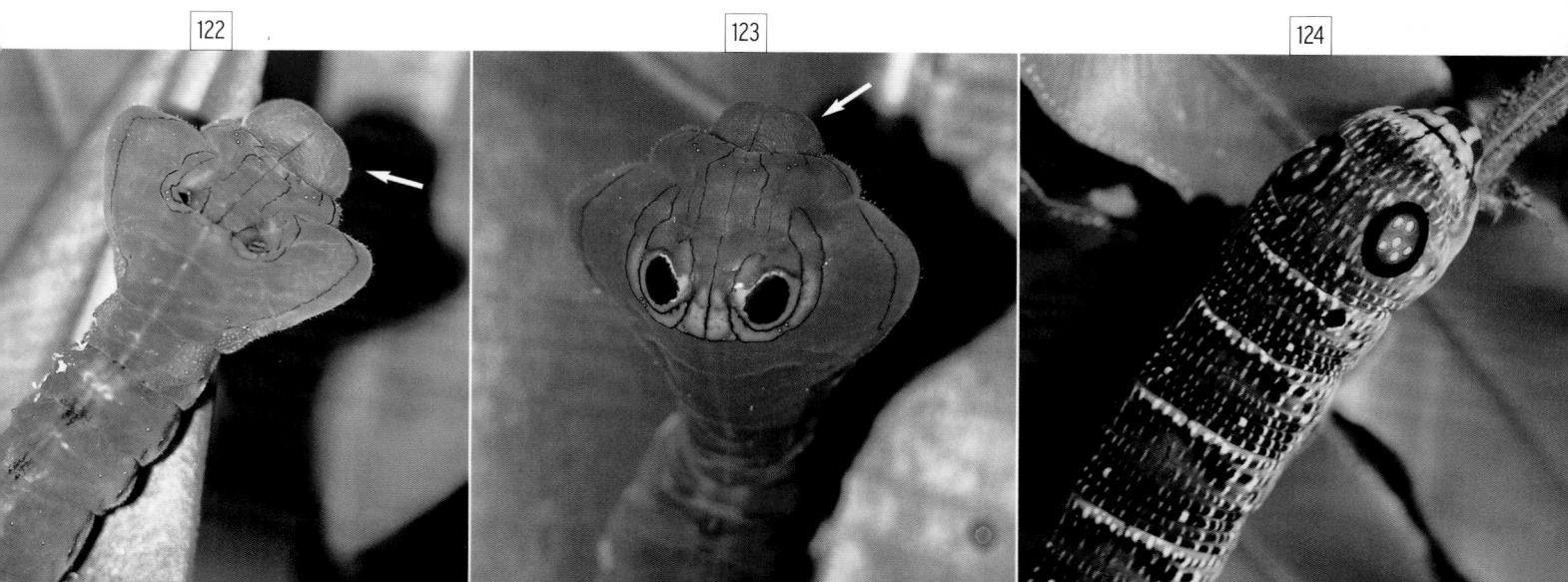

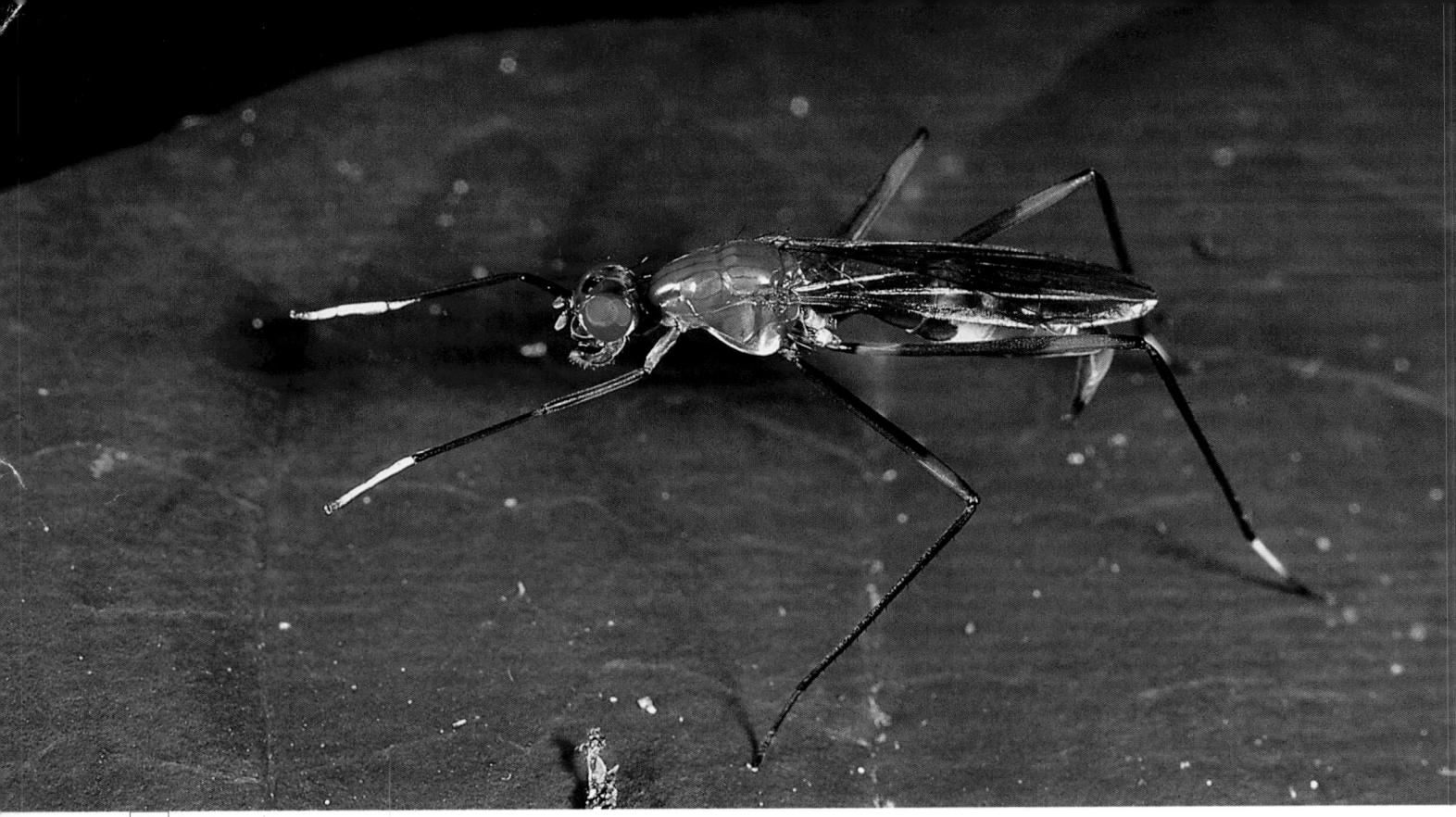

125

Photo 125 This fly, *Mimegralla*, inhabits forests in East and West Africa and appears to imitate a wasp. Its behavior, in particular, is very wasp-like, and involves a hesitant style of walking and a perpetual agitation of what seem to be long, wasp-like antennae. Flies normally have very short antennae. Here the fly's first pair of legs are raised into a horizontal position in order to obtain the desired effect; Shimba Hill Reserve, Kenya; length ¾ in/2 cm.

Photos 126-131 (opposite) These photos illustrate a more complex example of Batesian mimicry. The model, *Euploea mulciber* (Photos 126, 128 and 130), comprises two quite different sexes, the male (126 and 128) and the female (130), both of which are noxious. Each sex is mimicked by a different species of swallowtail butterfly. *Chilasa paradoxa* (129) closely resembles the male *Euploea*, while another species, *Chilasa clytia* (131), emulates the female *Euploea*. Central Malaysia; Wingspans all approximately 2¾ in/7 cm.

time sitting but wasps are nearly always on the move. Therefore, to emulate the wasp, the katydid must change its behavior; indeed, certain katydids and grasshoppers, although retaining their long, jumping legs have "learned" to fly in a very wasp-like manner.

Wasps are mimicked by many insects, including moths, flies (Photos 125, 132 and 133) and even beetles. This type of mimicry, in which both male and female copy a common model, is only one of many different forms of mimicry. In certain cases the male and female of a given species, whether it be model or mimic, are quite different. When several species are involved the situation becomes even more complex. Several combinations are possible. The first is a simple one-to-one relationship between mimic and model, as seen in Photos 121, 125, 132 and 133. The second occurs when only the female of the species mimics, and the male is unprotected. This may become very complicated when the female of the species has evolved a series of varieties. The classical example is that of a widespread African swallowtail butterfly, *Papilio dardanus*. While the pale yellow male remains constant from one region to another, the female varies radically; in each region the female variant mimics a different model. This remarkable infidelity was elucidated only after careful study and breeding.

In the third variation the potential model has two distinct sexes, both noxious. Both male and female may be mimicked by two different species of butterfly (Photos 126 through 131). This is the case for a common

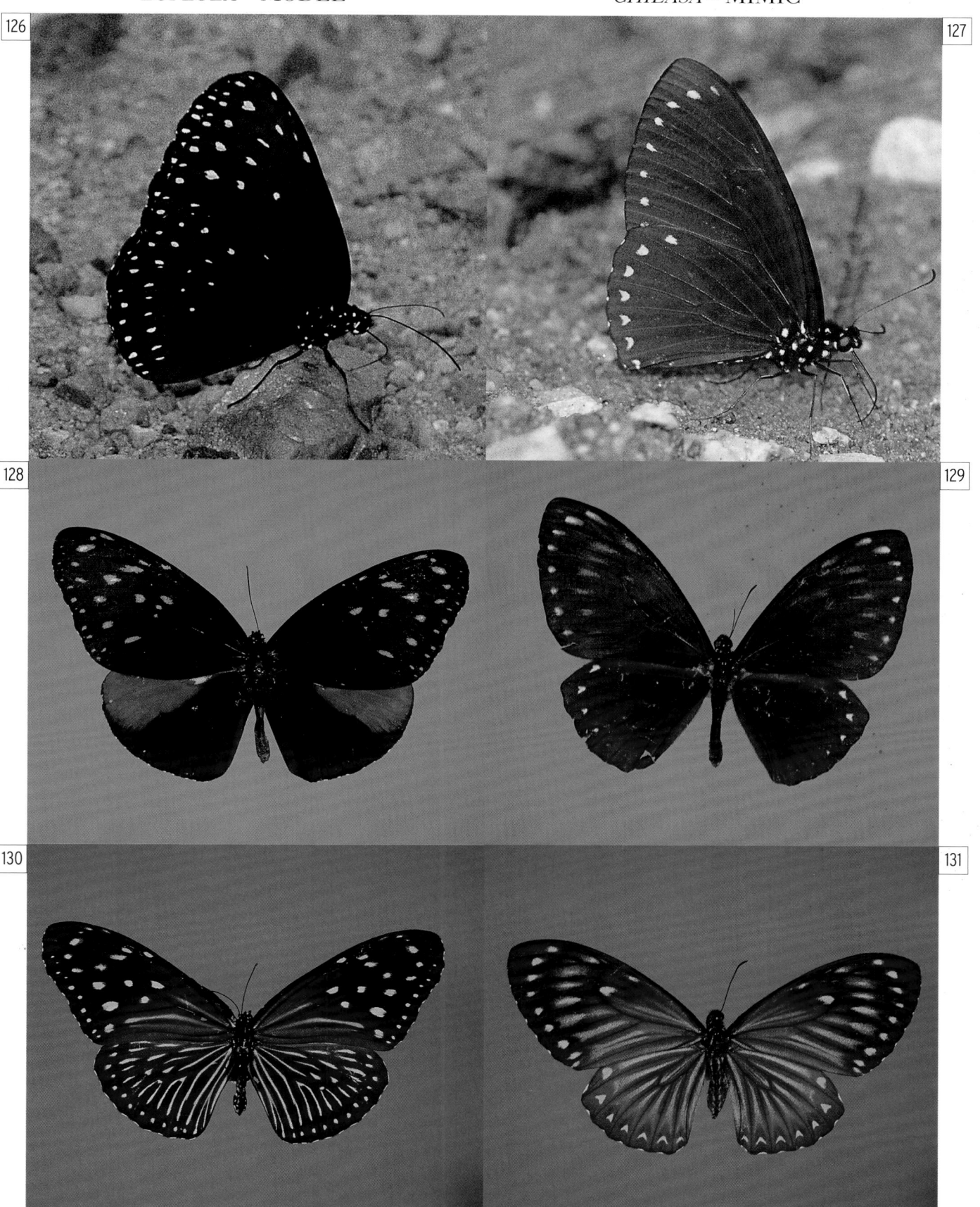

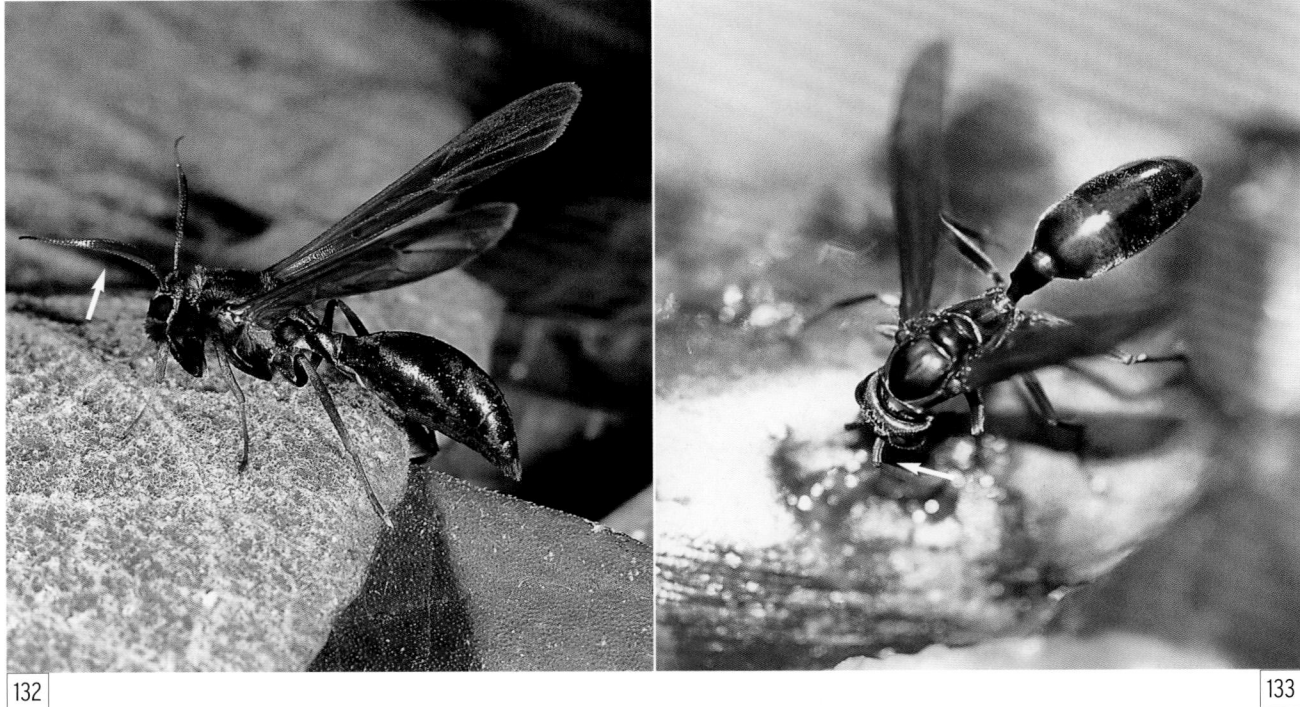

132

133

Photos 132, 133 Certain day-flying moths (Ctenuchidae), as seen in Photo 132, closely resemble stinging wasps, as seen in Photo 133. The moth has a slender, wasp-like abdomen, and the imitation is further enhanced by its narrow, wasp-like wings and by its wasp-like behavior. However, the true family affinities of both mimic and model are revealed by their antennae (arrows). Photographed near San Gerardo, central Costa Rica; wingspans about 1¼ in/3 cm.

Photos 134–137 (opposite) Clear-winged ithominiid butterflies are protected by unsavory body fluids and therefore make good models for other insects (Photo 135). Photo 134, a pierid; Photo 136, a castinid moth; and Photo 137, a riodinid butterfly. Although the wing patterns are all very similar, the number of legs (a better indicator of family affinity) varies. Photos 134 and 135 taken in French Guyana; Photo 136 in the Urubamba Valley, Peru; and Photo 137 at Saül in French Guyana. Wingspans 1¼ to 2¾ in/3 to 7 cm.

Asiatic butterfly *Euploea mulciber*, which frequents forest paths and public gardens throughout Malaysia. The metallic blue male is mimicked by a very similar *Chilasa paradoxa*, while the grey-blue female (of *E. mulciber*) is mimicked by a different species of *Chilasa clytia*.

In the field it is very difficult to distinguish between protected *Euploea* and the mimicking *Chilasas*, especially when they fly together. However, when menaced, the difference between model and mimic becomes very apparent; the two species of *Chilasa* revert to their true family habits and the rapid flight, typical of the swallowtail family to which they belong, favors their escape. In other words, the schizophrenic *Chilasas* resemble the noxious *Euploea* when it suits them, but can drop the disguise when necessary.

MIMICRY RINGS

A single species of toxic butterfly may be a model for many species of edible mimics. These "mimicry rings" are particularly well developed in the American tropics, where several important families of butterfly, including the heliconiids and the ithominiids, are toxic. Both these families, being protected, have a slow, fairly confident flight, and this is copied by the mimics shown in Photos 134–137. In the forest it is extremely difficult to distinguish not only between models and mimics but between the respective mimics; true family affinities require laboratory study.

We have seen that an insect protected by its noxious body fluids or sting may serve as a model for edible species, which gain protection through this Batesian mimicry. This similarity between toxic model and edible mimic, although often simple, may be extremely complex, involving several models and many different mimics.

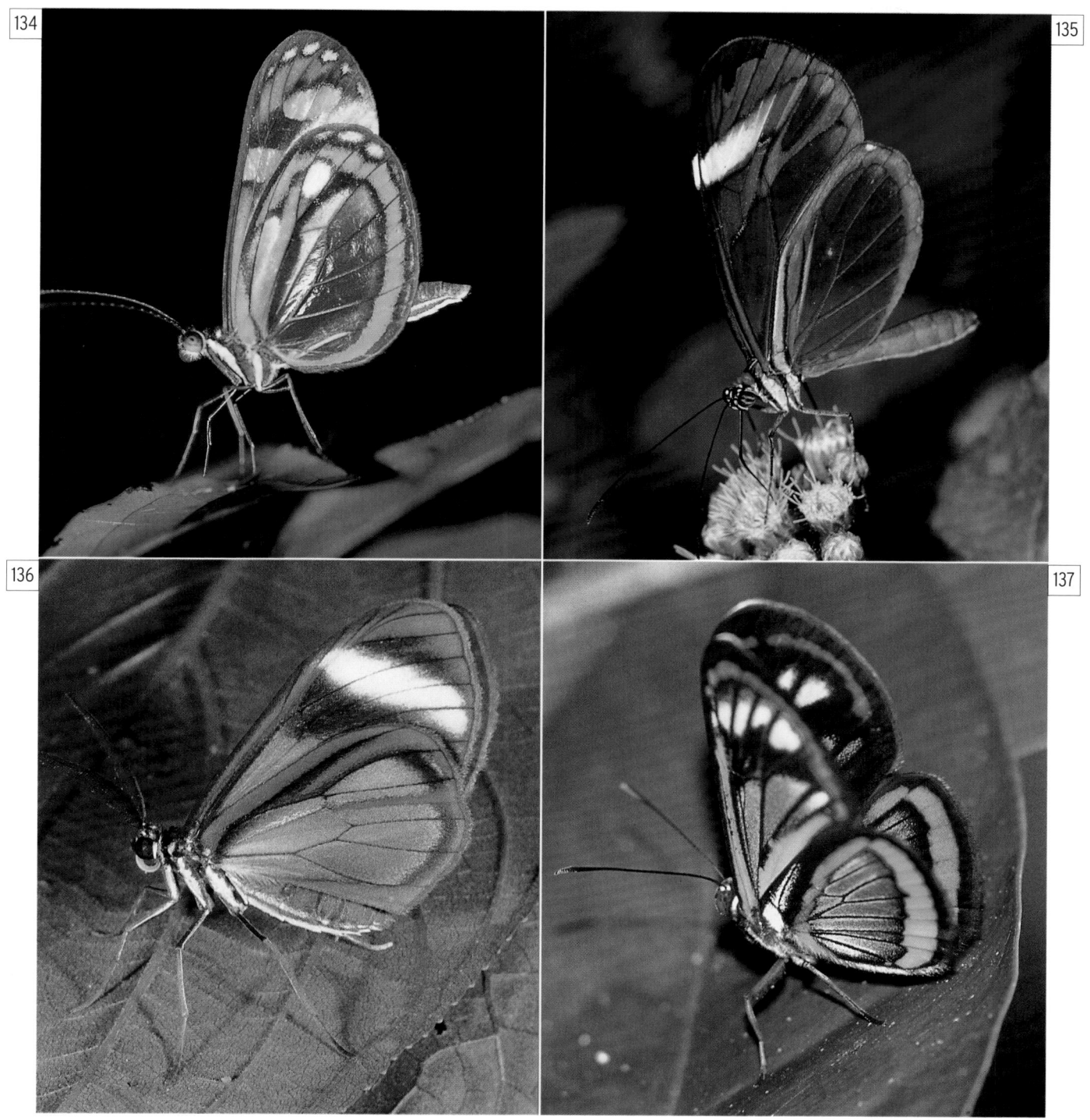

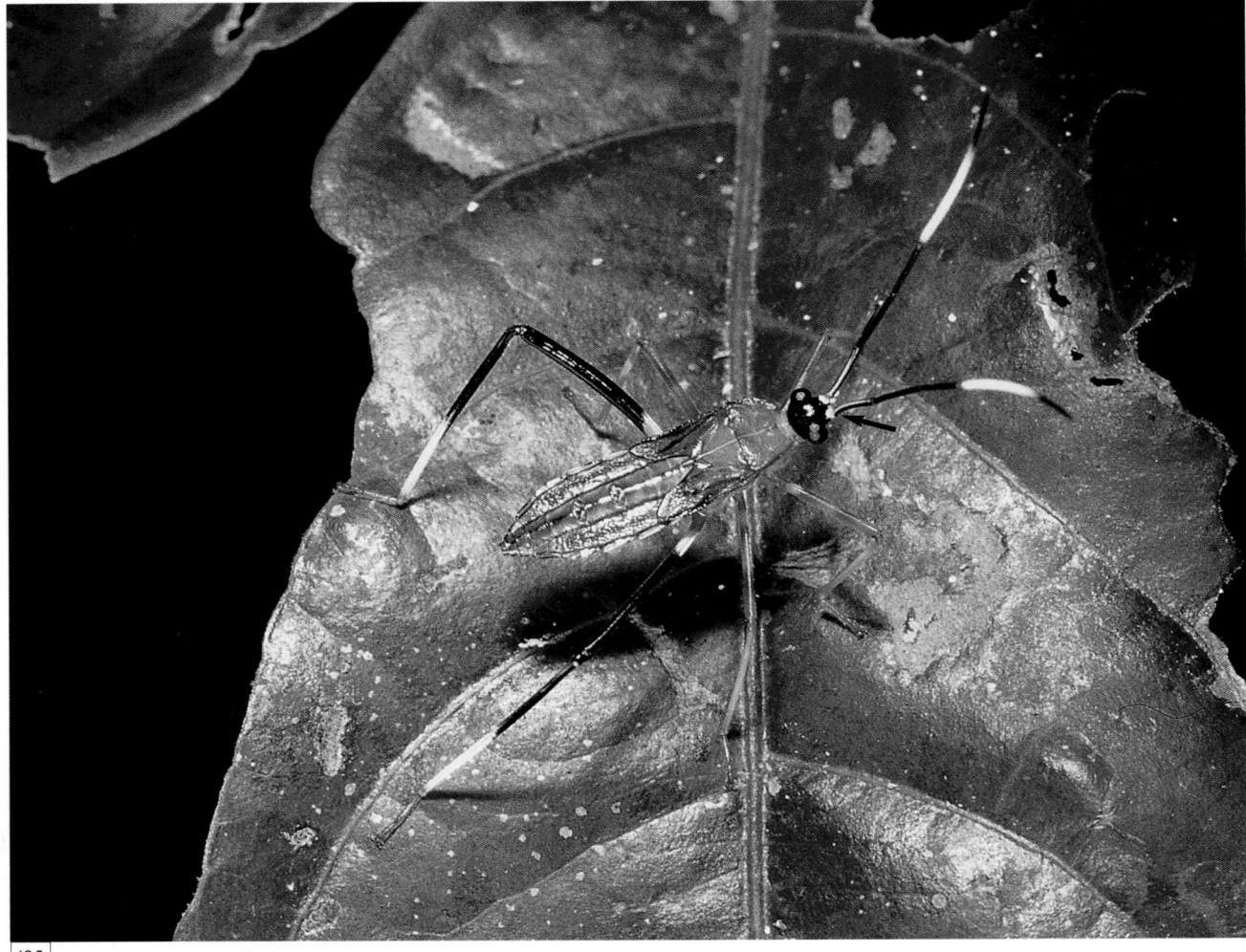

MÜLLERIAN MIMICRY

The situation becomes even more complicated when two or more families of insect, all toxic and thus potential models, are all very similar. In other words, because the noxious models resemble one another, one may wonder which insect is the mimic and which is the model. Fritz Müller's studies in 1879 in the Amazon led him to suggest that noxious (protected) insects would acquire mutual protection if they all resembled one another, this similarity making identification simpler for predators. In other words, a predator would have less trouble in learning which insect to avoid if all the noxious insects wore the same uniform. This phenomenon has been termed *Müllerian mimicry*.

INSECTS MIMIC ANTS

There are close similarities between wasps, bugs (Hemiptera) and ants, all three groups being protected, the wasps and ants by their stings and bites, the bugs by their offensive smell. Ants are a very successful family

Photo 138 True bugs (Hemiptera) generally have several forms of protection, including painful bites and horrible smells. Therefore, it is surprising that they seek to mimic other protected insects such as wasps. This picture, taken in Saül, French Guyana, provides a good illustration of Müllerian mimicry, which involves close similarity between a series of protected (biting or stinging) insects. With its long legs and twitching, white-tipped antennae, this bug (Coridae) could readily be mistaken for a wasp. However, the photo reveals its piercing rostrum or mouthpiece (arrow), which is typical of bugs, but not wasps. Length 1¼ in/3 cm.

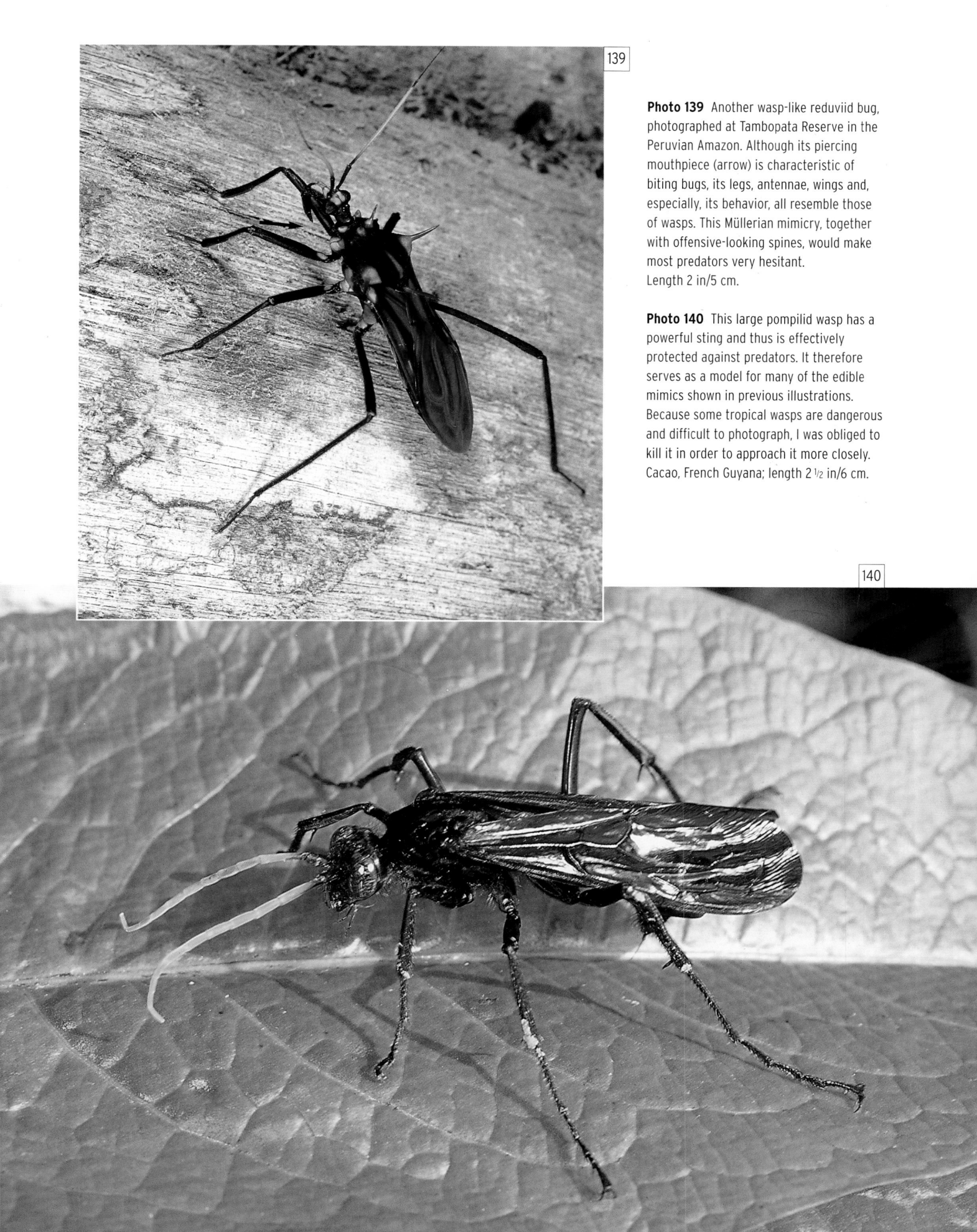

Photo 139 Another wasp-like reduviid bug, photographed at Tambopata Reserve in the Peruvian Amazon. Although its piercing mouthpiece (arrow) is characteristic of biting bugs, its legs, antennae, wings and, especially, its behavior, all resemble those of wasps. This Müllerian mimicry, together with offensive-looking spines, would make most predators very hesitant.
Length 2 in/5 cm.

Photo 140 This large pompilid wasp has a powerful sting and thus is effectively protected against predators. It therefore serves as a model for many of the edible mimics shown in previous illustrations. Because some tropical wasps are dangerous and difficult to photograph, I was obliged to kill it in order to approach it more closely.
Cacao, French Guyana; length 2 ½ in/6 cm.

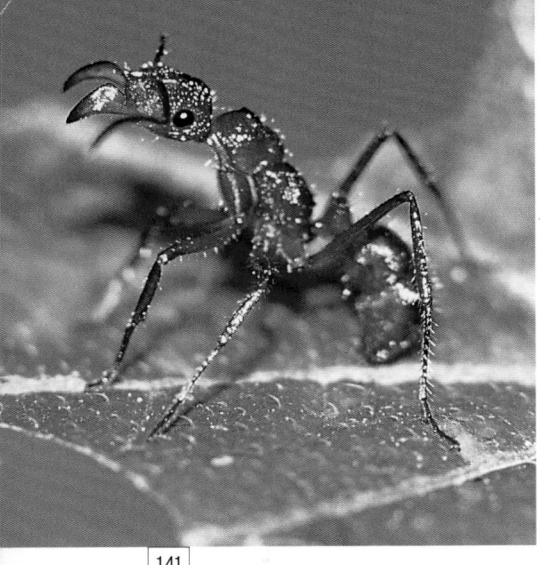

Photos 141, 142, 143 The two ant-like
insects in Photos 142 and 143 are in fact
broad-headed bugs (Alydidae), with no
family affinities with ants. These two
individuals were photographed on separate
continents: Photo 142 in French Guyana in
South America, and Photo 143 in Cameroon
in Africa. In spite of these considerable
distances, both insects appear to have
evolved the same type of mimicry. Both
bugs and ants (Photo 141) are protected
from predators by noxious body fluids.
Photo 141, of a true ant, shows the
considerable similarity between this model
and the mimics in Photos 142 and 143.
Peruvian Amazon; length ³/₄ in/2 cm.

of insects mainly because of their aggressive habits and noxious body
fluids. They are rarely attacked by other insects. Therefore, it is not
surprising that ants are mimicked by many edible insects and spiders
that seek protection through masquerade. The small, wingless alydid
bugs shown in Photos 142 and 143 are good examples.

Certain beetles also resemble ants and these even penetrate into the
ant colony, where they obtain food. Theoretically, their acceptance by
the ants with which they live, is favored by their ant-like appearance.
This form of deception has been termed *Wasmannian mimicry*, in honor
of Erich Wasmann, who first described the phenomenon. However, the
similarity between the ant hosts and the invading mimic may be fortuitous, for many ants are blind and their acceptance of the beetles and
other insects may depend mainly on odor; these wolves in sheeps'
clothing even smell like sheep!

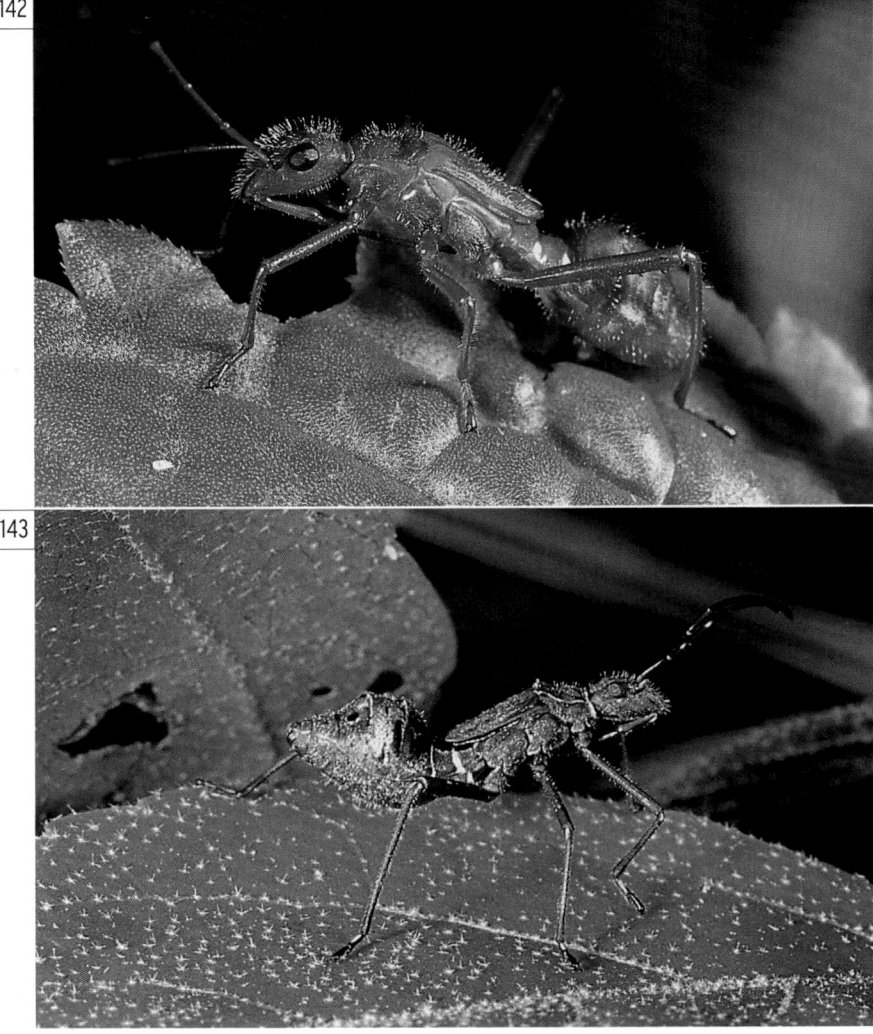

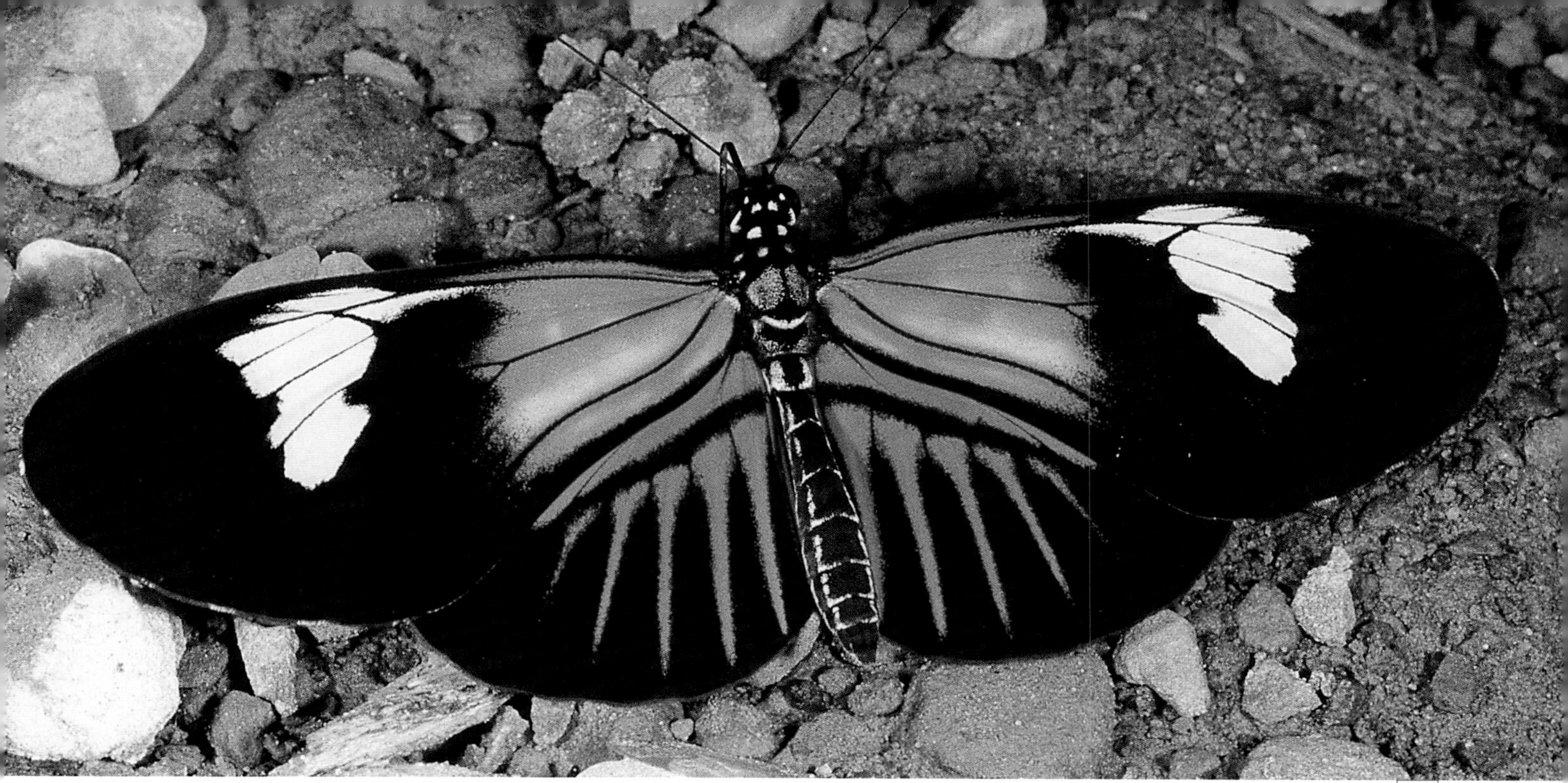

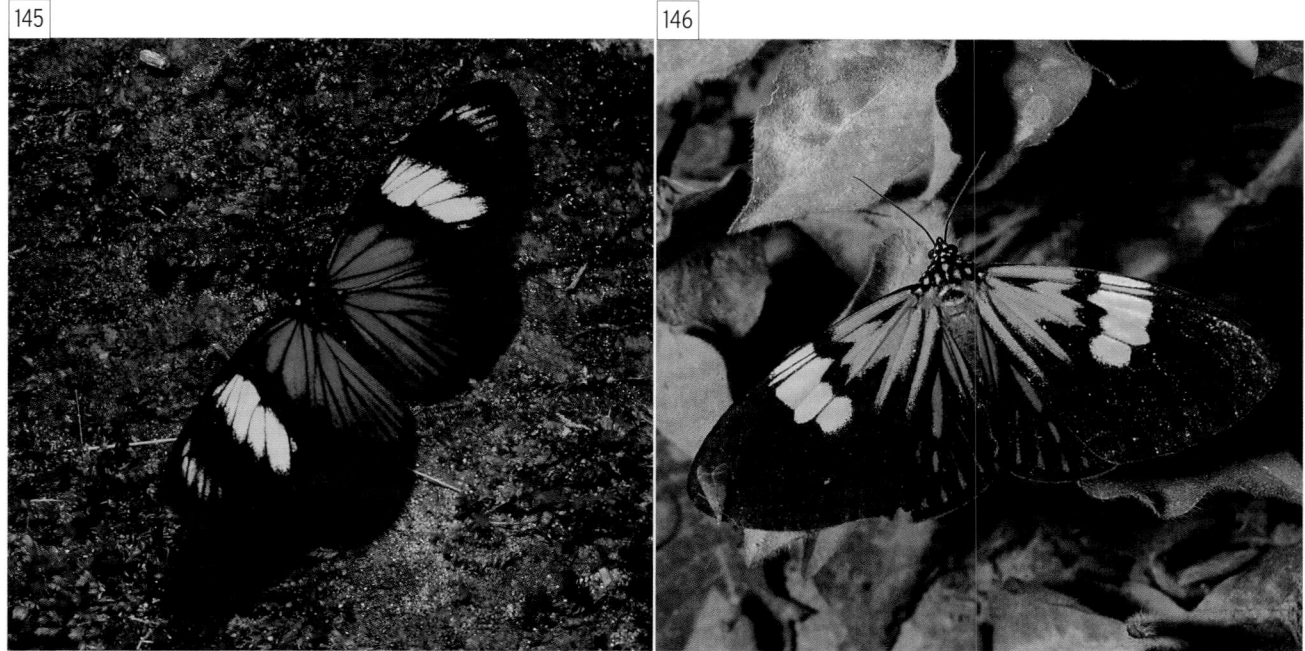

MIMICRY CLANS

Mimicry can be a fairly simple affair involving a noxious model and an edible mimic. However, mimicry often is complicated by the intimate association of several models and numerous mimics; these are commonly referred to as "clans," with all members of the clan sporting a common tartan. Thus, in a given region, the butterflies, although genetically different, superficially may be very similar. A classical complex is the *Heliconus melpomene* clan of tropical America. Three of its many members are illustrated in Photos 144, 145 and 146.

Photos 144, 145, 146 Three members of the *Heliconius melpomene* clan that are all protected by noxious body fluids. The similarity of this form of protection is thought to cause predators to avoid all members of the clan, even those that are not protected by noxious fluids. It has been termed "Müllerian mimicry." Photo 144, *Heliconius melpomene* (Heliconiidae), 2 ¾ in/7 cm; Photo 145, genus *Actinote*, 2 in/5 cm; Photo 146, castinid moth, 2 ½ in/6 cm. All from Madre de Dios Valley, Peruvian Amazon.

145

146

INSECTS MIMIC ANIMALS

Insects sometimes assume very bizarre forms that resemble certain verte-brates: snakes, frogs and even crocodiles. To human eyes, it seems as though these frightening models afford a measure of protection for the insect concerned. Although these analogies are not totally convincing, the most intriguing element of these strange phenomena is the behavior of the insect mimic. The snake-like caterpillars not only change color but they stand up and display various body contortions that resemble those of a snake. And the little toad bug (Photo 147) not only resembles a minute frog, but actually jumps like one, rather than running like a "normal" insect.

Photos 147, 148, 149 Certain insects appear to imitate vertebrate animals. In Photo 147, the small "toad bug" *Gelastocoris* from the Peruvian Amazon looks and behaves like a small frog. It lives among the gravel on the edges of tropical mountain streams, where it jumps about in a frog-like manner. Its eyes face forwards, like those of a frog. Length 3/16 in/5 mm.
Photo 148 shows the caterpillar of an unknown sphinx moth seen in the forests of central Malaysia. When it rotates its body, the front segment seems to resemble the head of a snake.
Photo 149 illustrates the head of *Lanternaria*, a cousin of the cicadas from French Guyana. This strange appendage seems to resemble the head of a crocodile, complete with eyes, teeth and nostril. The arrow indicates the true eye of the insect, which lives in small groups on tree trunks in primary forests. Length 2 3/4 in/7 cm.

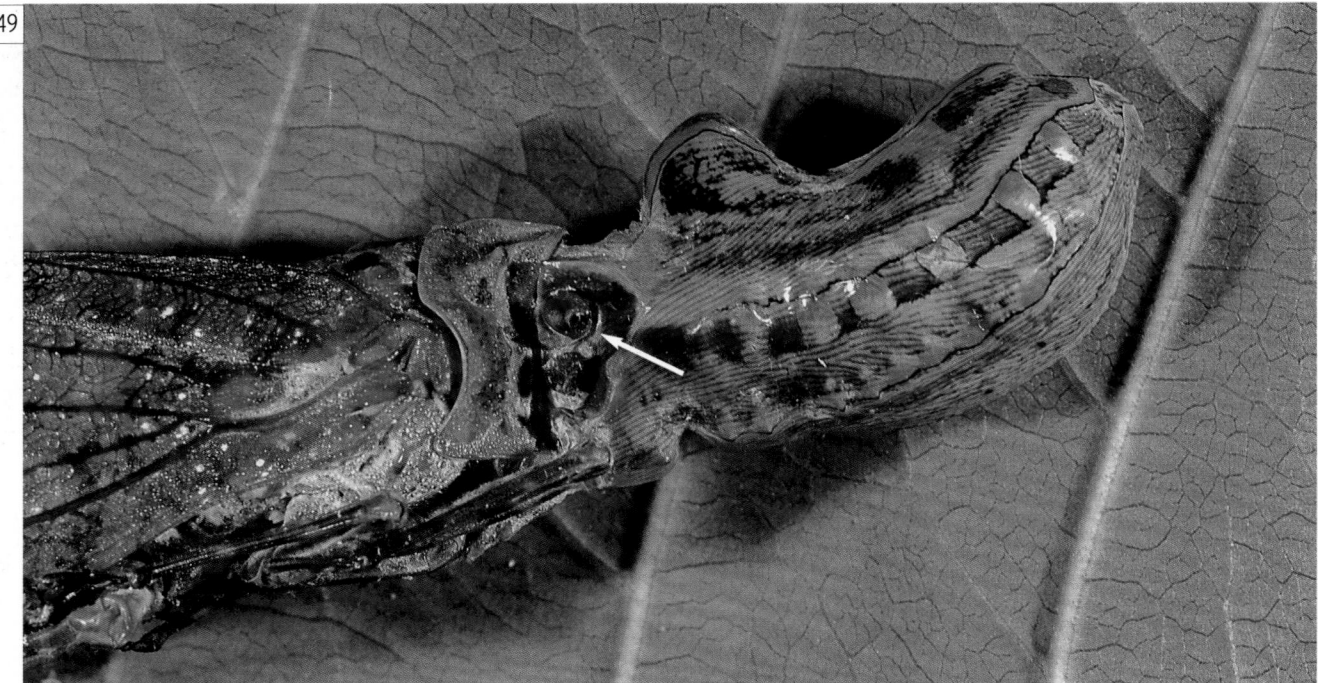

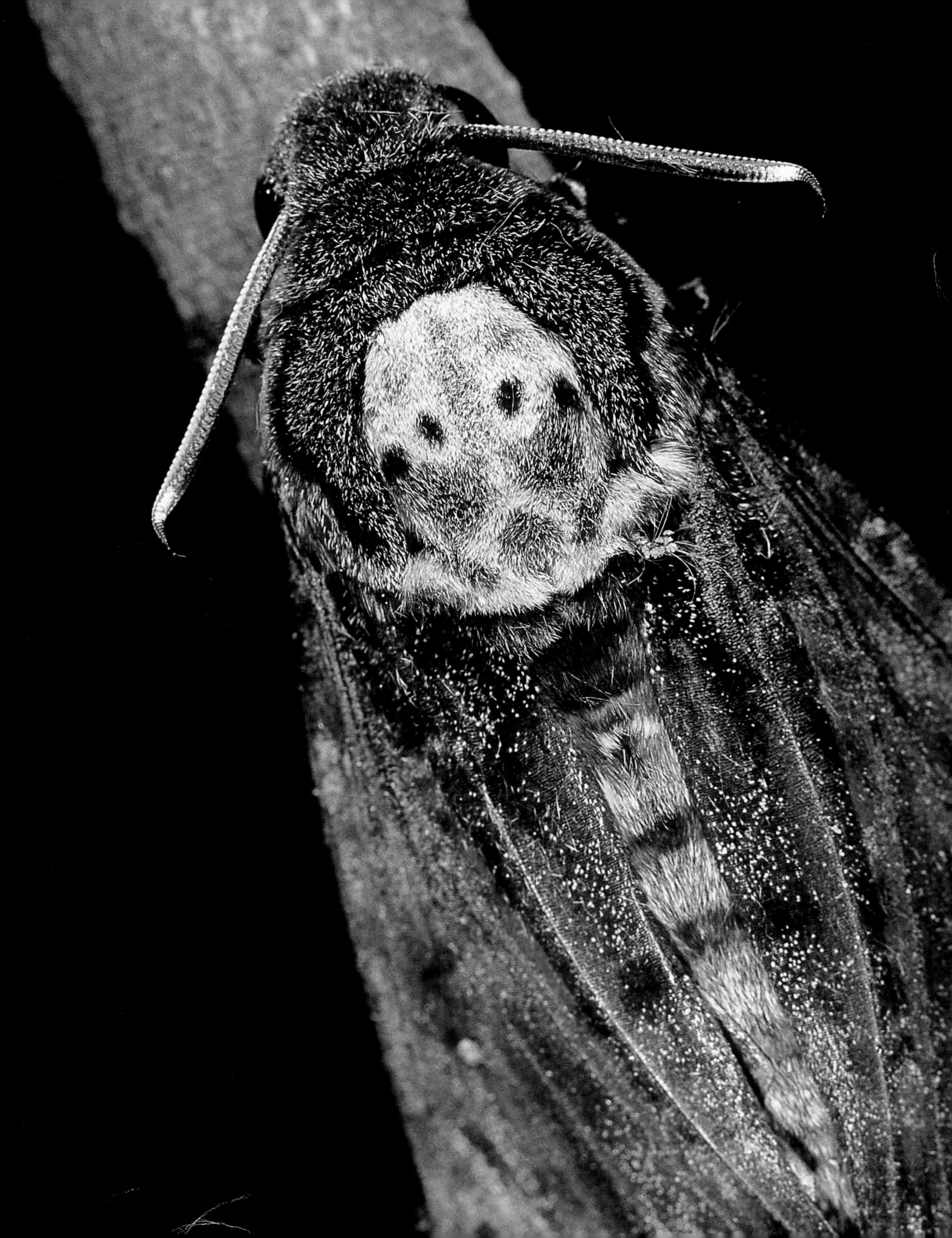

WEIRD COLOR PATTERNS

Insects may have very weird shapes and patterns. While the snake-like caterpillars are rather convincing, it is difficult to understand what a small, tree-inhabiting insect like *Lanternaria* could possibly gain from resembling the head of a crocodile. Some of these unusual patterns, notably the false eyes, do intimidate aggressors, but mainly because they are striking in appearance. Patterns such as those exhibited by the sphinx moth or the *Callicore* butterflies (Photos 150, 151), while decorative, may have little or no protective function.

Photos 150, 151 The color patterns decorating insect bodies or wings sometimes assume very original shapes. For example, this sphinx moth (Photo 150, previous page) (Sphingidae), photographed in the Dja Forest of Cameroon, carries a pattern closely resembling a human skull. Diameter of "skull", ½ in/12 mm. The small nymphalid butterfly, *Callicore* (Photo 151), photographed in the Peruvian Amazon, displays wing patterns that look like numbers. Length 1¼ in/3 cm.

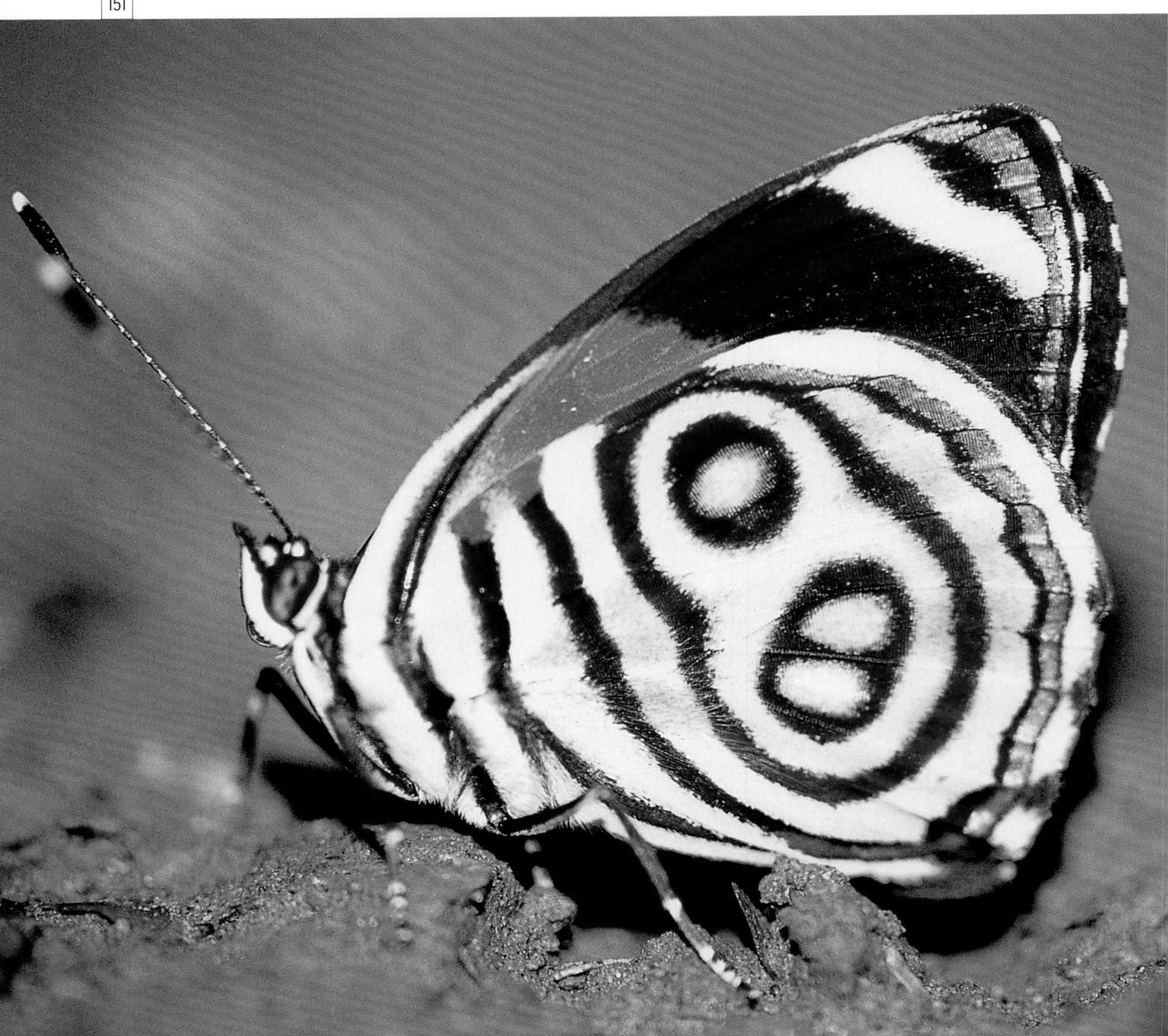

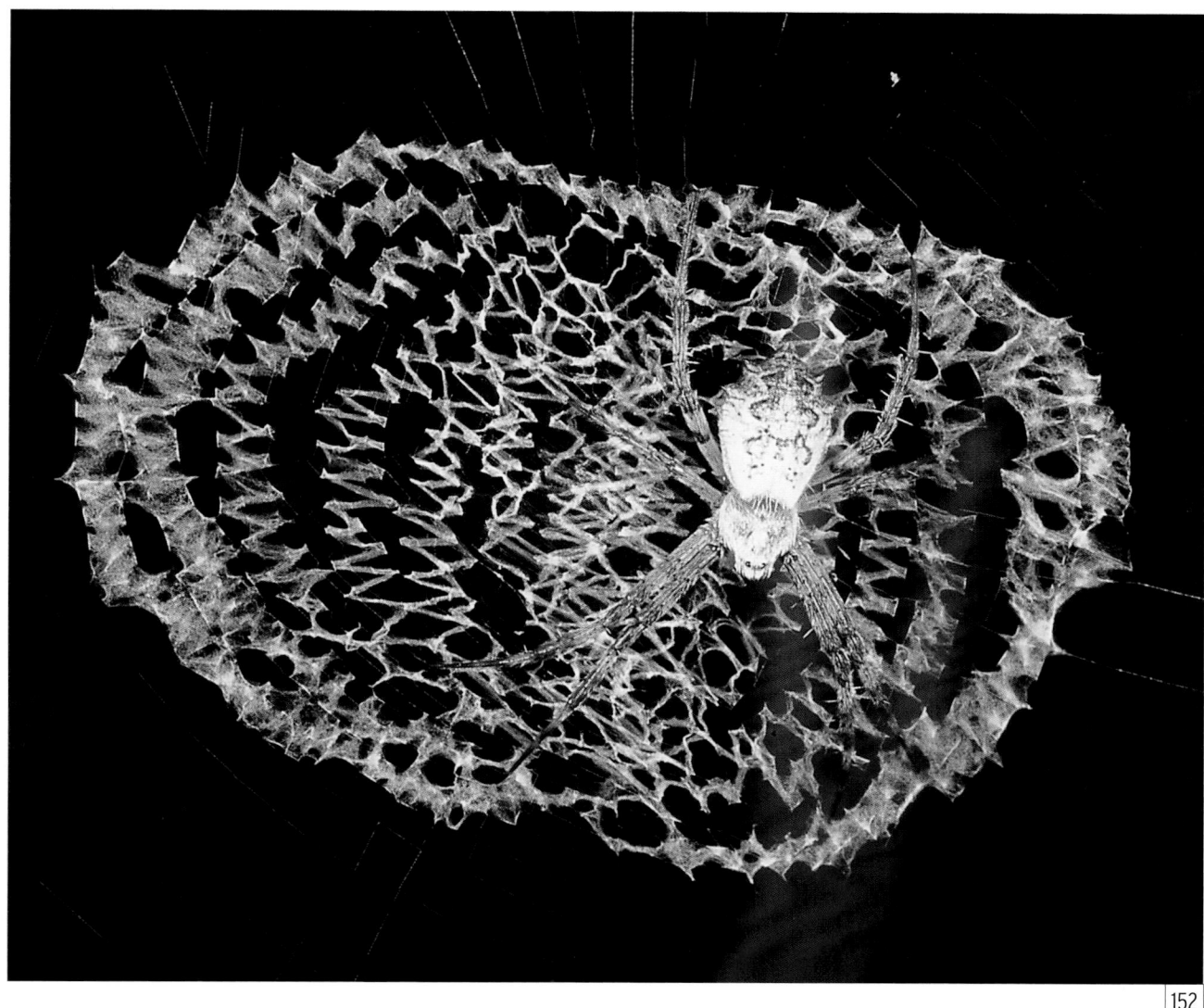

SPIDERS

I have included spiders because their behavior enables us to extend the intriguing story of camouflage and mimicry. Spiders are not actually insects because they have eight legs, while insects have only six.

Because web-building spiders are suspended in space, they are extremely vulnerable; most are easily seen and therefore suffer from bird and insect attack. And because they are suspended, they have great difficulty in camouflaging themselves. However, a number of spiders seem to have overcome the situation by developing their own artificial surroundings, within which they hide. These substrates, in the form of webs, are designed both to catch insects and help dissimulate the spider. These webs take many different forms, depending on the species and age (juvenile or adult) of the spider. This ingenious form of protection, in which the spider constructs an artificial substrate within which it camouflages itself occurs on most continents, including Europe.

Photo 152 A juvenile *Argiope* has built a dense circular network within a larger web. By placing itself on this substrate it perhaps acquires a certain camouflage that offers more protection than a position within its relatively transparent web. Shimba Hills Reserve, coastal Kenya; length ⁵/₁₆ in/8 mm.

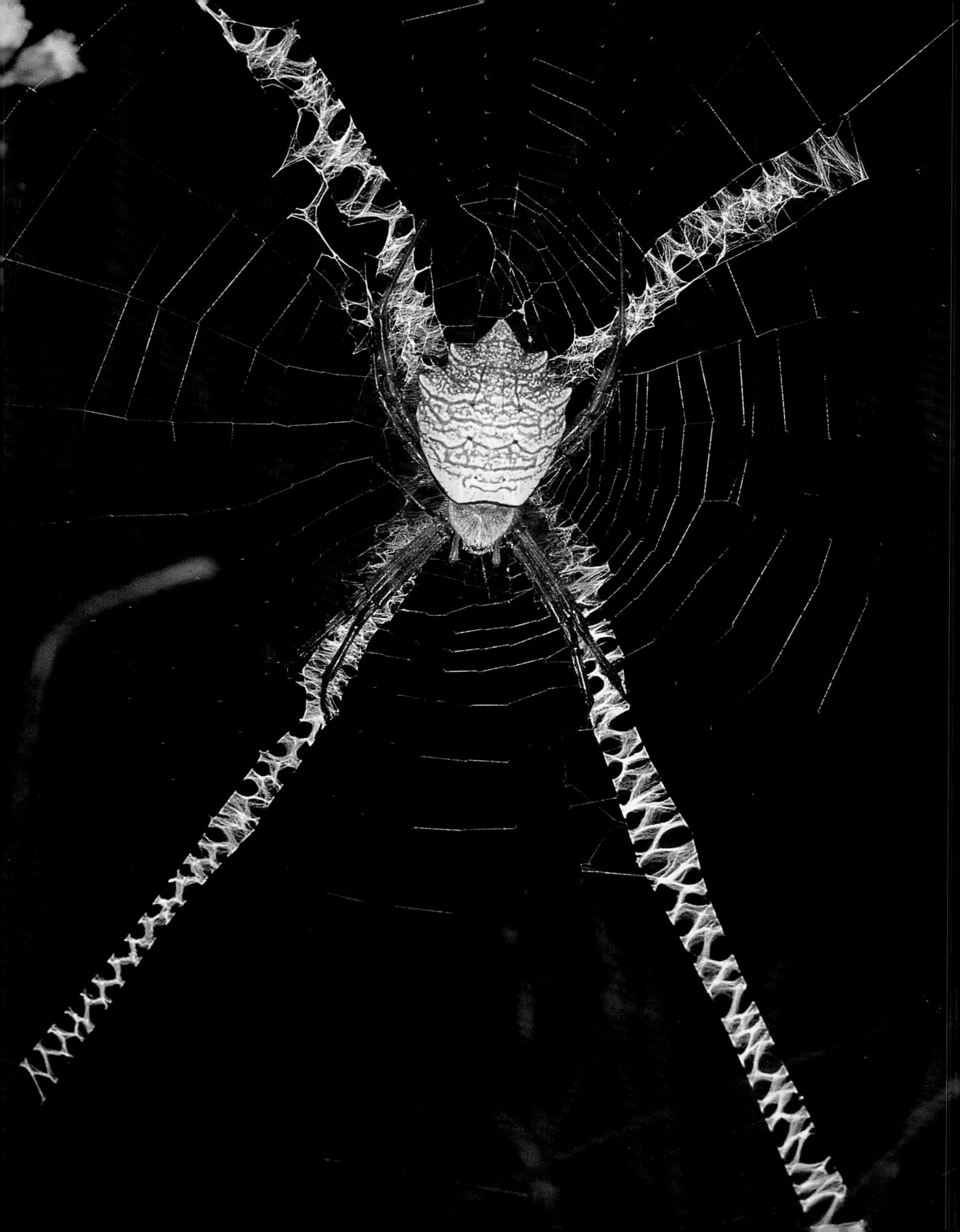

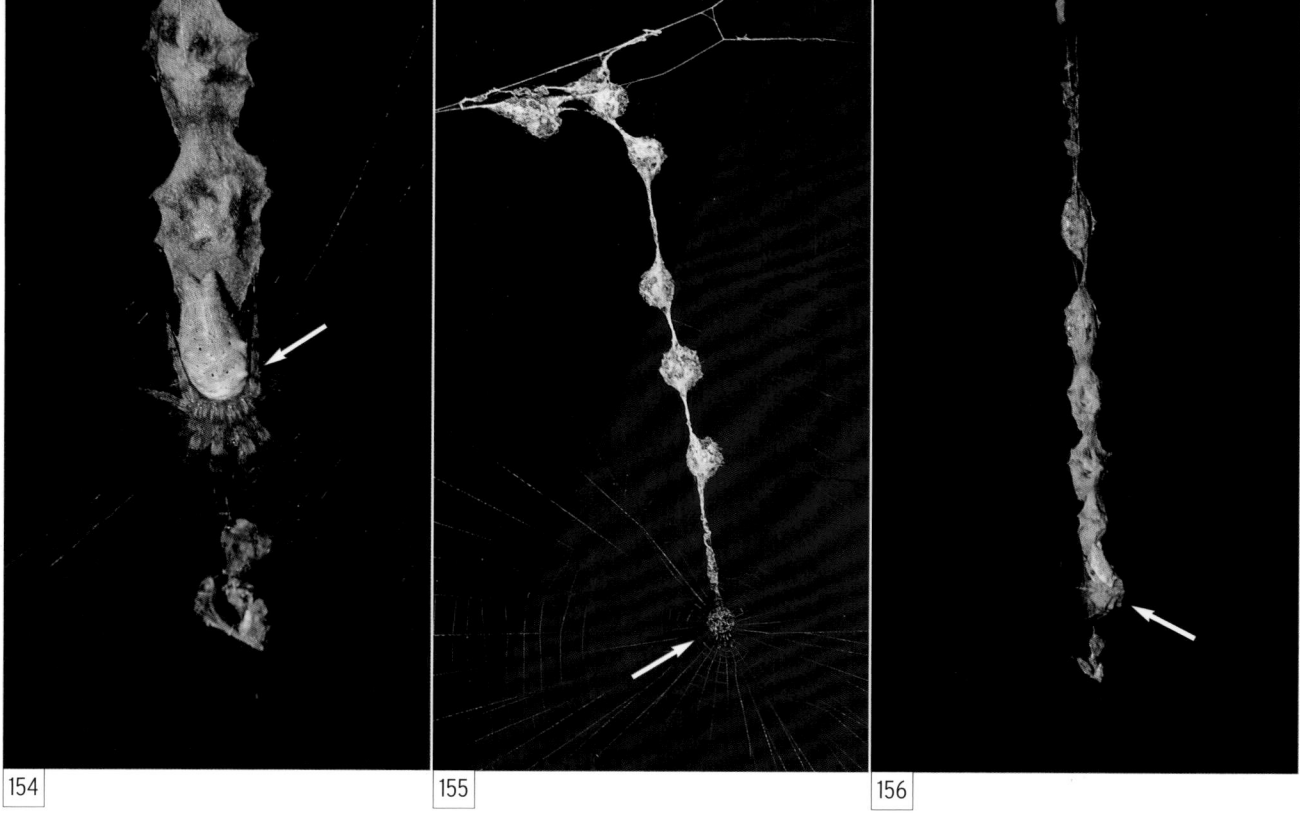

154　　　155　　　156

Spiders of the genus *Argiope* construct a dense white web in the form of a cross (Photo 153, opposite page). This structure is suspended within the normal circular web, where it is clearly visible. The spider then places itself on the cross, carefully arranging each of its four pairs of legs along each segment of the cross. This may have two effects; not only does it dissimulate the spider but it exaggerates its size and thus dissuades predators. Other species of *Argiope* construct a dense white web designed to hide its owner, as shown in Photo 152.

Spiders not only create their own system of camouflage by constructing special webs, but they have also devised systems of automimicry. Many small spiders belonging to one or two specific families have acquired the techniques of building their own models, which they then mimic. This is called automimicry. The spider constructs dummy spiders and places them in various patterns within its web.

The most common is a series of ovoid pods constructed by the spider. Made from densely woven silk, they are suspended in chains, generally within the spider's normal web (Photos 155, 156). The spider, which closely resembles one of the pods, places itself at the end of the chain, where it is very effectively dissimulated.

Photos 154, 155, 156 Another group of spiders construct dummies. In this case, each dummy is constructed of fine insect debris and may contain the eggs of the spider. These dummies are suspended in a chain, the spider forming the lowest element (see arrow, Photo 155). Photographed near the foot of Mount Kilimanjaro, Tanzania; length 1/8 in/3 mm.

The spider shown in Photos 154 and 156 has suspended debris at the end of the chain. This debris may represent the spider as a "master dummy." Photographed on the shores of Lake Peten, Guatemala; length 3/16 in/5 mm.

Photo 153 (opposite page) In this photo a fairly large *Argiope* spider has constructed a distinct cross in the center of its web. The spider has carefully adjusted itself to coincide with the shape of the cross. The cross may help to hide the spider and thus protect it from predators, or the cross may appear to increase the size of the spider and thus intimidate predators. Photographed in Kakamega Forest, western Kenya; length 3/8 in/1 cm.

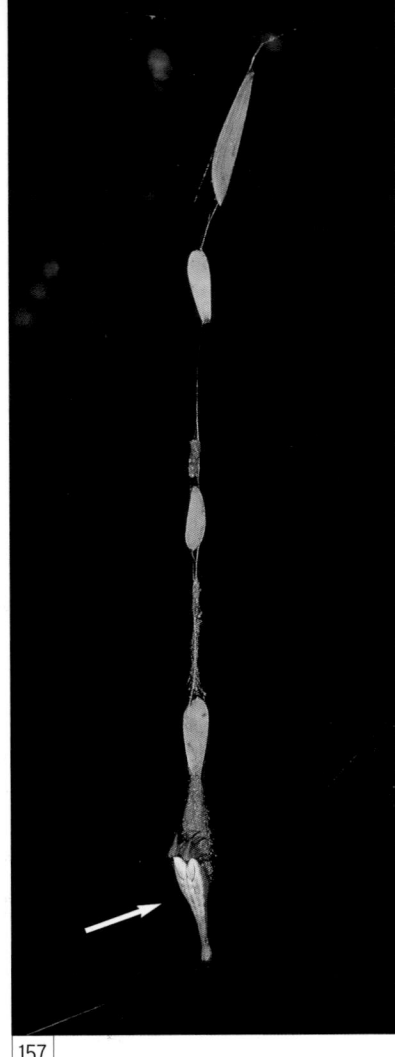

The example shown in Photo 159 is particularly interesting since the similarity between the spider and the six dummies is very convincing. This particular style of mimicry has been observed at several localities. In every case the living spider occupied exactly the same position. In other words, the construction is not haphazard. Although it would almost seem that the spider knows what it is doing, this is an illusion. Because the system is probably common to most, if not all individuals of this particular species, it is hereditary and the spider has not learned the trick from experience.

Where else in the animal kingdom could one find a more subtle form of mimicry? It is difficult to understand how it has developed, not through any calculated attempts at perfection but, on the contrary, through the effects of organic evolution, over which the spiders have had no control.

Photos 157, 160 This little spider uses small leaves as dummies, placing itself at the end of the chain (arrows). The similarity in size, shape and color between the spider and the manuka leaves is remarkable, and the spider was discovered only by accident. Photographed near Rotorua, New Zealand; length 3/16 in/5 mm.

Photo 158 The difference between the dummy and the real spider (arrow) is not immediately evident. The artificial spider (top) is made of insect debris, with the imitation perfected by the addition of its own circular web. Shimba Hills Reserve, Kenya; length 3/16 in/5 mm.

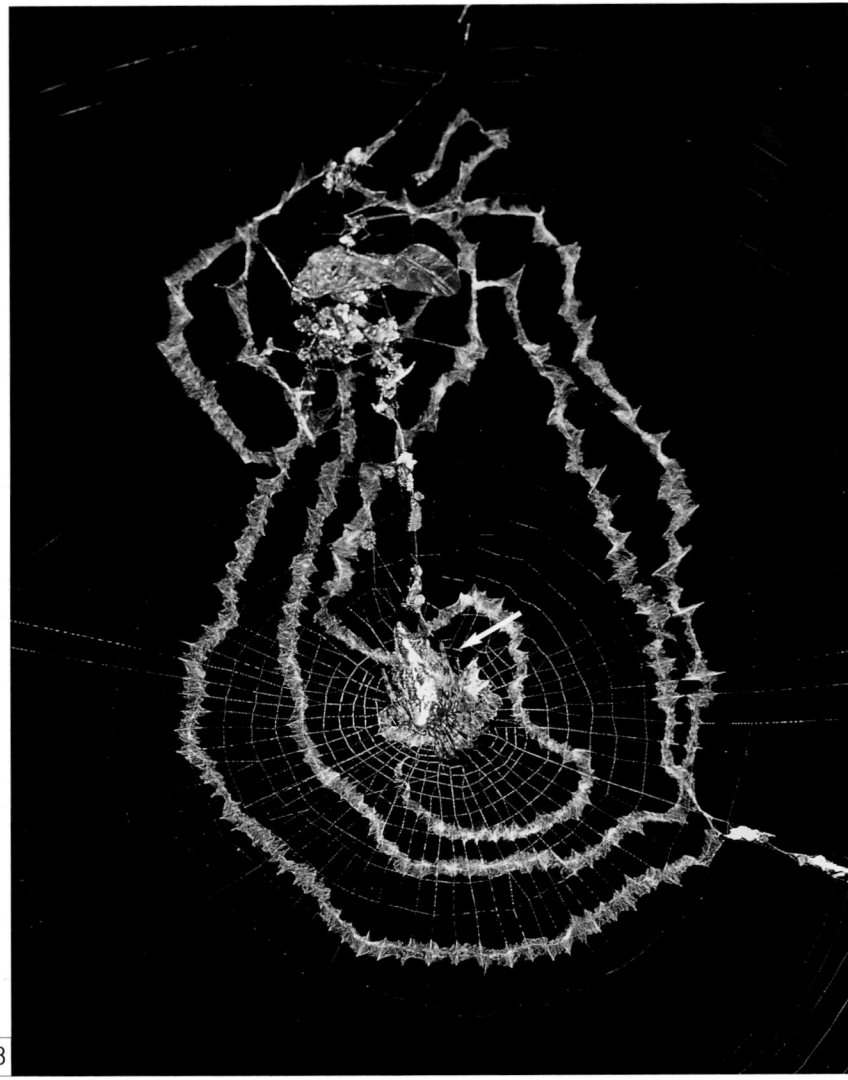

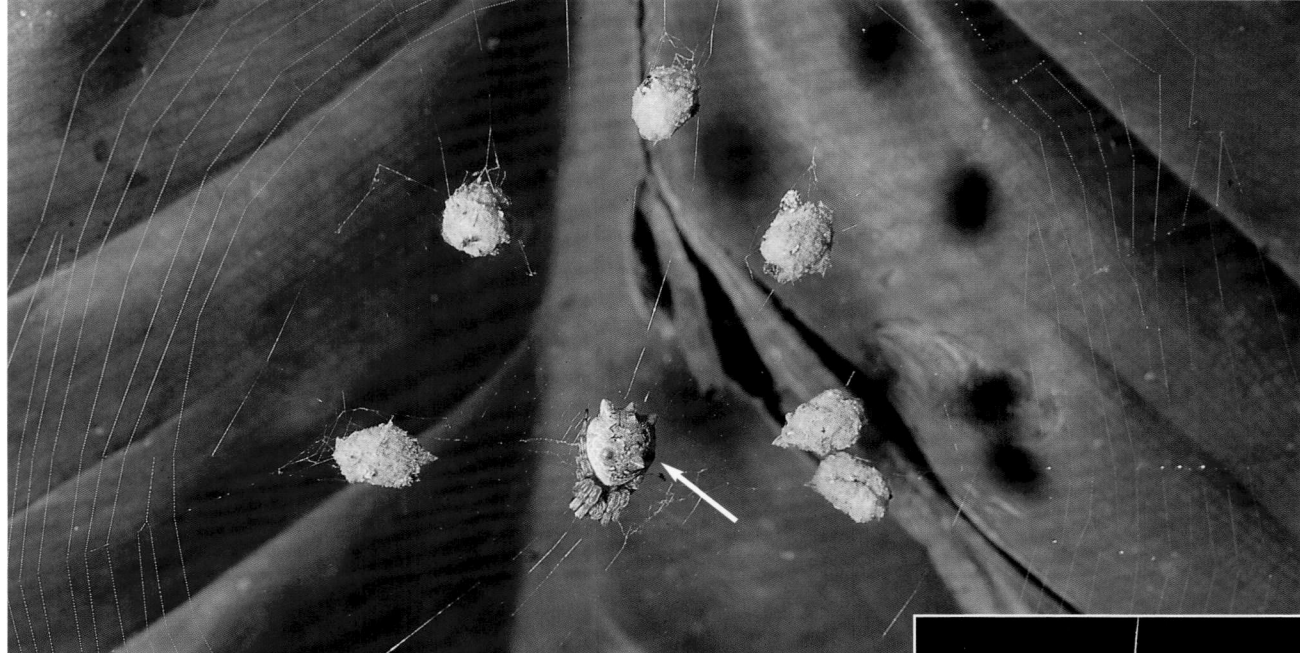

Photo 159 This small spider has opted for an curved system of dummies, with the spider (arrow) placing itself in the center. The ovoid balls, which may contain its eggs , are identical in size and color to the spider. Presuming that the ruse is effective, the spider has six chances out of seven in escaping if attacked. Photographed in Yanachaga National Park, central Peru; length ³/₁₆ in/5 mm.

160

SUMMARY

We have examined, very briefly, some of the many intriguing aspects of camouflage and mimicry. While the simplest forms may be coincidental, the deliberate efforts made by other insects to improve their camouflage, by actively adjusting themselves to better conform with their surroundings, should convince us that camouflage, indeed, is a specific product of organic evolution. The complexity of this fascinating phenomenon, unequaled in the animal kingdom, culminates in the various forms of mimicry. To the motivated observer, the manner in which a harmless katydid gains protection by resembling a wasp is thought-provoking. The katydid's extraordinary behavior gives the impression that it knows what it is doing.

However, as noted repeatedly, the diverse ruses, clearly aimed at self-protection, are all instinctive. They do not express an exceptional form of intelligence, for they are inherited from one generation to another. Through geological history repeated variations (mutations) of a given species interact with the multiple constraints of nature — notably predatorial menace. Those insects that develop forms of camouflage are privileged; they are more likely to survive and to reproduce the favored mutant. Natural selection promotes or eliminates.

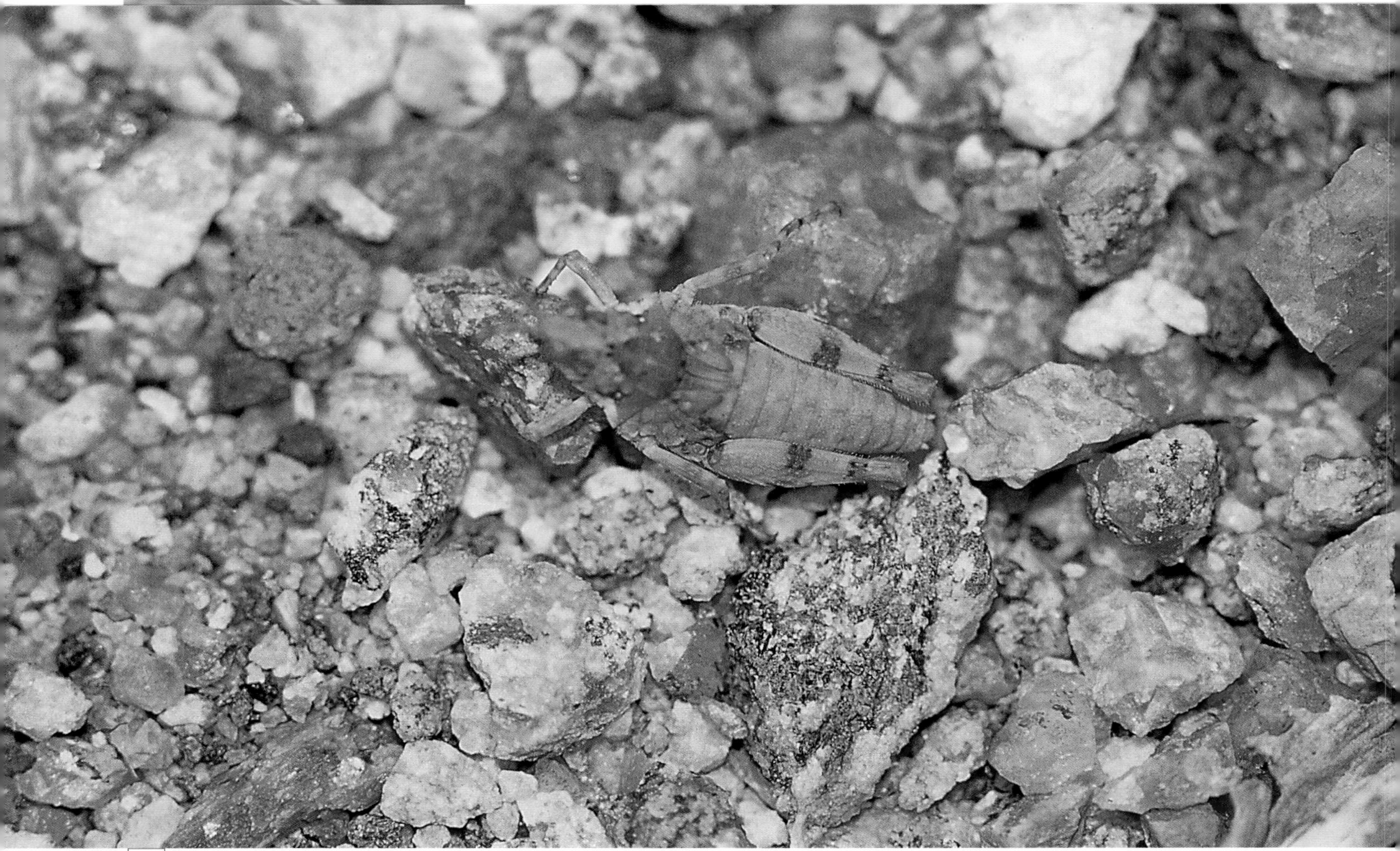

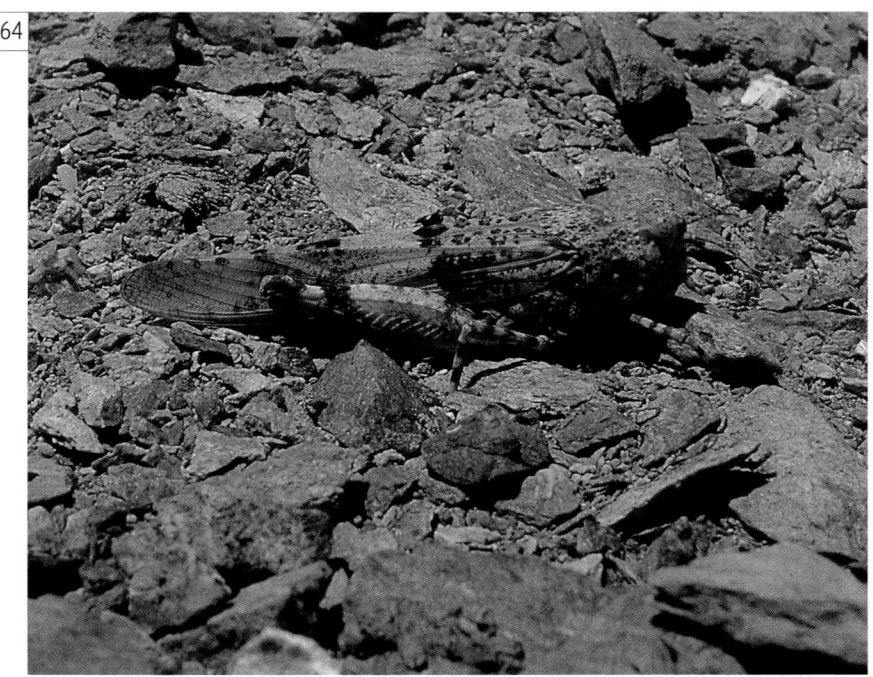

Photos 163, 164, 165 Among ground-living grasshoppers there often exists a close relationship between their color and that of their surroundings. In Photo 165 (Yemen) (opposite) the desert gravels are beige limestone; in Photo 164 (Egypt) the gravels are grey volcanic materials; and in Photo 163 (Tanzania) the substrate is rust-colored quartzite.

between insects and their habitats in terms of camouflage. We will compare insects that spend most of their time on the ground with those that live above, usually on vegetation. To accentuate these differences we compare two contrasting environments, the tropical forest and the dry lands (deserts and dry savannas) .

164

CAMOUFLAGE ON THE GROUND

The majority of insects that live on the ground are well camouflaged. On the forest floor most tend to be brown and they often take the shapes and colors of dead leaves or sticks.

Insects living in desert or other dry-land environments occupy sandy or stony habitats whose color depends on the geological nature of the region (as shown in Photos 163, 164 and 165). In limestone areas this detritus is often beige, while in volcanic regions it may be dark grey or black. Granite or quartzite regions are rust-colored or rose. In these dry, sandy or stony habitats grasshoppers, mantids and beetles are the most common insects. Where the color of the rock detritus changes rapidly (over a few hundred yards), a given species of desert grasshopper may exhibit corresponding changes. These relationships between the mineral and the animal worlds are fascinating. Furthermore, because desert detritus is often rounded or without rough edges, the insects that live in this environment are more regularly shaped compared with the leaf-shaped inhabitants of the forest floor.

In savanna regions the ground is littered with dry grass and small thorny sticks, much of which is light grey in color. It is not surprising, therefore, that the insects and spiders living in these habitats are nearly all light grey. Their shapes are thin and wispy, closely resembling those of the dried grasses among which they live.

165

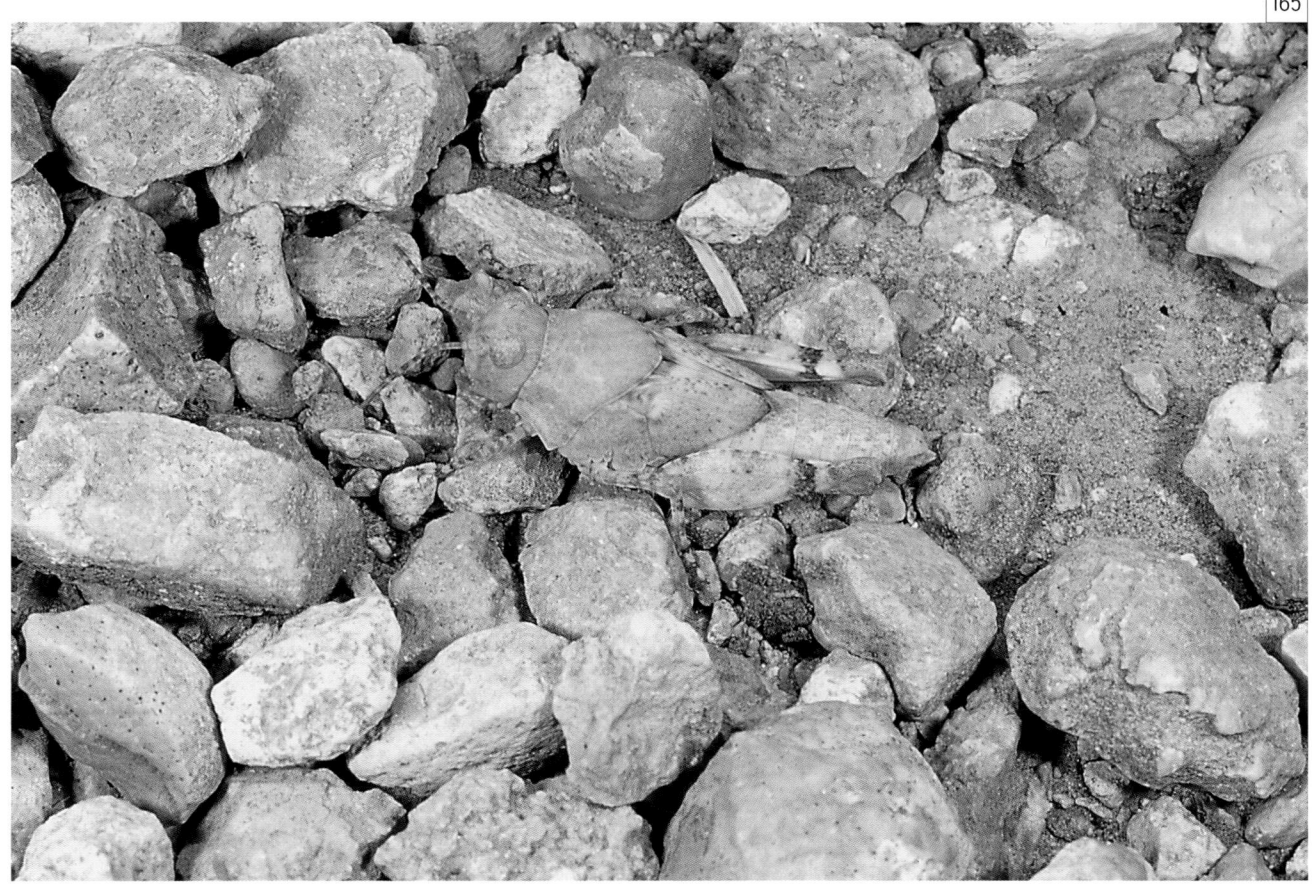

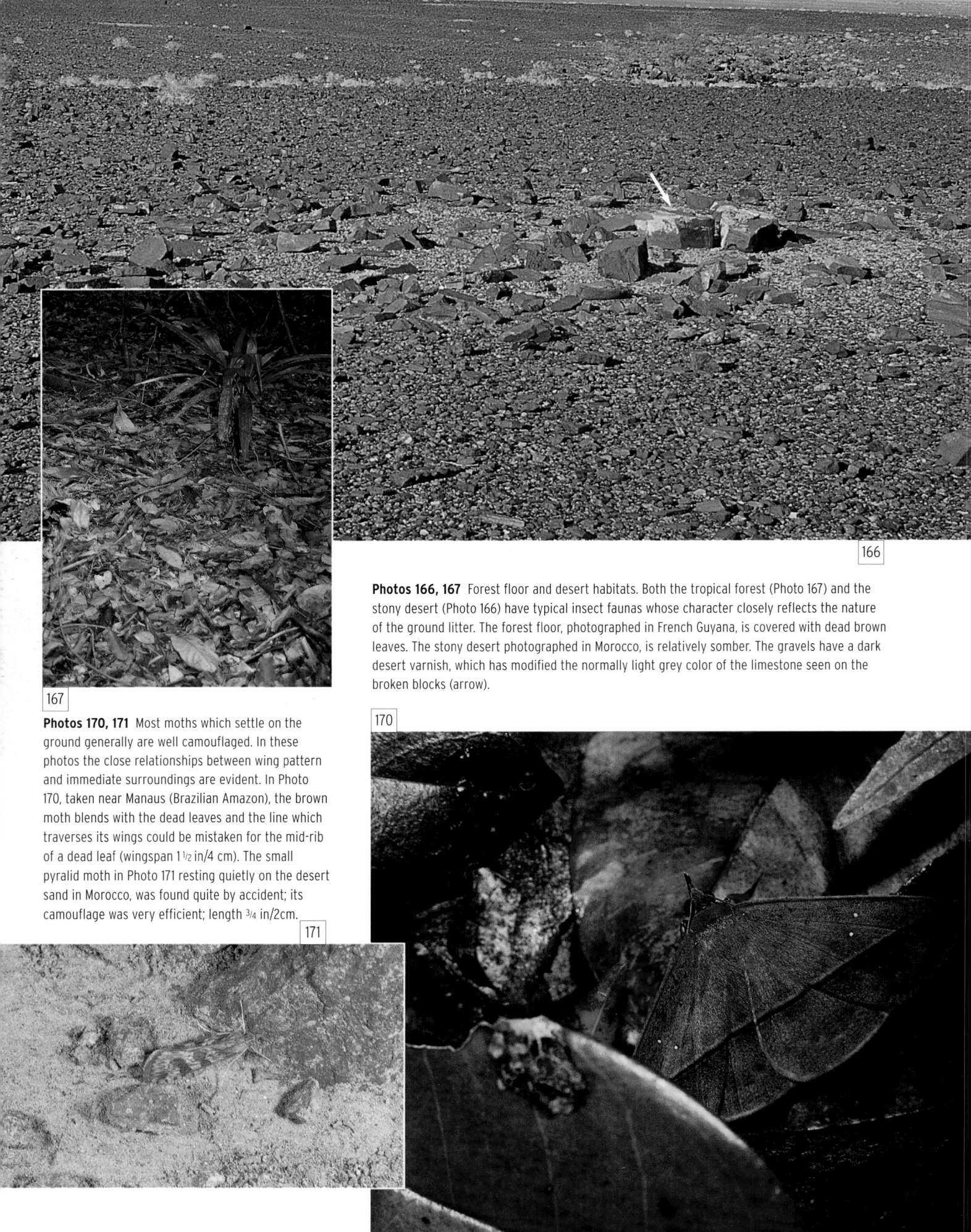

Photos 166, 167 Forest floor and desert habitats. Both the tropical forest (Photo 167) and the stony desert (Photo 166) have typical insect faunas whose character closely reflects the nature of the ground litter. The forest floor, photographed in French Guyana, is covered with dead brown leaves. The stony desert photographed in Morocco, is relatively somber. The gravels have a dark desert varnish, which has modified the normally light grey color of the limestone seen on the broken blocks (arrow).

Photos 170, 171 Most moths which settle on the ground generally are well camouflaged. In these photos the close relationships between wing pattern and immediate surroundings are evident. In Photo 170, taken near Manaus (Brazilian Amazon), the brown moth blends with the dead leaves and the line which traverses its wings could be mistaken for the mid-rib of a dead leaf (wingspan 1 1/2 in/4 cm). The small pyralid moth in Photo 171 resting quietly on the desert sand in Morocco, was found quite by accident; its camouflage was very efficient; length 3/4 in/2cm.

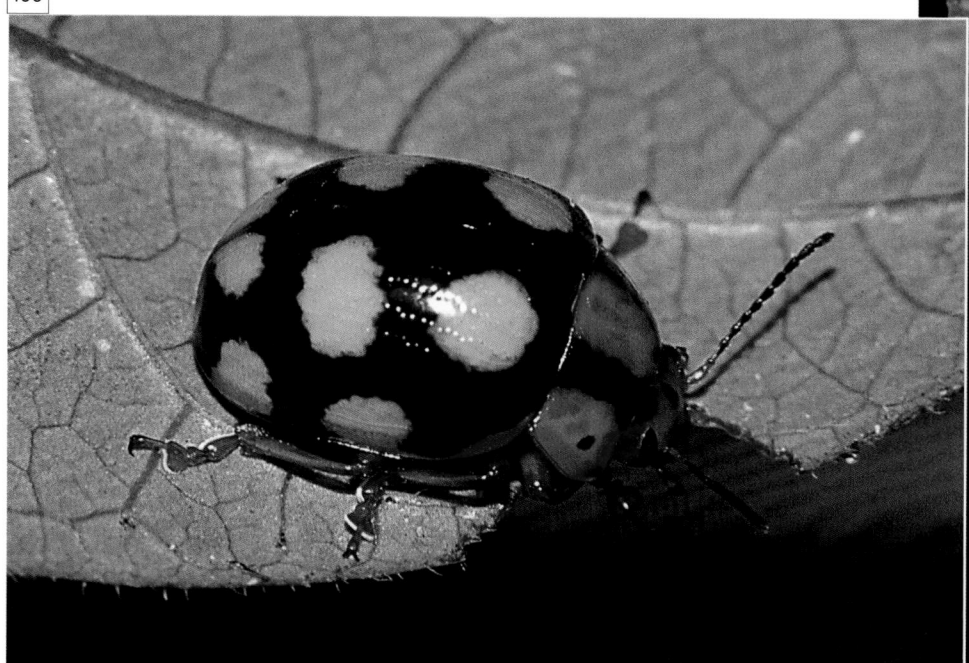

Both forest floor and stony desert are littered with detritus that often houses a varied insect fauna. Those that live on the surface are generally immobile and finding them requires careful search. Within the forest, the lack of sunlight favors those insects whose brown colors blend perfectly with the dead leaves among which they sit (Photo 170). In desert areas, the insect fauna is abundant during spring when the seasonal vegetation encourages both butterflies and beetles. For the remainder of the year one must search carefully between stones, where grasshoppers and mantids are carefully hidden. These insects differ both in color and shape from their cousins that inhabit the forest floor.

Beetles are seen frequently in tropical forests. Many are brightly colored, often a warning to predators of their noxious, inedible qualities. But the majority are brown or black and have little need for camouflage, for they are usually hidden in plant detritus. The minority that seek camouflage, including many weevils and the occasional longhorn, generally resemble the bark or lichens on which they rest.

Within the tropical forest there are many habitats, each having its particular color and form. The forest floor, as seen in the preceeding photos, is nearly always brown in color and the dead leaves and sticks that carpet the surface are irregular in shape. Jungle insects, including moths (Photo 170), take advantage of this habitat, within which they may be perfectly camouflaged. Often they are discovered by accident. When I walk slowly through the forest, a moth may suddenly flutter away and I must note very carefully the exact point at which it lands if I wish to photograph it. The same situation occurs in the desert although moths are relatively rare. Small pyralids

Photos 168, 169 The striking contrast between these two beetles expresses their means of defence. Photo 168 shows a brightly colored chrysomelid beetle that advertises its noxious flavors, while the edible longhorn beetle (Photo 169) seeks protection through camouflage.

Photographed respectively in Tikal Reserve, Guatemala (length ¼ in/6 mm) and Madre de Dios in the Peruvian Amazon (length ¾ in/2 cm.).

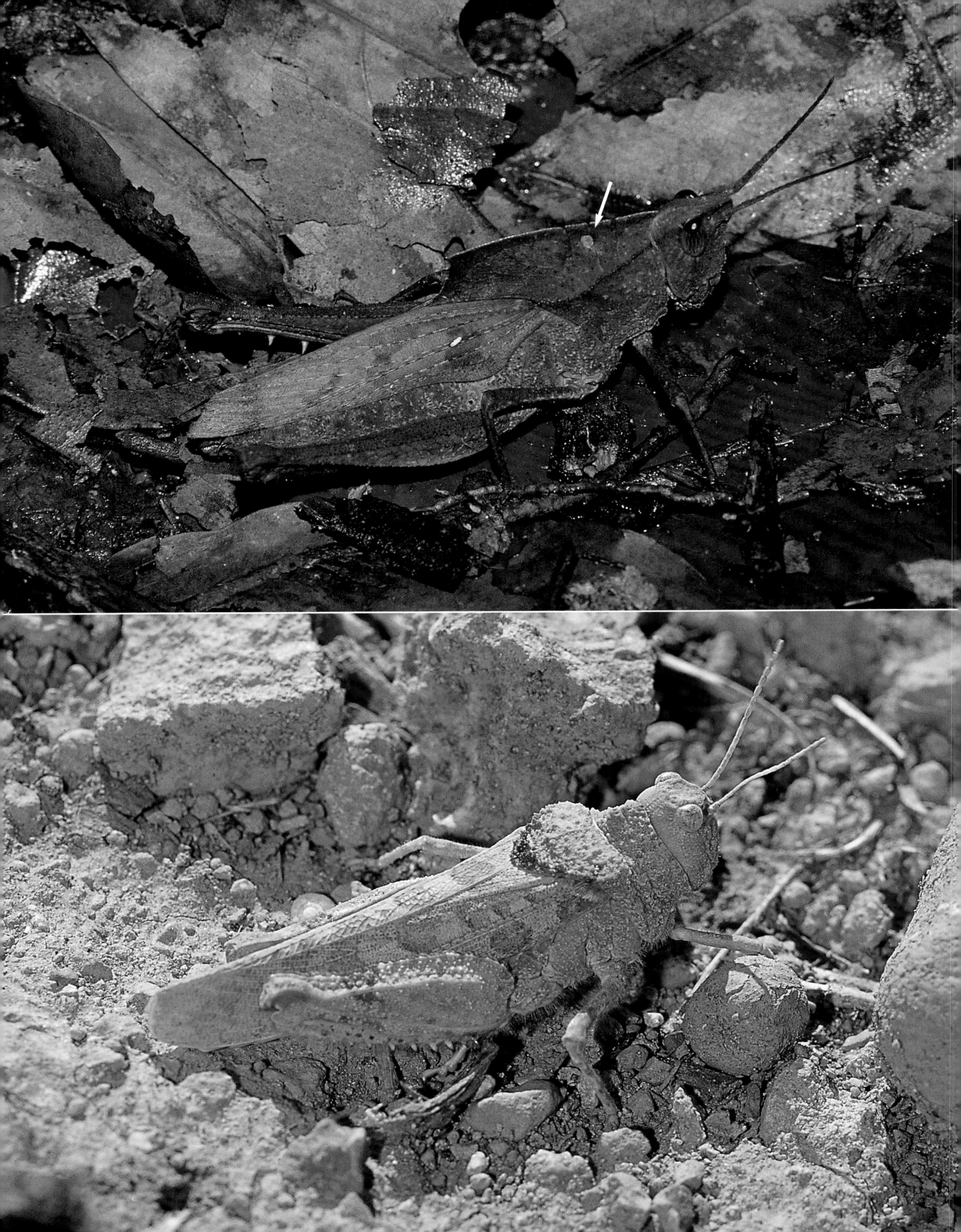

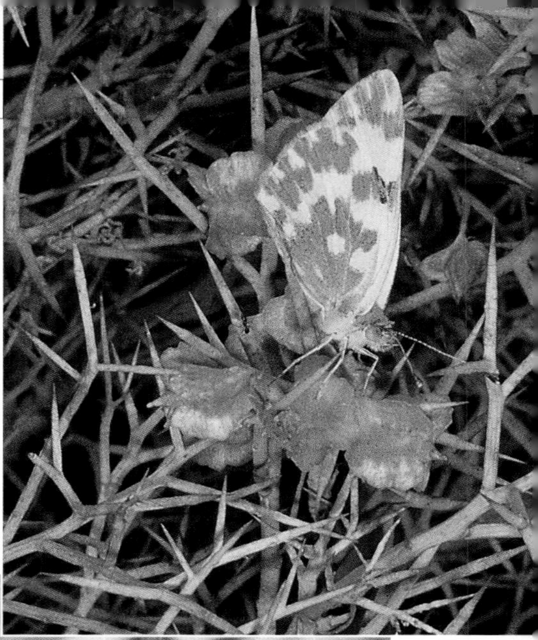

and noctuids may nestle between stones (Photo 174), where their beige colors blend well with the desert detritus. During the day moths are not apparent but at night they are relatively abundant, especially when one lights a strong lamp.

Most butterflies are mobile creatures and therefore rarely seek camouflage. However, those that spend most of the day on the ground or on low vegetation may blend with their surroundings. Jungle moths, in particular may be green or brown while the butterflies which live in dry savanna scrub generally lack color, being white or beige (Photos 174 and 175).

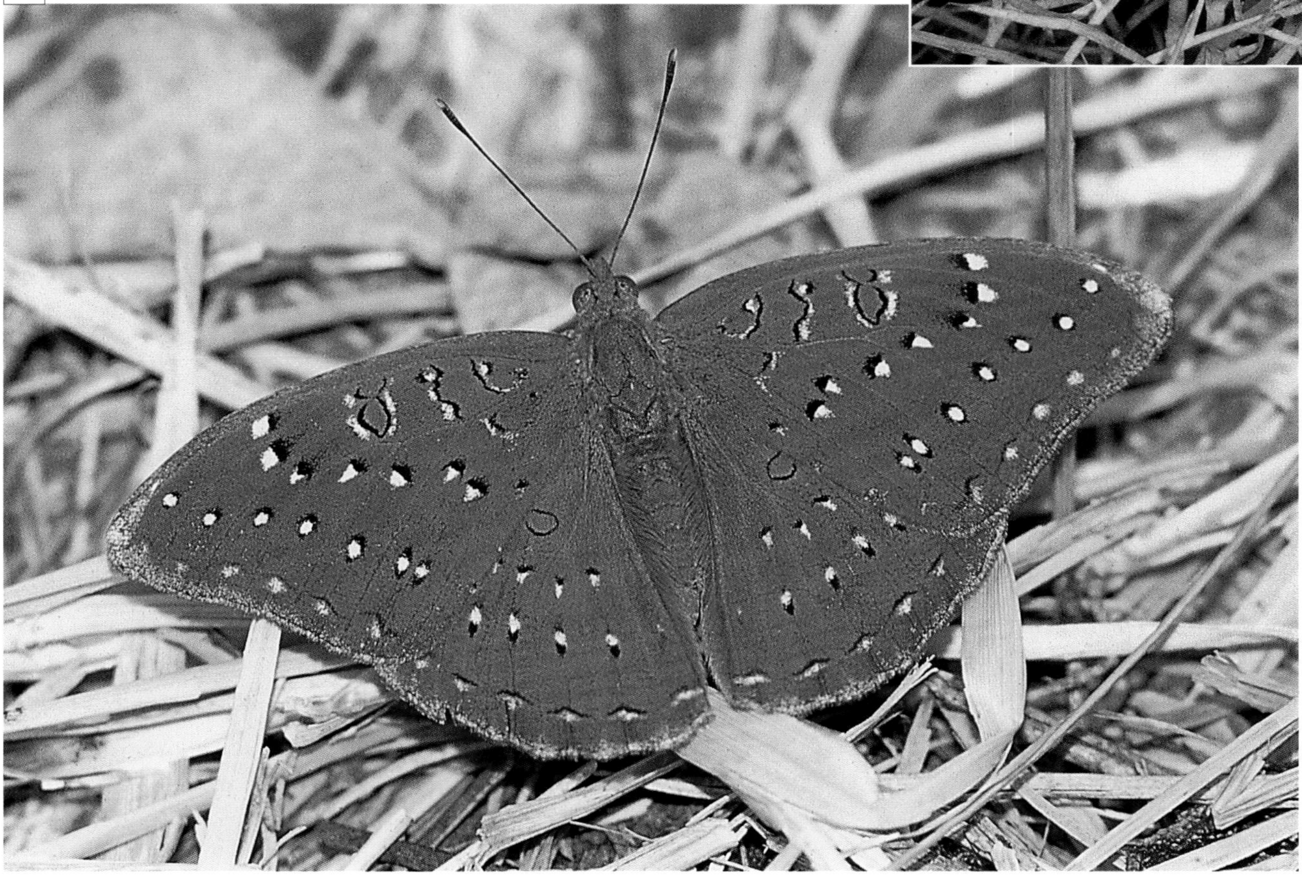

Photos 172, 173 (opposite page) Grasshoppers usually blend well with their immediate surroundings. In Photo 172, (upper) taken in the Peruvian Amazon, the brown acridid grasshopper has a leaf-shaped pronotum (arrow) and wings. Like the leaves among which it sits, these are smooth.

In Photo 173 (lower), taken in southern Morocco, the desert acridid grasshopper is beige in color and its pronotum and legs are decorated with small bumps. These give a body texture that closely resembles that of the limestone gravels among which it sits.

Photos 174, 175 These butterflies, in dry savanna habitats, contrast with the moth in Photo 176 (next page). The small pierid butterfly (*Pontia*), in Photo 175, is fairly well camouflaged on the thorny bush, while the larger grey butterfly (*Humanumida*) tends to blend with the dry savanna scrub in which it lives. Photographed respectively in southern Morocco and in Tanzania.

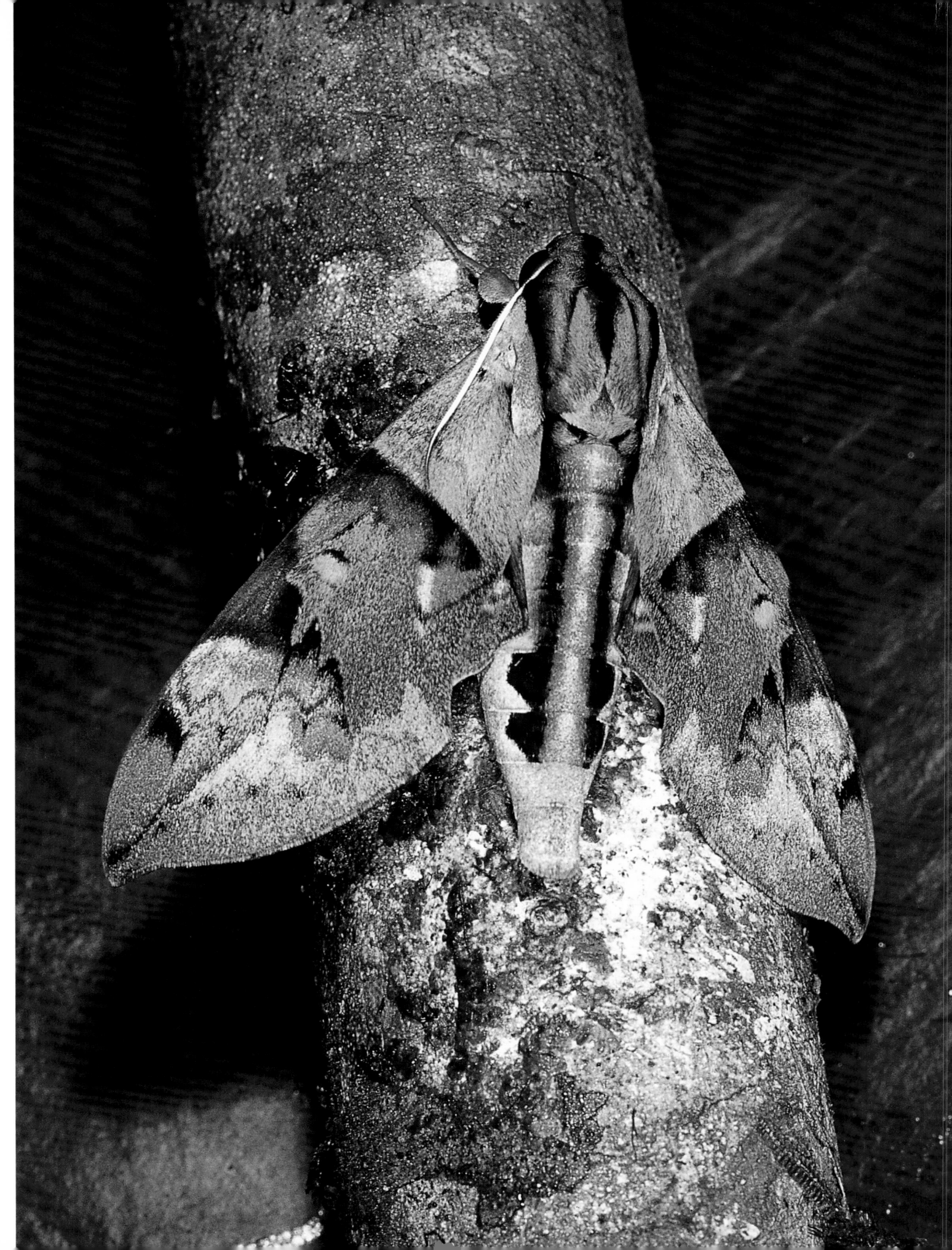

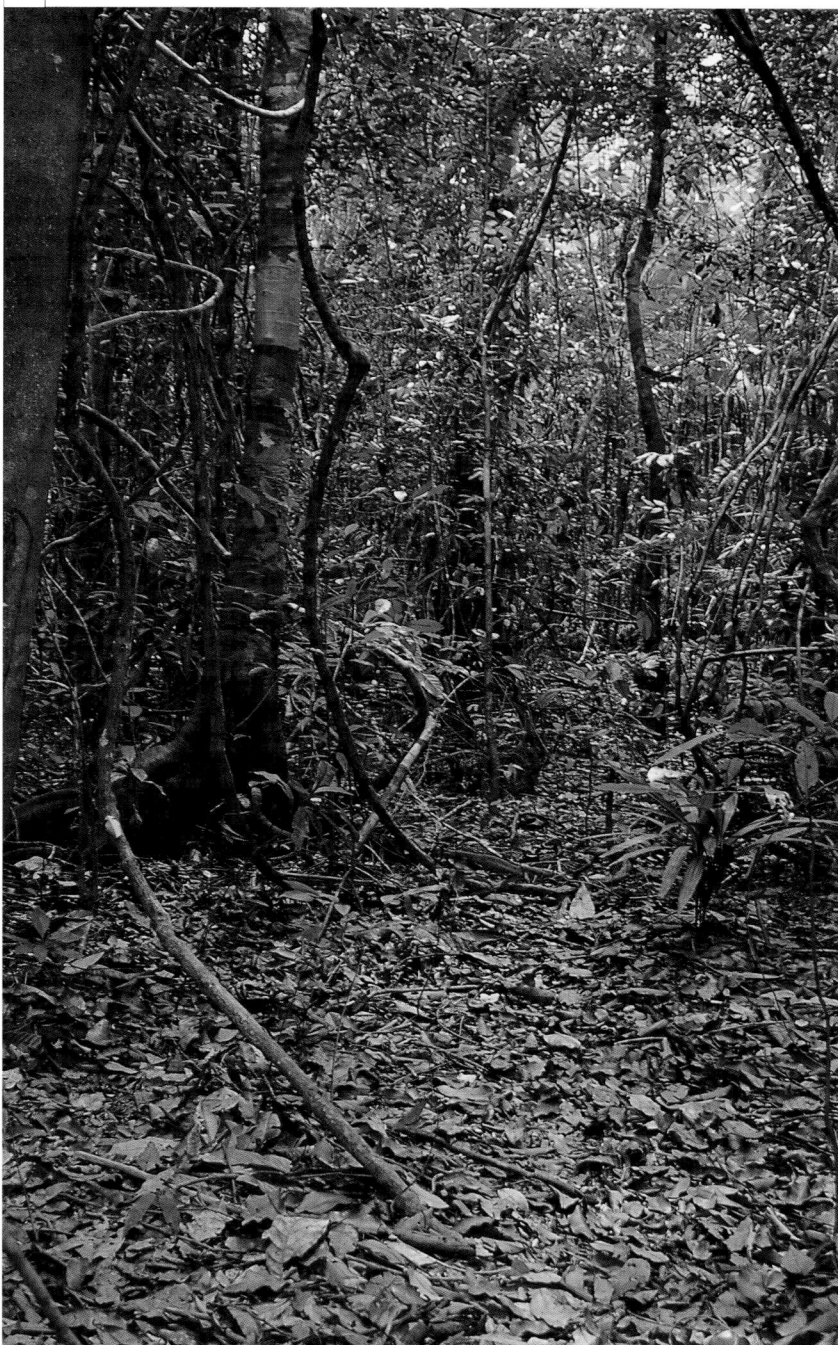

Photo 176 (opposite) This splendid sphinx moth (*Eumorpha*), would be perfectly camouflaged when resting on green vegetation. Its camouflage depends mainly on the series of disruptive green bands, whose oblique orientation with respect to the wings tends to optically modify the shape of the moth. French Guyana; wingspan 3½ in/9 cm.

Photos 177, 178, 179 (this and following pages) These photos show the mantids of a typical rain forest. In Photo 177, taken near the Maroni River in French Guyana, green vegetation and brown detritus litters the forest floor. The latter is relatively poor in large insects as most of the large insects live in the green vegetation above. Most mantids (Photo 179, page 117) and grasshoppers are green in color, but the exceptional brown mantids (Photo 178, page 116) closely resemble dead leaves suspended temporarily among the living vegetation. Length, both mantids 2½ in/6 cm.

There are marked differences between the mantids and bugs which live in forest or in dry-land habitats. Their shapes and colors closely reflect those of the leaves on which they are camouflaged. This same situation also applies to the katydids and grasshoppers shown in Photos 182 and 183. A green, leaf-like katydid would be completely out of place in a dry savanna, where it would rapidly be eaten by a bird or lizard. Dry-land, thorny vegetation is inhabited by other families of grasshoppers, whose beige colors and thin bodies are well adapted to these habitats.

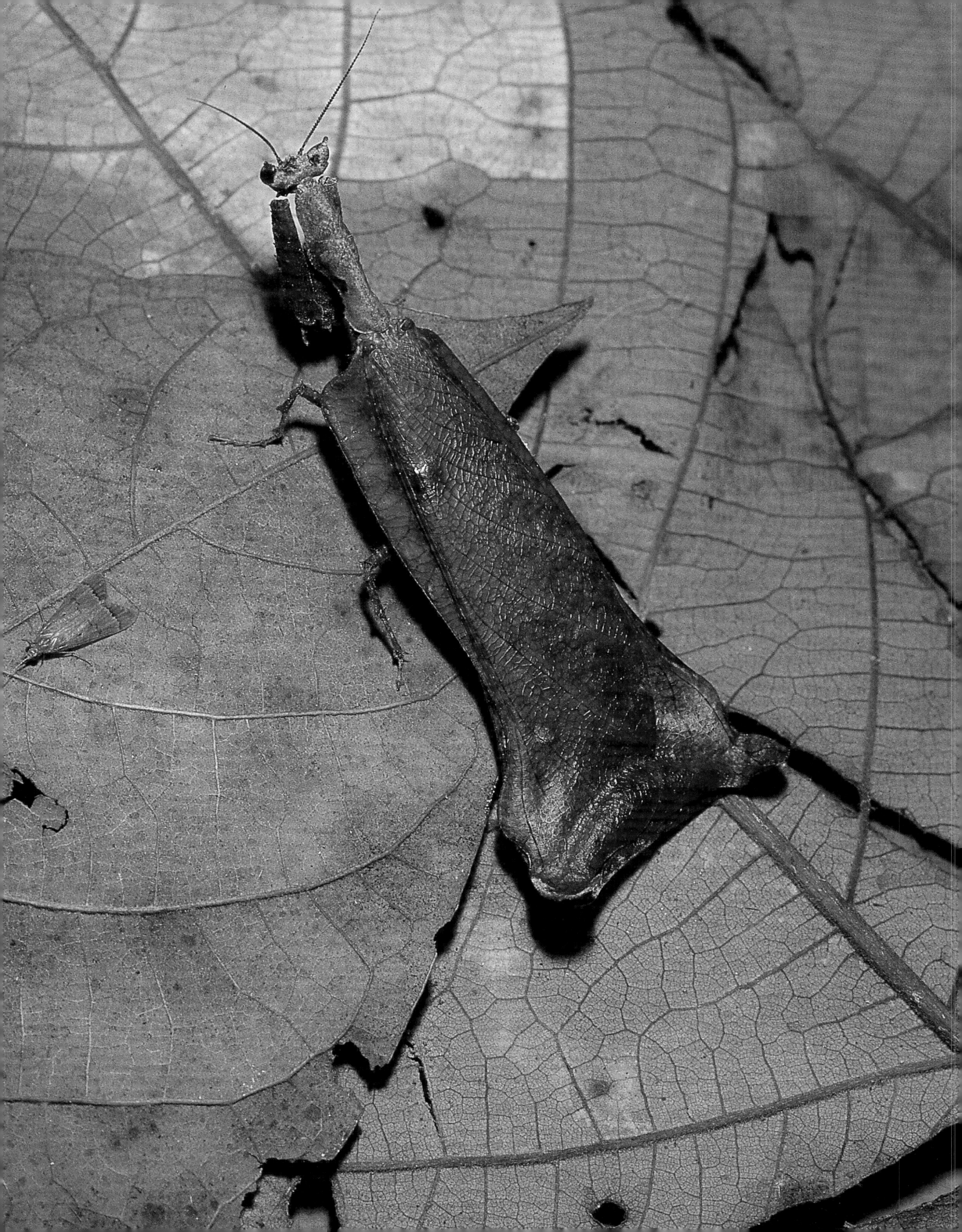

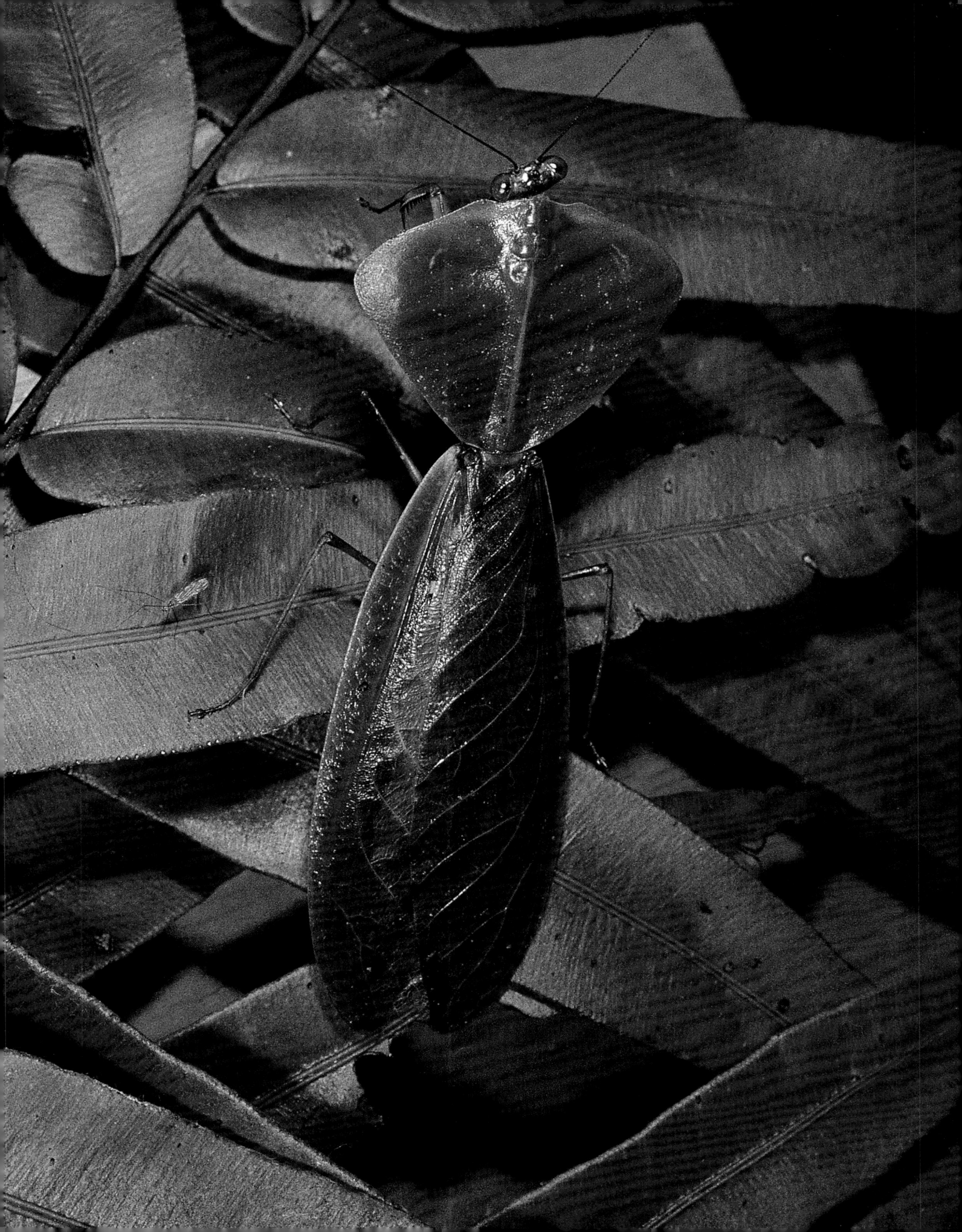

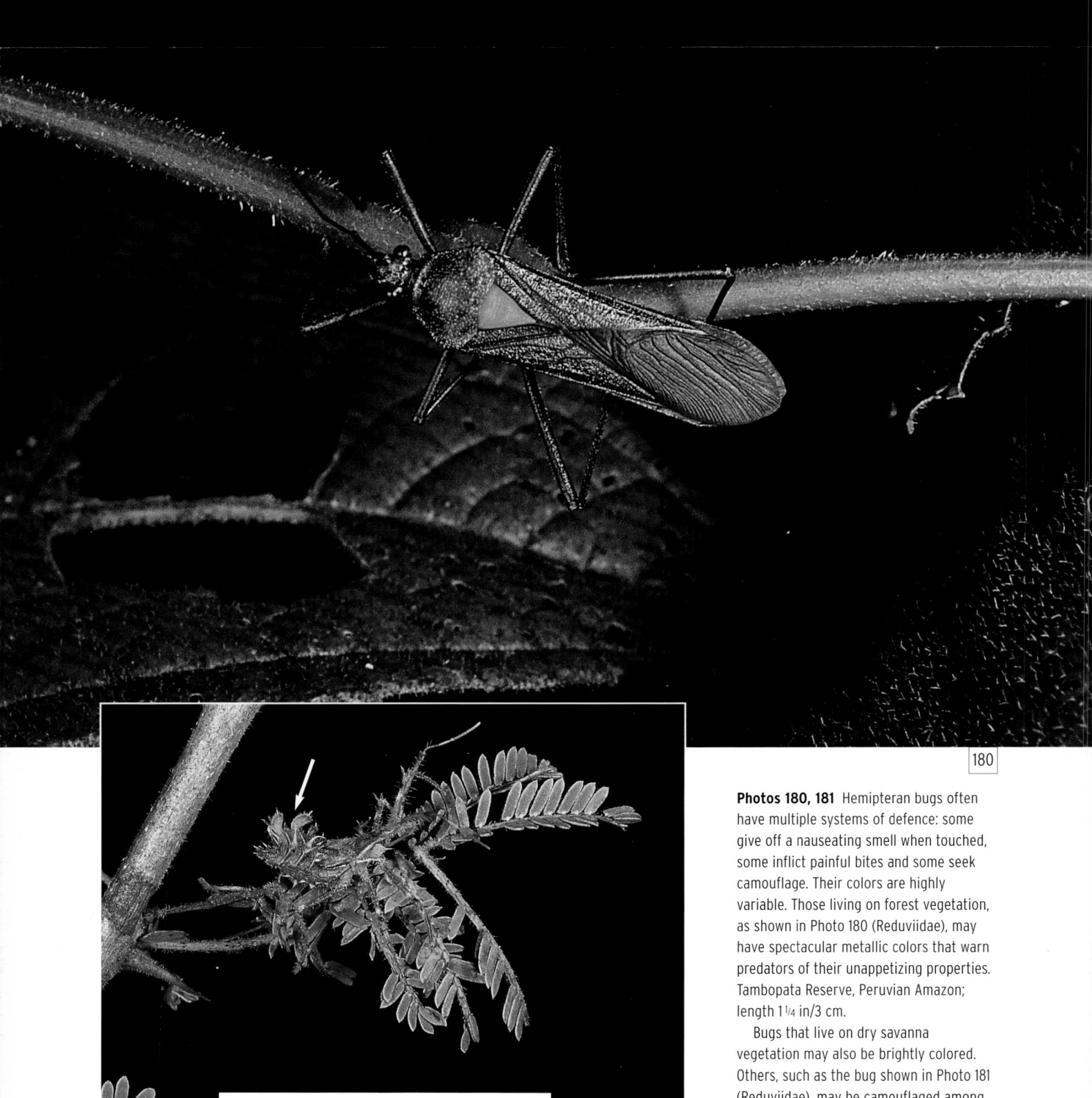

Photos 180, 181 Hemipteran bugs often have multiple systems of defence: some give off a nauseating smell when touched, some inflict painful bites and some seek camouflage. Their colors are highly variable. Those living on forest vegetation, as shown in Photo 180 (Reduviidae), may have spectacular metallic colors that warn predators of their unappetizing properties. Tambopata Reserve, Peruvian Amazon; length 1 ¼ in/3 cm.

Bugs that live on dry savanna vegetation may also be brightly colored. Others, such as the bug shown in Photo 181 (Reduviidae), may be camouflaged among the small leaves of acacia trees. Note the very close correspondence between the shape of the body (arrow) and that of the acacia leaves (see sketch, inset). Northern Tanzania; length ³⁄₄ in/2 cm.

181

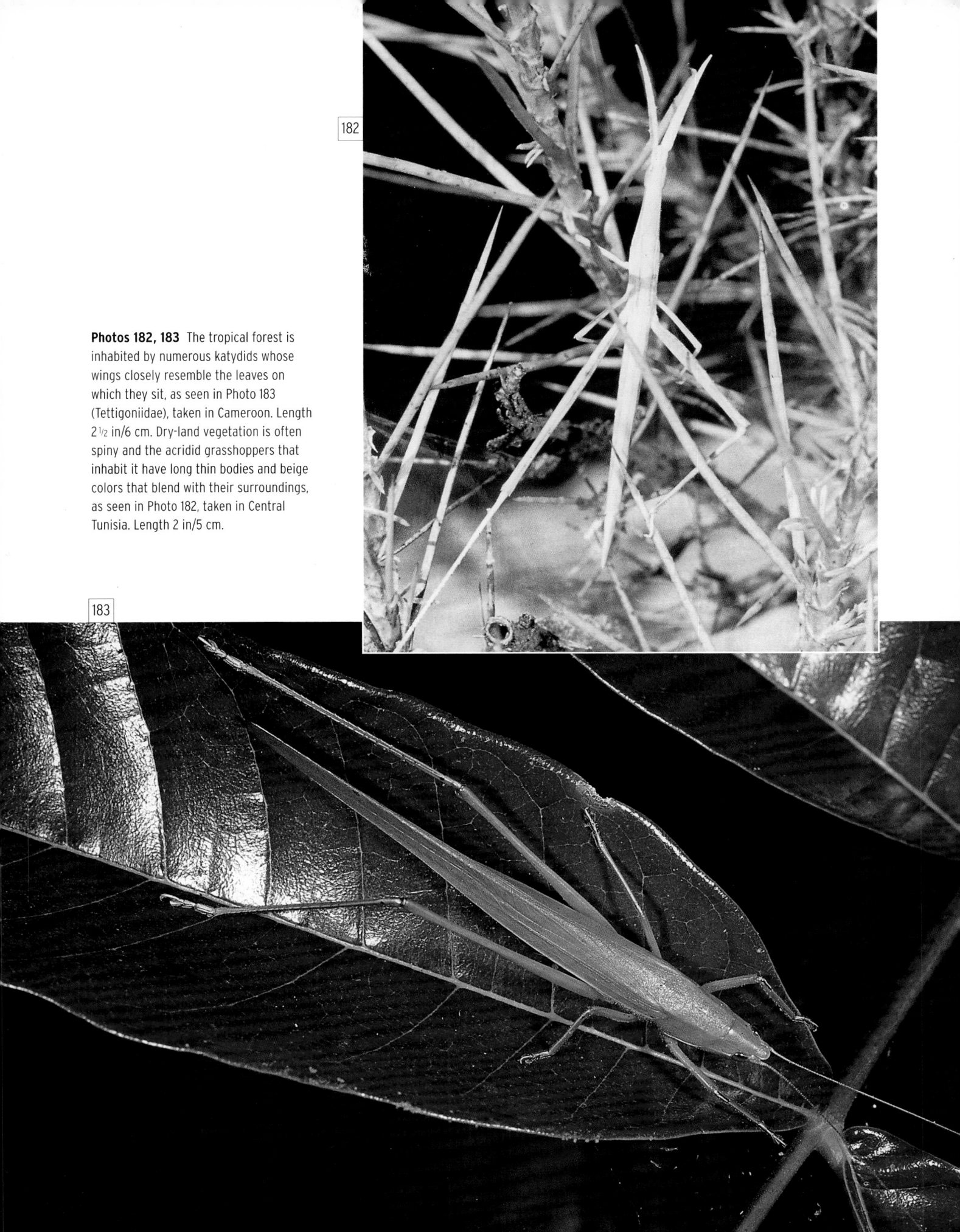

Photos 182, 183 The tropical forest is inhabited by numerous katydids whose wings closely resemble the leaves on which they sit, as seen in Photo 183 (Tettigoniidae), taken in Cameroon. Length 2½ in/6 cm. Dry-land vegetation is often spiny and the acridid grasshoppers that inhabit it have long thin bodies and beige colors that blend with their surroundings, as seen in Photo 182, taken in Central Tunisia. Length 2 in/5 cm.

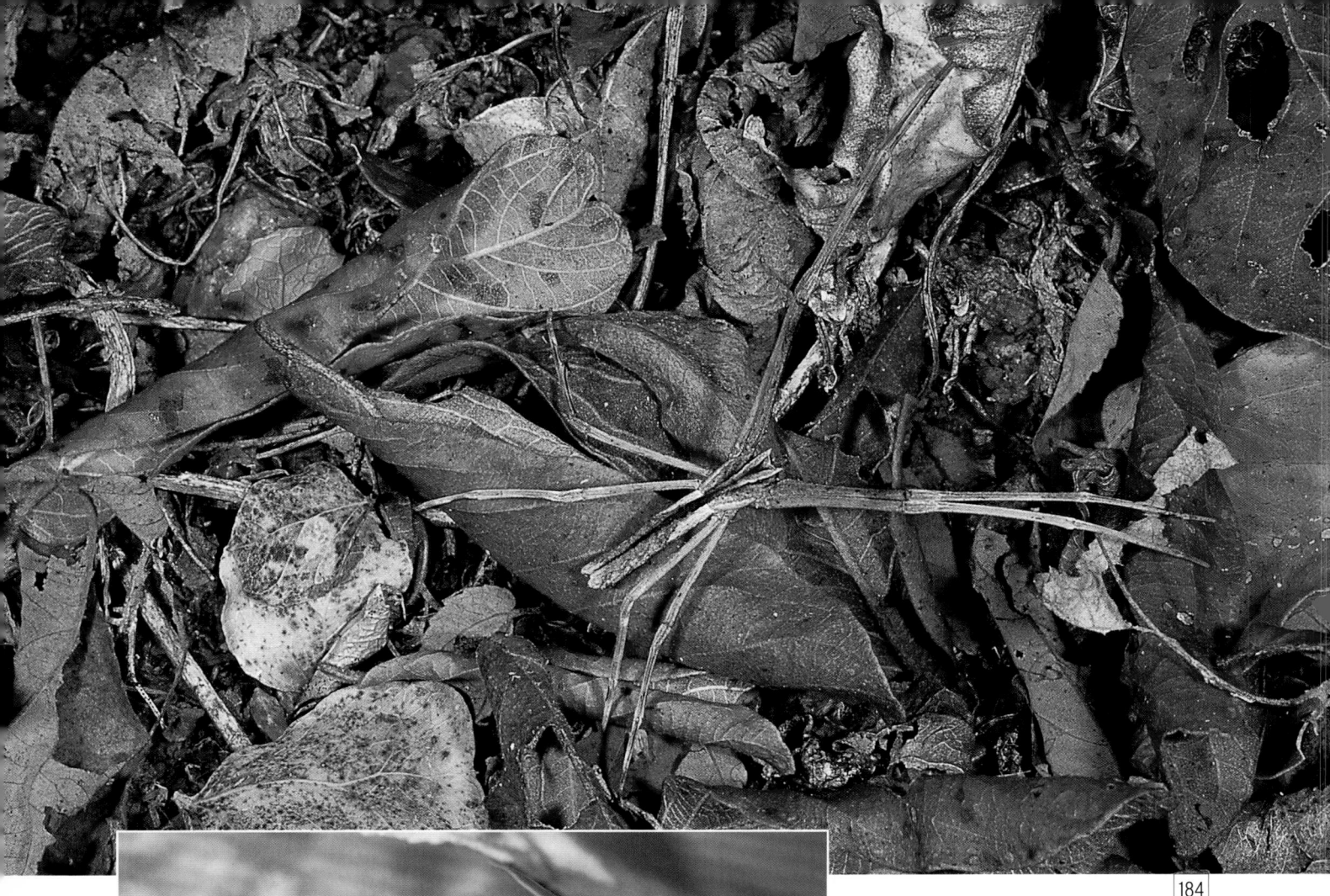

Photos 184, 185 In general, forest spiders
are bigger and darker in color than their
desert equivalents, as illustrated by the
hairy *Avicularia* in Photo 185, photographed
in the Venezuelan forest. Width 2 3/4 in/7 cm.
Spiders living among dry savanna detritus
(Photo 184) are often beige in color and
match the colors of the surrounding
grasses and leaves. Photographed near the
Pare Mountains, Tanzania; width 2 in/5 cm.

Photos 186, 187 (opposite page) Low
vegetation, both in tropical forest and in
dry savanna, usually houses a rich insect
fauna. In Photo 186, a track through Hutan
Lipur Forest in Malaysia is bordered by
secondary vegetation, where I
photographed mantids, grasshoppers and
passing butterflies. Photo 187, in contrast to
the photo above it, shows the typical beige,
thorny acacia shrubs and stony desert in
the Dra Valley, Morocco.

185

Most spiders do not require camouflage, for they are hidden between leaves or in burrows. However, spiders that are exposed on the ground or suspended in webs may seek protection. The forest dwellers are usually bigger and are often massive in shape, the migales and araneids being typical. In desert or dry savanna, spiders are less common and many have thin wispy legs and bodies that blend with the dry vegetation. They may run very quickly and are very difficult to photograph.

CAMOUFLAGE ABOVE THE GROUND

In *tropical forests* above-ground habitats are very numerous for, unlike deserts, there is a significant vertical dimension. Tree trunks, in particular, are an important habitat for insects. These trunks are often covered with a complex system of mosses, small ferns and lichens, which generally has a delicate, finely branched structure often imitated by its insect inhabitants.

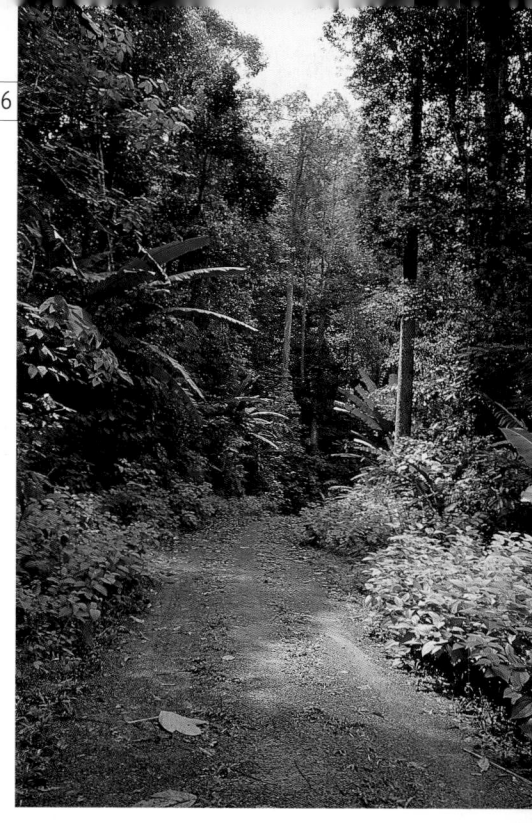

186

187

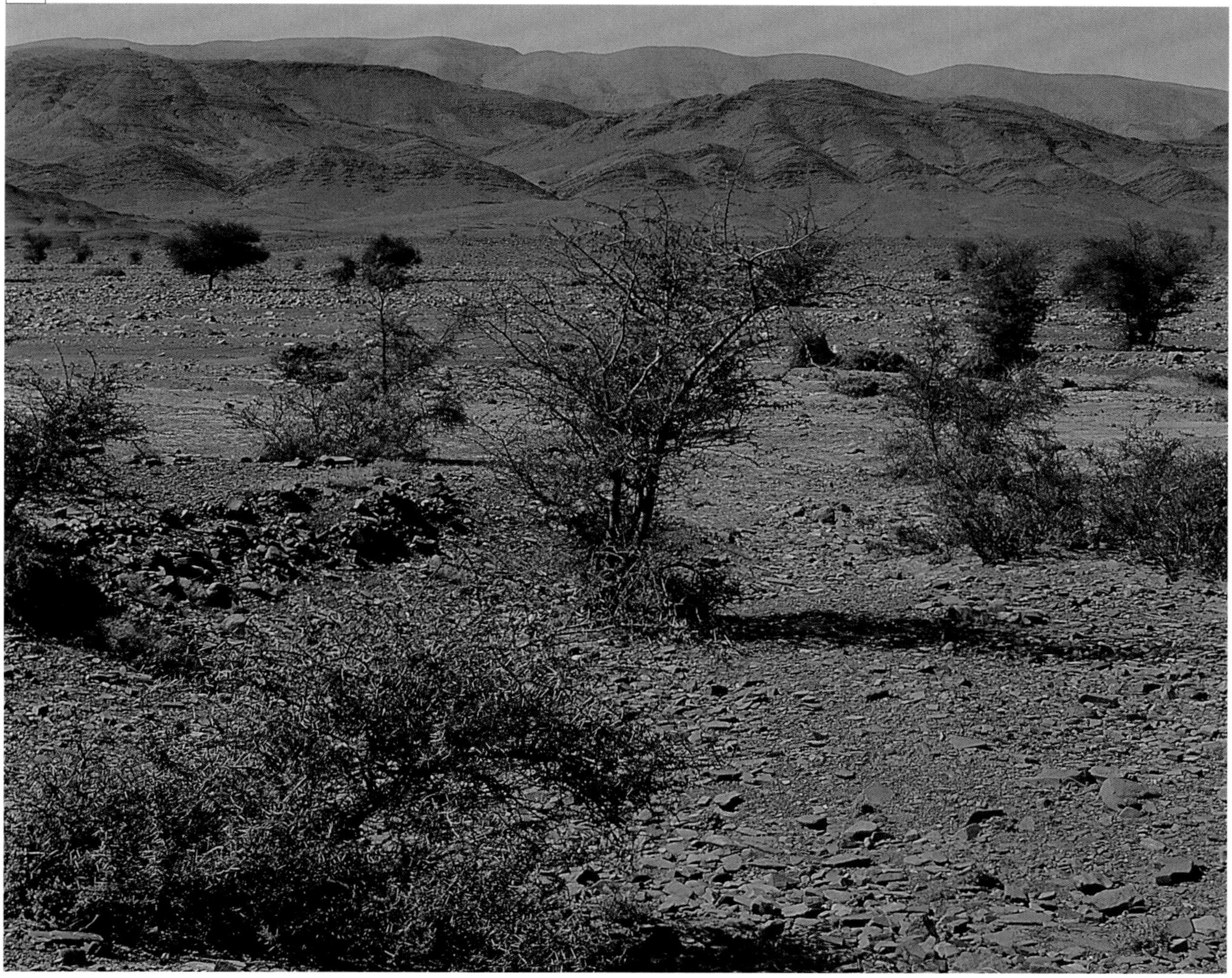

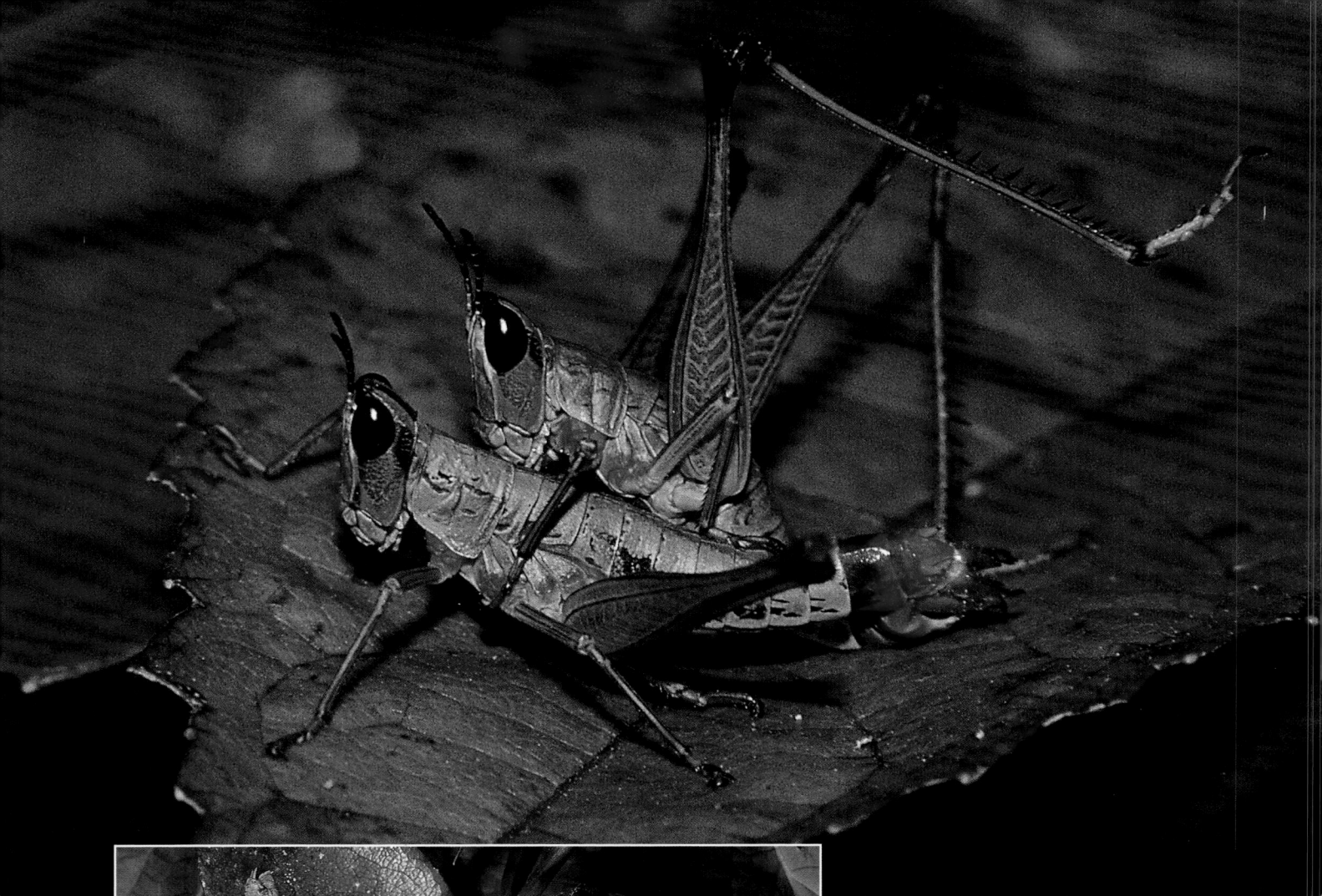

Photos 188, 189 Low, secondary vegetation fringing forest trails and narrow roads is a good place to find grasshoppers and mantids. These insects may be carefully camouflaged to match the green leaves and fallen twigs. In Photo 188, a pair of colorful acridid grasshoppers on secondary vegetation in Tikal Reserve, Guatemala. Length 1 1/4 in/3 cm. Mantids may resemble leaves or sticks. In Photo 189 a thin mantid hangs from a roadside plant where it closely resembles a fallen stick (arrow indicates head). Shimba Hills Reserve, Kenya; length 3 1/4 in/8 cm.

Photos 190, 191 (opposite page) Insects inhabiting dry savanna very often resemble dry grass. These two photos, both taken at the foot of the Pare Mountains in Tanzania, clearly show the very close relationships between the insect fauna and its habitat. In Photo 190, a phasmid resembles a blade of grass. Length 2 1/2 in/6 cm. In Photo 191, a mantid (arrow) is virtually invisible between tufts of dead grass. Length 1 1/2 in/4 cm.

189

Branches, whether these be situated close to the ground or high in the canopy, are dominated by leafy greens. These are matched by the green or brown, leaf-shaped grasshoppers, mantids and, especially in Asia, by large leaf-like phasmids.

In dry-land environments there are few trees and the tree-living insect fauna is correspondingly reduced. Because of the climate, the acacia trees have no epiphytes and the vegetation is often spiny. However, these habitats may have a surprisingly rich fauna, which includes many of the families found in tropical forests. Because the vegetation is dry, the light-green foliage of the forest is replaced by darker green or beige-colored spines and small leaves. The insects, whether they be mantids, grasshoppers or bugs, are often thin and their legs may be pointed (Photo 182); most are beige in color. They tend to blend perfectly with the dry, spiny vegetation.

In dry savanna and stony desert habitats, low vegetation in the form of grasses and thorny bushes may be quite green during the short spring, but this vegetation dies rapidly and the grass becomes beige. However, many insects remain and these often match the colors of the dry vegetation, as seen in Photos 190 and 191. Finding and photographing these insects requires systematic search, generally on hands and knees. In the heat of early summer this can be hard work.

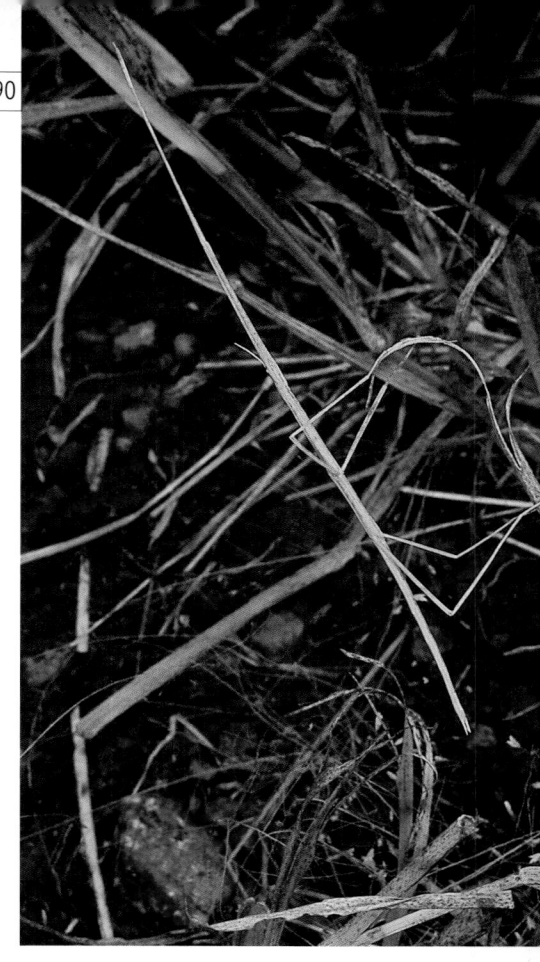

190

191

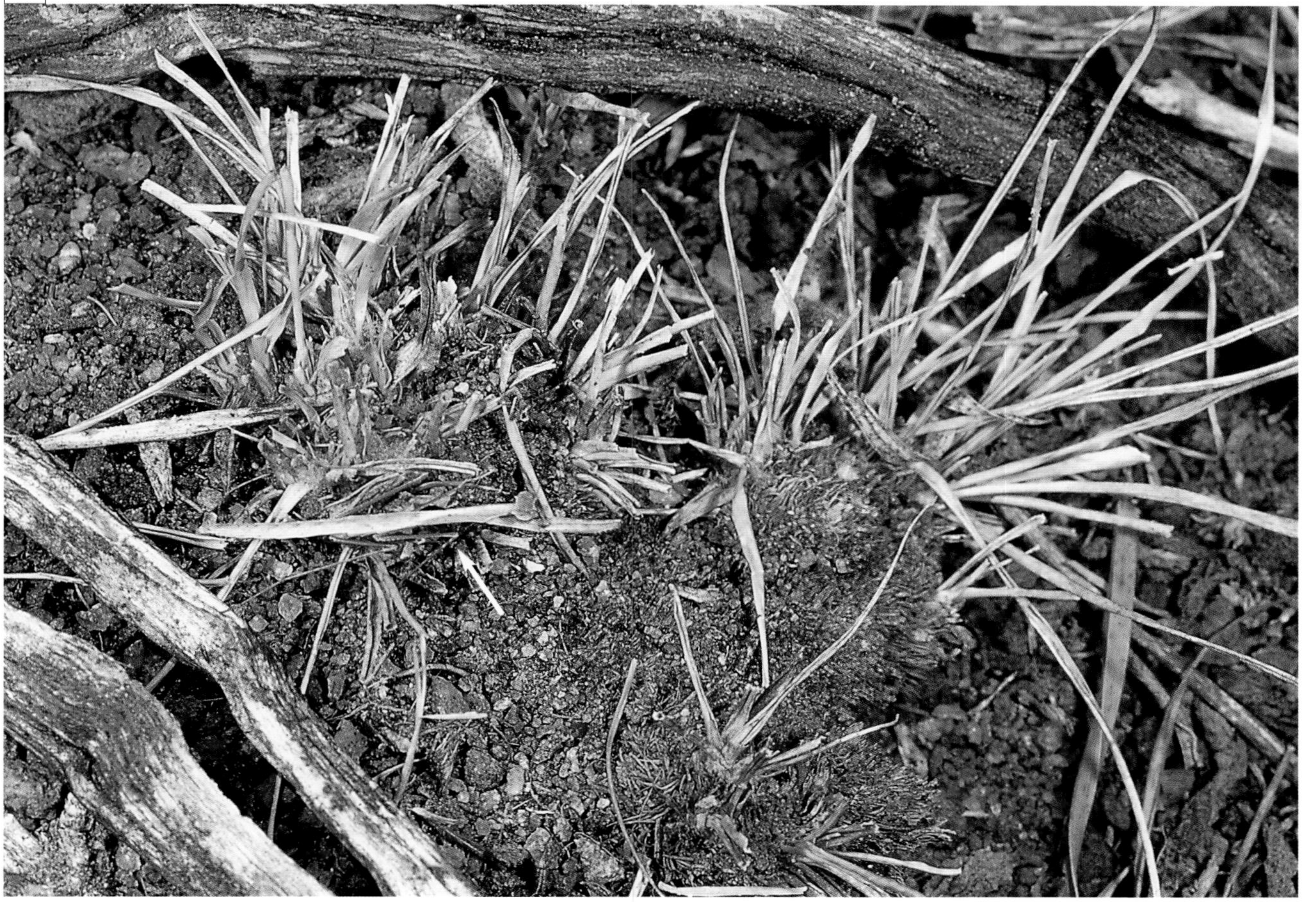

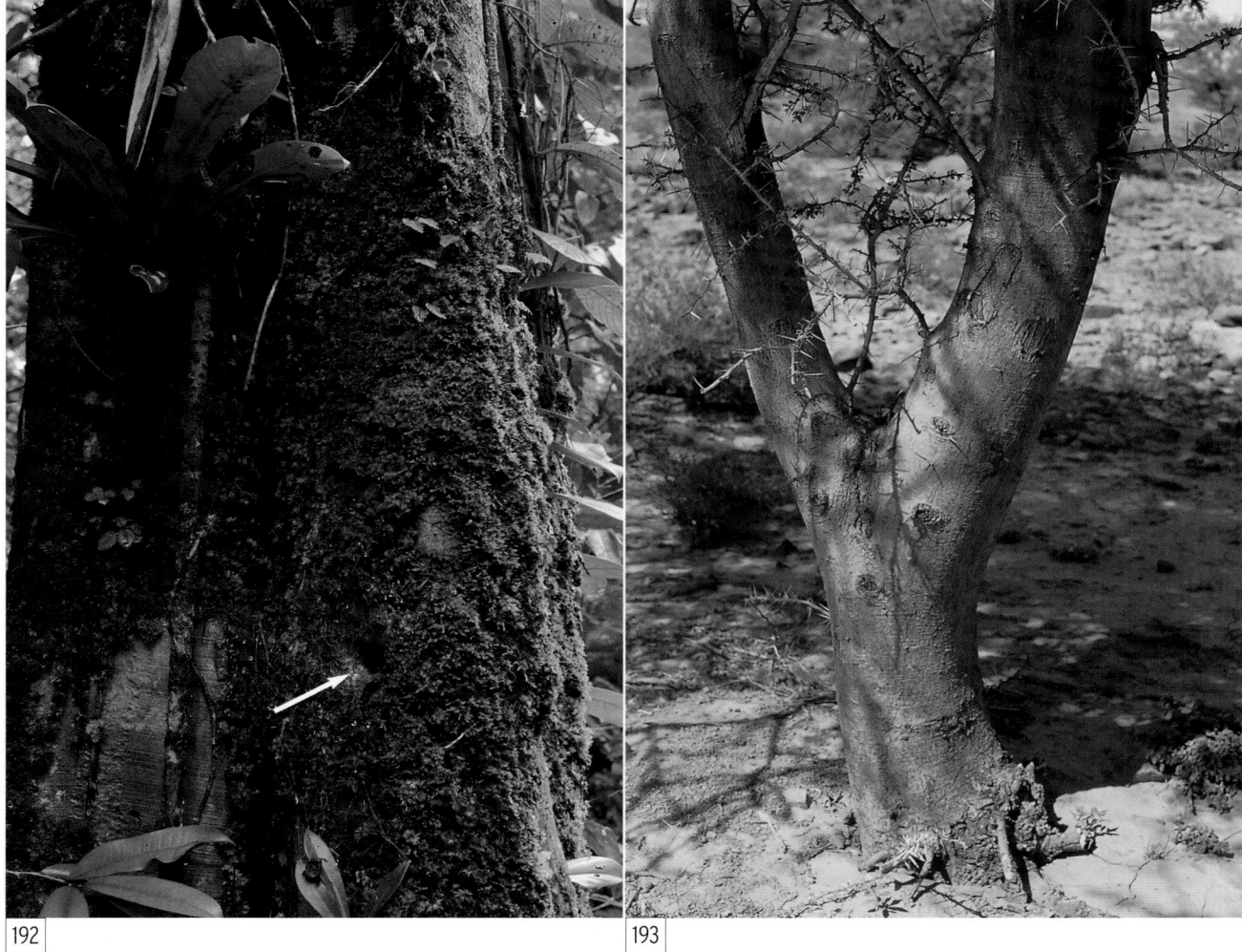

192

193

Photos 192, 193 Tree trunks provide habitats for a rich insect fauna that is usually camouflaged among the dense epiphytic vegetation encrusting the tree. Photo 192, taken in the Kaw Hills of French Guyana, shows a typical tree trunk. It is occupied by a large spider that lives in a hole (arrow) that was probably abandoned by a beetle. The trunks of acacia trees that grow in dry savannas and deserts have no epiphytic plants, as shown in Photo 193 taken in southern Morocco.

Photo 194 (opposite page) The large grey katydid (*Acanthodis*) in Photo 194 blends well with the grey lichens, the light and dark grey colors of its legs and body matching the different shades of grey on the bark of the tree. The insect is flattened against the tree trunk in order to reduce shadow and thus help it to merge with the surrounding bark.

THE TREE-TRUNK HABITAT

Insects which spend most of the day sitting quietly on the trunk of a forest tree are usually hidden within the epiphytic vegetation or, when exposed, well camouflaged. The density and variety of the epiphytic cover depends on humidity, attaining a maximum within cloud forests at altitudes of several thousand feet above sea level. These very wet forests are festooned with mosses, on which katydids and mantids may be nearly invisible. In rain forests, situated below about 3280 feet (1000 meters) above sea level, there are fewer epiphytes. Insects, including moths and katydids, sit directly on the bark where they are usually cryptically camouflaged (Photos 194, 195, 196).

In areas of low humidity, such as dry savanna, the scattered trees are devoid of epiphytic vegetation and, although the smooth trunks may hide scattered moths, most insects are camouflaged within the thorny branches above.

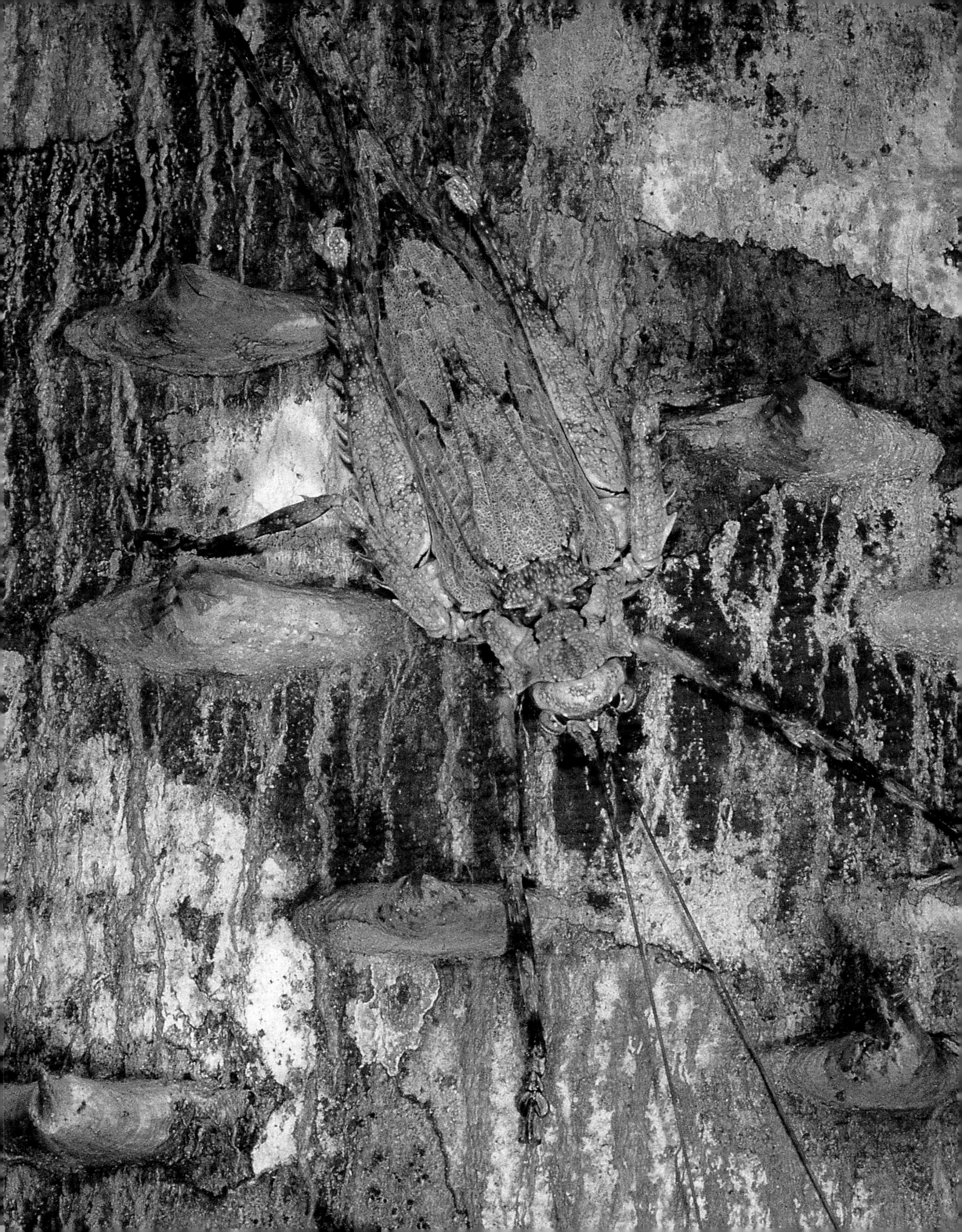

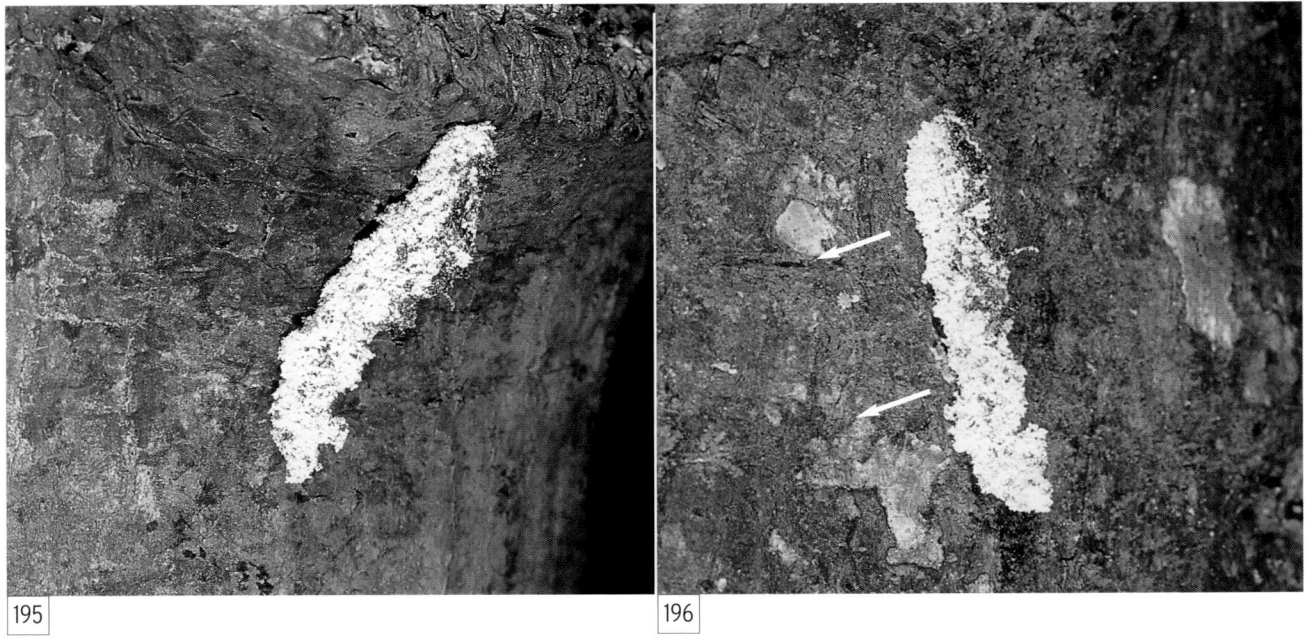

195

196

SUMMARY

Through geological time natural selection favors or eliminates. This selection is demonstrated in a convincing manner if we compare the faunas of two quite distinct environments: the jungle floor and the dry savanna. In each of these

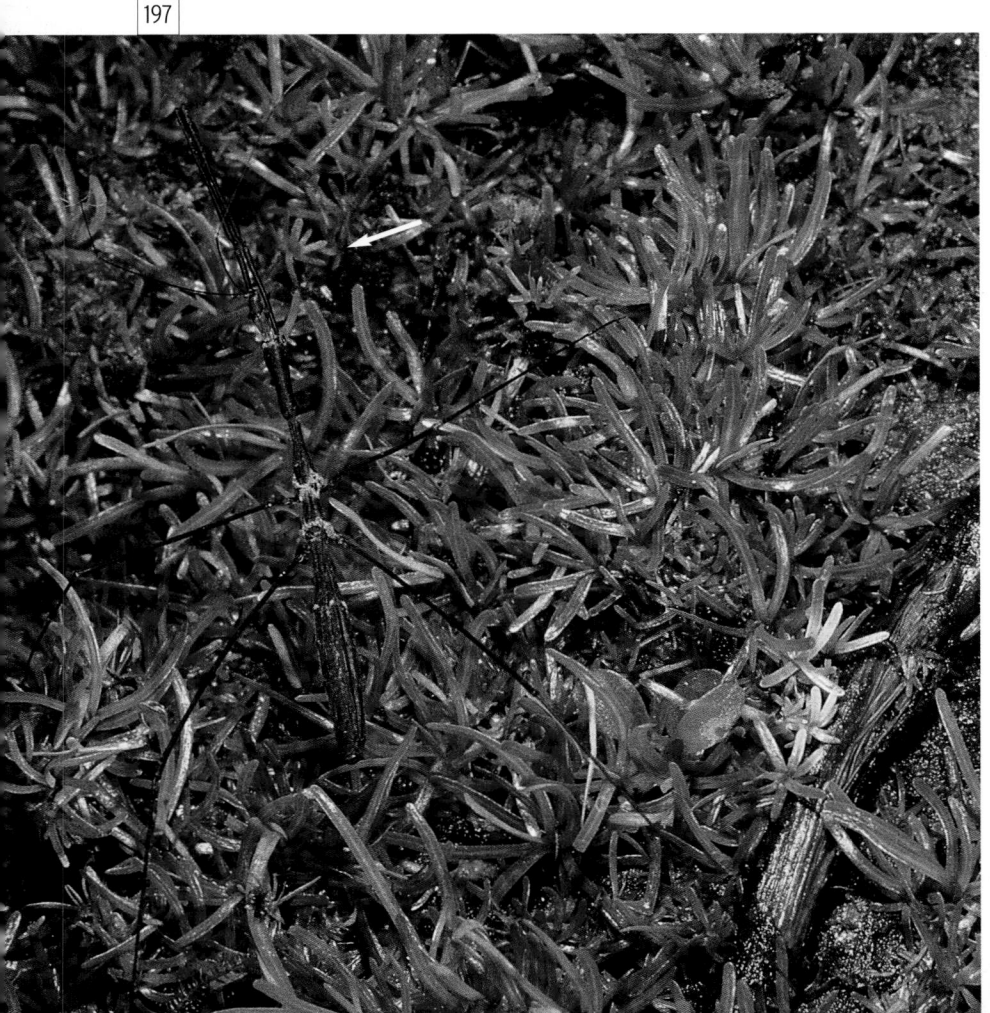

197

Photos 195, 196 These photos show different positions of a small caterpillar that looks like a piece of bark. Fortunately, this strange little object moved sideways (see two arrows) and revealed itself. Hutan Lipur Reserve, central Malaysia; length ¾ in/2 cm.

Photos 197, 198 These two photos illustrate the considerable difference between insects inhabiting the trunks of trees (Photo 197) and those living somewhat higher among the leaves (Photo 198, opposite page). The former (197) is thin and wispy, resembling a stick insect (arrow). In fact it is an unusual hydrometrid bug whose long narrow legs and body blend with the narrow-leaved epiphytic vegetation. Kaw Hills, French Guyana; length 1½ in/4 cm. The mantid opposite is more massive. Its pronotum (arrow) blends with the leaves on which it sits. This mantid is typical of tree-inhabiting mantids. Malaysia; length 2 in/5 cm.

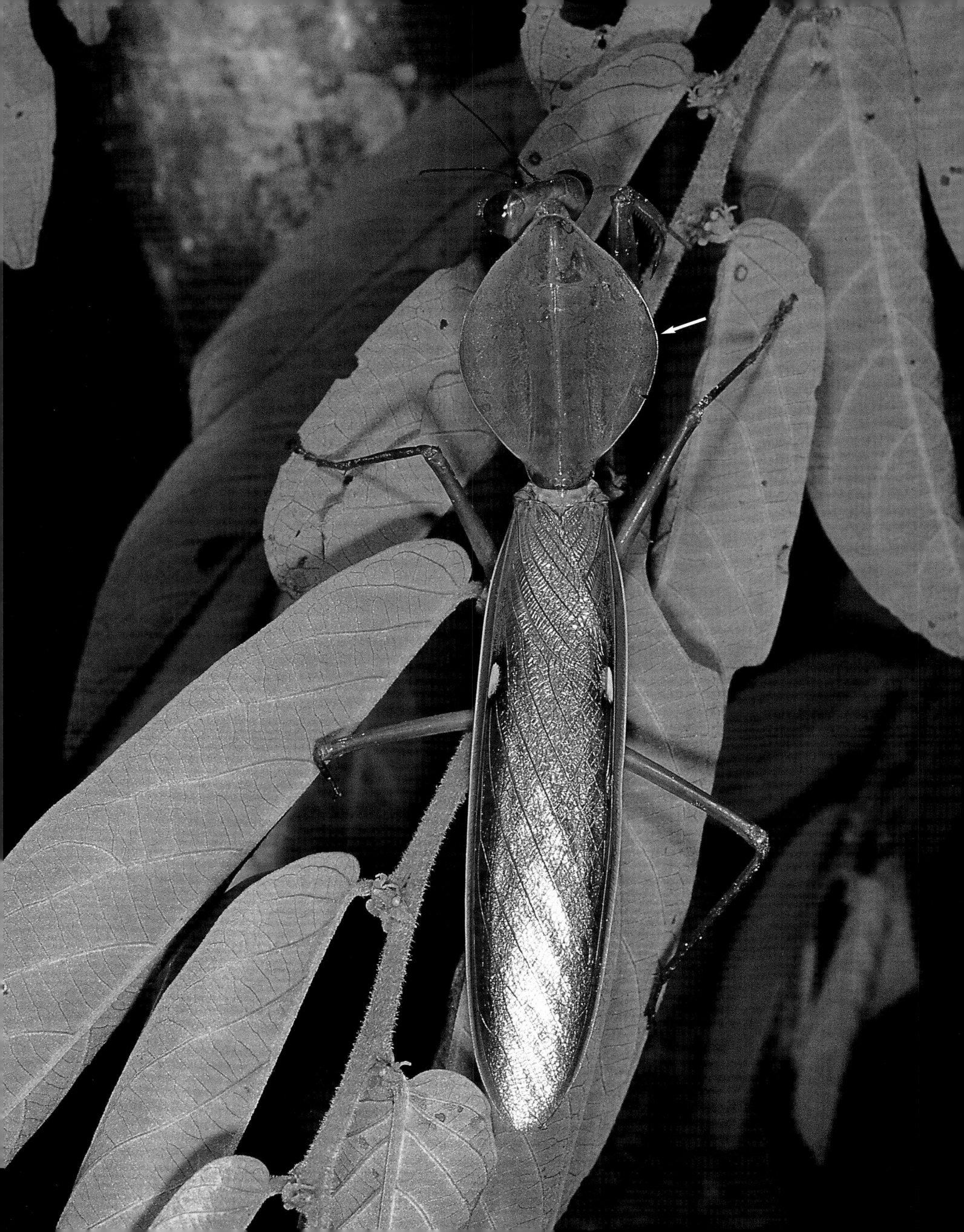

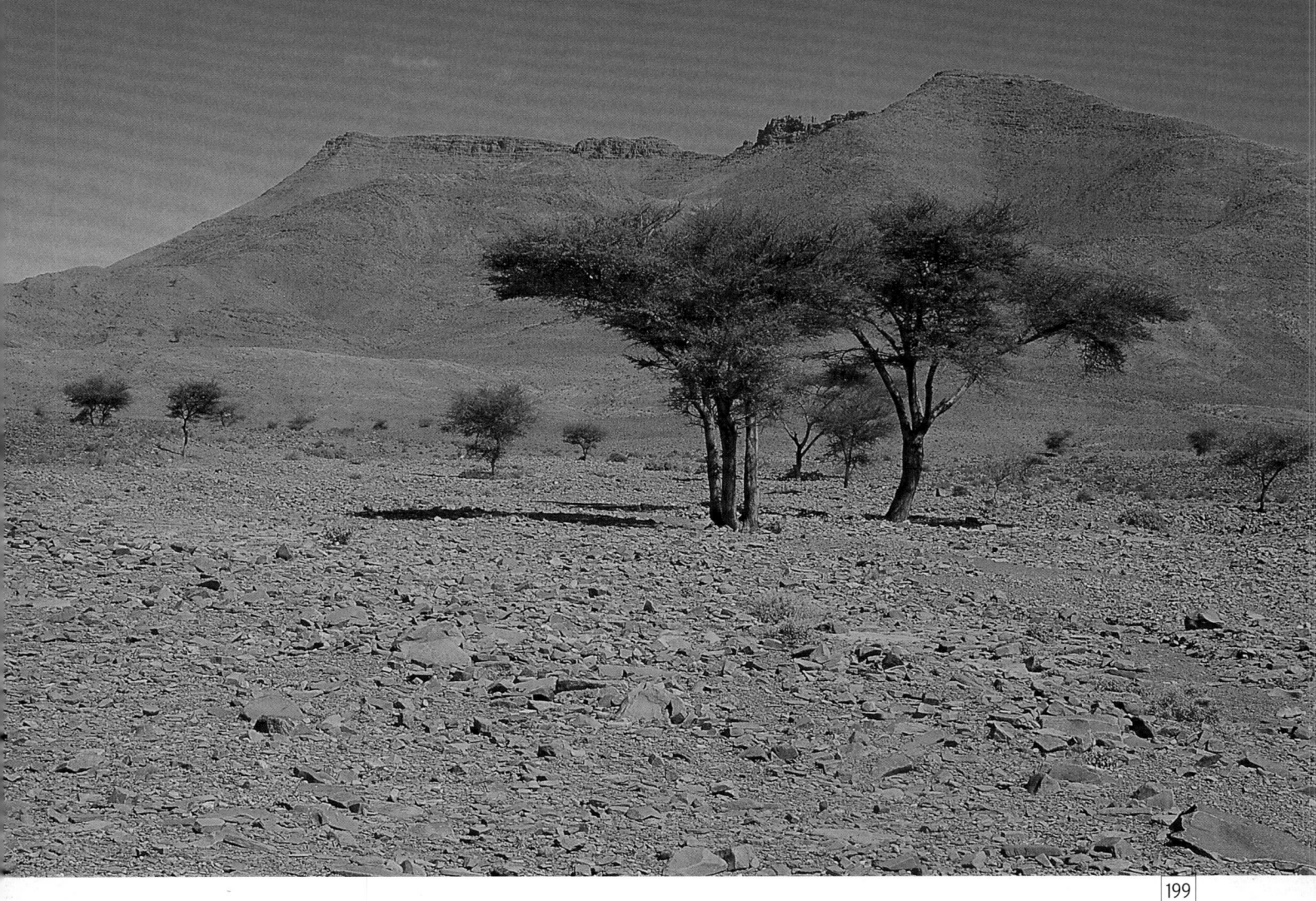

199

Photos 199, 200 These photos illustrate the obvious differences between tropical forest and dry savanna environments, which are reflected by the colors and shapes of their insect inhabitants, these being adapted to these settings through the process of natural selection. Photo 199, taken in the Dra Valley in southern Morocco, illustrates the two major habitats found in dry-land savanna: the stony soil with small dry shrubs and the spiny acacia trees. Photo 200 (opposite) shows typical hill forest at Creek Voltaire, French Guyana. It includes three major habitats: forest litter, tree trunk and living foliage. In spite of their hostile appearance, both these habitats may have a moderately rich insect fauna.

settings insects have suffered the constraints associated with that particular environment, and there has been selective preservation of species whose camouflage and other attributes are best suited to that particular setting.

In the case of insects, this convergence is due mainly to camouflage; many forest dwellers are brown or green and often have shapes resembling leaves or sticks, while in deserts and savannas insects tend to be grey or beige and resemble stones or dry grass. The magnitude of this natural selection becomes dramatically clear if we imagine the consequence of some magic transfer of the forest-dwellers to the dry savannas, while moving the savanna-dwellers to the forest. This transfer obviously would produce a very sharp color contrast between each environment and its new inhabitants. The clash, no doubt, would be disastrous for the insects; no longer camouflaged, they would be devoured rapidly by local predators. This impossible scenario highlights the nature and importance of natural selection in general, and camouflage and mimicry, in particular.

Camouflage and mimicry are among the most intriguing aspects of insect life. We are witnessing only a very small part of a very long and fascinating story.

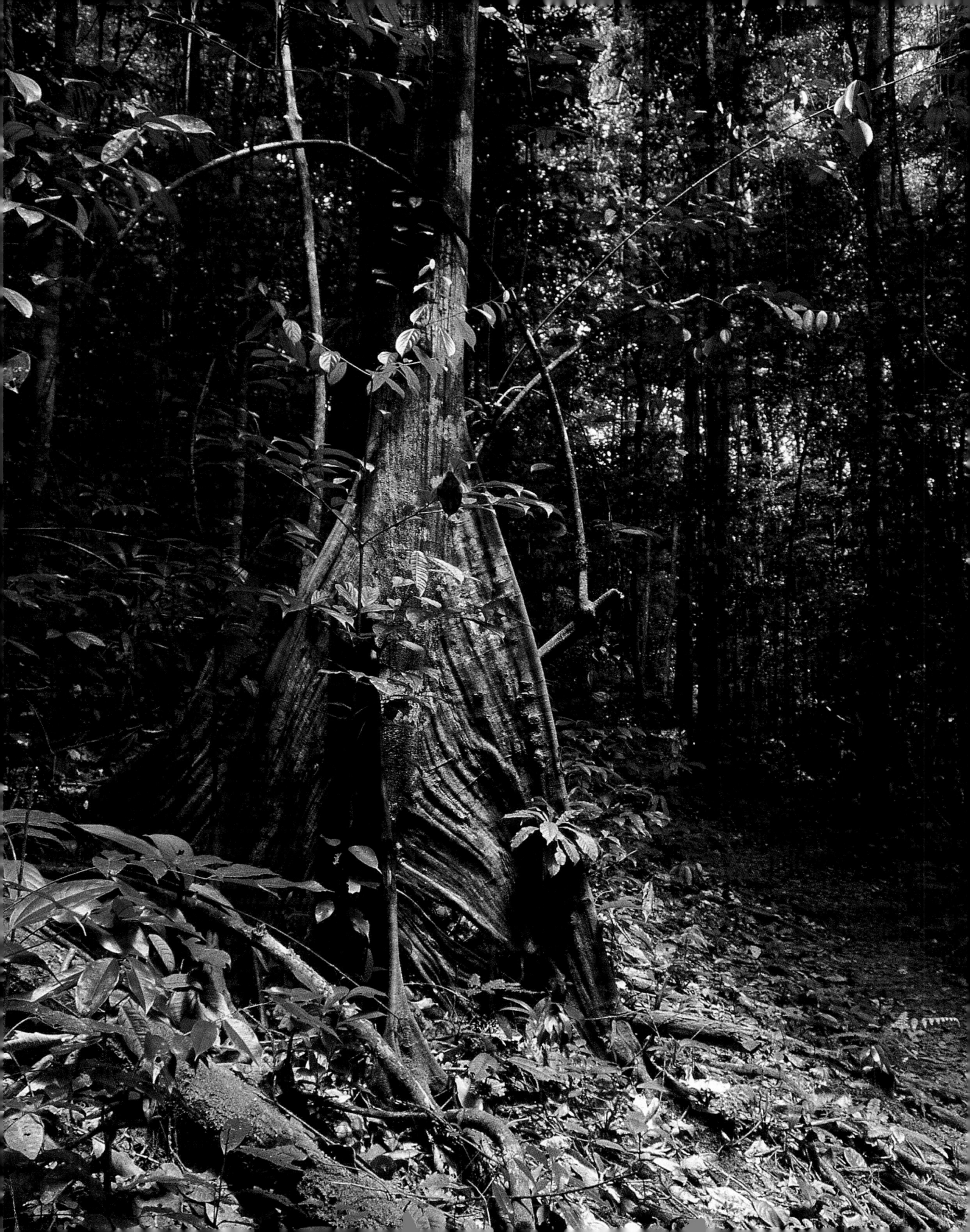

Photos 201, 202, 203, 204

(opposite page) These four photos show the basic differences between tropical forest and dry-land insects. Although quite different, they all blend well with their immediate surroundings, a behavior that has undoubtedly helped in their successful evolution. Photos 201 and 202 show typical forest insects: two *Siliquofera* katydids (1 ¼ in/3 cm) in Papua New Guinea in Photo 201, and a brown acridid grasshopper in Photo 202 (2 ½ in/6 cm) sitting among brown detritus in French Guyana. Photos 203 and 204 illustrate the typical beige colors of desert mantids. The mantid in Photo 204 (2 in/5 cm) lives on dry vegetation in North Africa, while the mantid in Photo 203 (1 ¼ in/ 3 cm) lives in the stony deserts of the Middle East. Photographed in central Tunisia and Abu Dhabi.

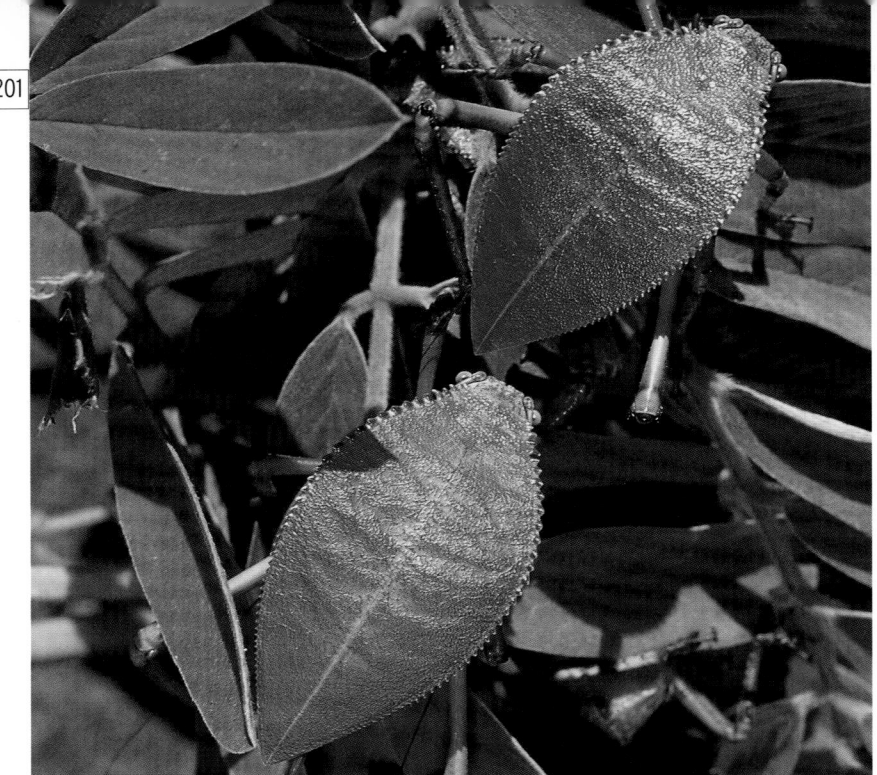

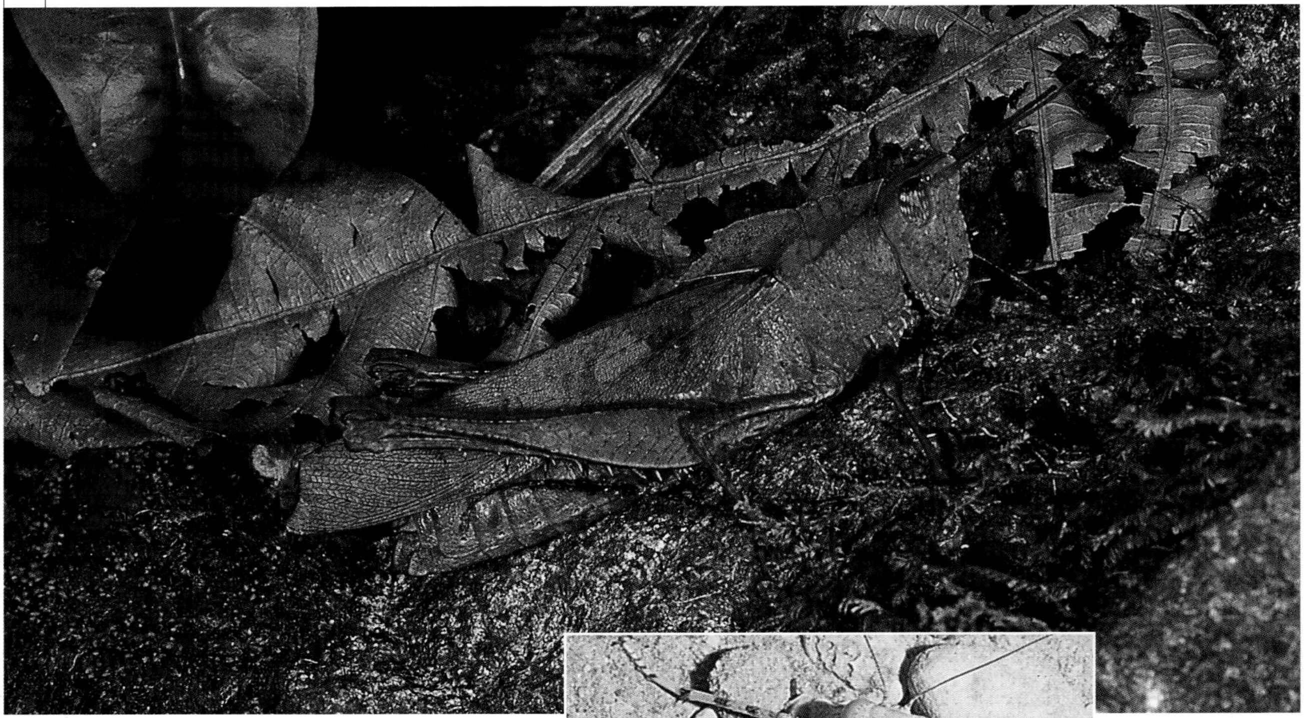

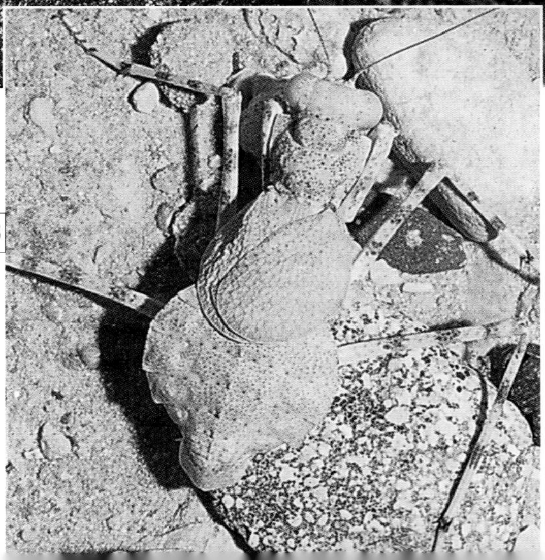

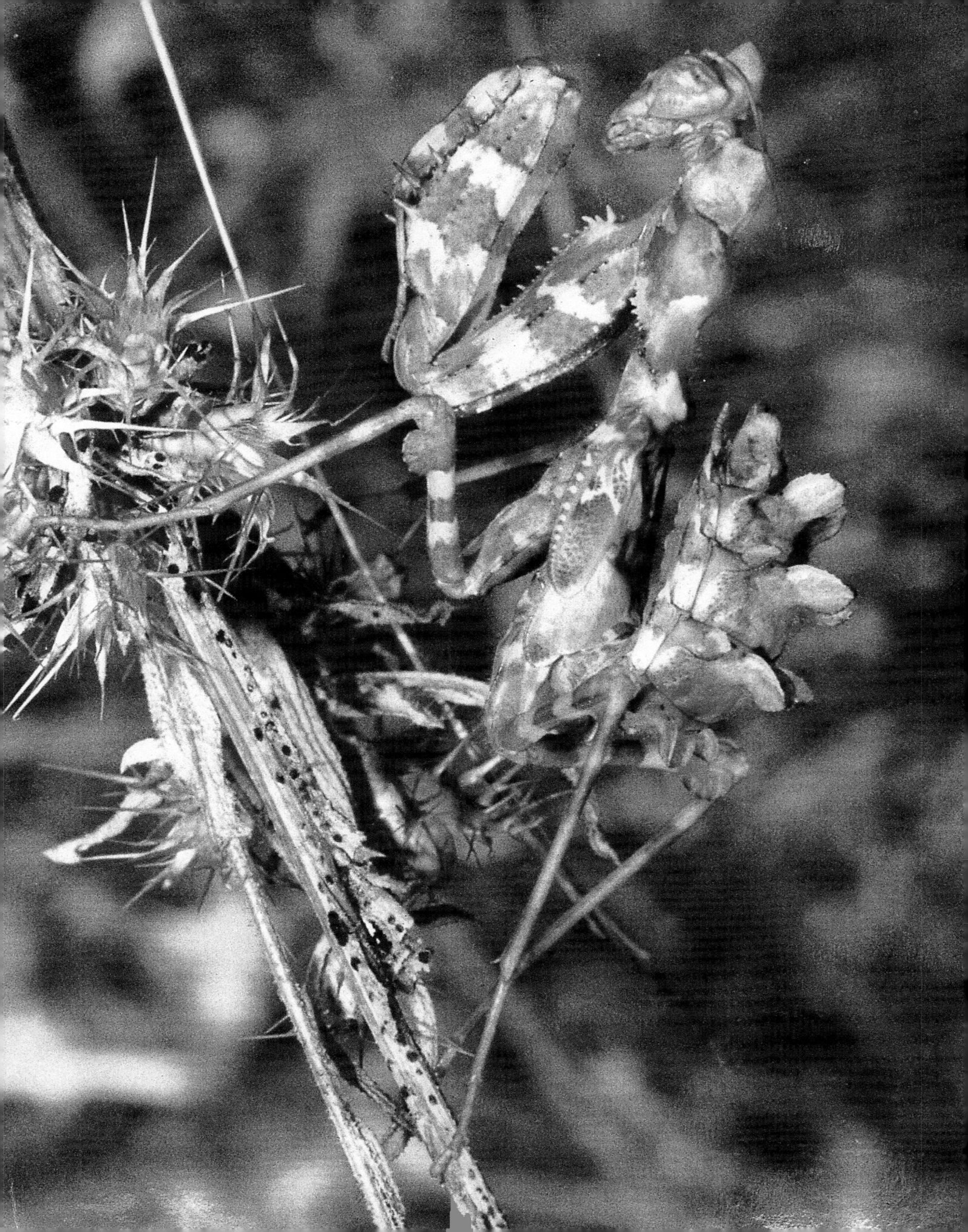

GLOSSARY

active camouflage: occurs when an insect deliberately seeks to improve its camouflage and therefore the loss of identity is not coincidental: see Photos 65 and 66.

Acrididae: a particular family of grasshoppers characterized by short antennae; certain species occur in large, migratory swarms: see Photo 33.

Alydidae: family of "bug" that often mimics ants. Because of their structure (notably their mouth-parts or rostrum), they belong to the order Hemiptera, commonly refered to as "bugs": see Photos 141, 142 and 143.

antlion: clear-winged insect belonging to the family Neuroptera. They tend to resemble dragonflies: see Photos 11 and 12.

aposematic: bright, usually red or orange colors, designed to warn that the insect is unpalatable ("red for danger"): see Photos 45 and 46.

Araneidae: a large family of spiders (including the genus *Argiope*) which build classical orb webs: see Photo 153.

automimicry: occurs when an insect or spider constructs a dummy, presumably in order to confuse predators: see Photos 154, 155 and 156.

Batesian mimicry: when an insect seeks protection by resembling a protected (noxious or otherwise dangerous) model. For example, a harmless moth may resemble a dangerous wasp: see Photos 132 and 133.

bug: has two meanings: a common term applied to any small insect or spider. In this text it is a scientific term applied to insects belonging to the order Hemiptera: see Photos 180 and 181.

carapace: a hard layer or shell that protects the soft material beneath it.

Chrysomelidae: a family of beetles, including "ladybugs"; usually brightly colored and noxious: see Photo 168.

color asymmetry: occurs when upper and lower surfaces of a butterfly's wings have contrasting colors; generally, lower surface is more somber, providing camouflage when butterfly folds its wings: see Photos 88 and 89.

crypsis: a form of camouflage involving close similarity between color pattern of the insect and that of its substrate: see Photo 7.

cloud forest: a tropical forest that occurs at higher altitudes where its humidity is derived directly from cloud vapors (i.e., it is bathed in clouds).

detritus: dead leaves and twigs on the forest floor in varying states of decay that have dropped from the trees above.

disruptive coloration: a form of camouflage involving bands of color that modify the appearance of the insect, protecting it by making its shape hard to identify: see Photo 40.

epiphytes: plants that live perched on trees, independent from the ground; a common insect habitat: see Photo 192.

exoskeleton: the rigid skin that contains the soft body of the insect.

evolutionary convergence: when unrelated insects tend to resemble one another. This happens when different families of insect occupying the same habitat, evolve a common color or form best suited to that habitat through natural selection: see Photos 31, 32 and 33.

false heads and eyes: form of mimicry involving a pattern or structure that resembles a head or eyes; a form of protection: see Photo 111.

Fulgoridae: plant suckers characterized by strange heads (that sometimes resemble crocodile heads): see Photos 148 and 149.

Geometridae: family of moths characterized by slender bodies and triangular-shaped wings: see Photo 7.

grasshoppers: a very general term often applied to the family Acrididae: see Photos 172 and 173.

gymnasty: term proposed by the author to describe the unnatural positions adopted by insects, notably moths, in order to modify their identity; presumably a form of protection: see Photos 101, 102 and 103.

habitat: the place occupied by specific animals and plants; not to be confused with "environment," which includes both geographic and non-geographic parameters such as temperature and humidity; tree trunks or a stony desert are habitats.

Hemiptera: a large order of insects; includes "bugs.": see Photos 180 and 181.

Heliconiidae: a family of butterflies, very abundant in the American tropics, characterized by bright colors, slow flight and noxious body-fluids; often serve as models for Batesian mimics: see Photo 144.

Katydid: a large family of grasshoppers characterized by exceptionally long antennae; frequently chirp (sing) at night: see Photo 56.

Leaf insect: a form of phasmid that closely resembles a leaf: see Photo 16.

Lepidoptera: order of insects comprising butterflies, moths and skippers.

lichen: plant made up of fungus and algae that grows on trees, rocks and walls.

longhorn: type of beetle belonging to the family Cerambycidae, characterized by long antennae. This family includes the world's largest beetles: see Photo 169.

Lycaenidae: large family of small butterflies often characterized by blue colors and false eyes on hind-wing: see Photo 113.

Lymantriidae: family of moths frequently characterized by long, hairy front legs: see Photo 85.

Membracidae: or tree-hoppers, a family of small, plant-sucking insects related to cicadas; often characterized by strange pronotum giving them an "extra-terrestrial" appearance: see Photos 36 and 37.

mimicry: the art of modifying one's identity by resembling the color, shape and (especially) the behavior of another, generally unrelated animal; a form of protection: see Photos 107 and 108.

Morpho: large, generally brilliant, metallic-blue butterflies belonging to the family Morphinae, limited to the American tropics: see Photos 90 and 91.

Müllerian mimicry: occurs when two or more protected (noxious) models resemble one another; a form of mutual protection: see Photos 144, 145 and 146.

Natural selection: theory proposed by Darwin to explain organic evolution via the elimination of certain natural variants (mutants) and the selective preservation of others better suited to the natural constraints of the environment.

Noctuidae: the largest family of moths, generally characterized by massive bodies and rather elongate wings with rectangular terminations: see Photo 8.

Nymphalidae: large family of butterflies characterized by robust bodies and only four functional legs; includes many well-known species such as the "admirals": see Photos 59 and 60.

Orthoptera: an order of insects that includes grasshoppers and crickets.

ovoid: rounded

ovipositor: a rigid appendage used for laying eggs. Situated at the extremity of the abdomen, it is often sword-like in shape: see Photo 56.

Papilionidae: swallowtail butterflies; a large family of generally large, colorful butterflies whose hindwings may be extended as "tails."

passive camouflage: occurs where there is no evidence that the insect has deliberately camouflaged itself. Passive camouflage may be coincidental: see Photo 8.

phasmids: a family of insects in the order Phasmatodea. They generally resemble sticks or leaves: see Photo 3.

proboscis: tube-like mouthpiece characteristic of butterflies and moths, used for sucking fluids: see Photo 107.

pronotum: the rigid, horned or hump-like appendage developed on the thorax of membracid and orthopteran insects: see Photos 36 and 37.

Proscopidae: a small family of grasshoppers limited to the American tropics, characterized by long slender bodies and very strange heads: see Photo 32.

protective resemblance: a form of camouflage in which the insect closely resembles a natural object such as a leaf, stick or stone; not to be confused with mimicry: see Photos 18 and 19.

Pyralidae: a family of small moths that usually have long narrow wings; includes certain fruit moths and cloth-destroying moths: see Photo 170.

rain forest: a tropical forest, often growing to more than 100 feet (30 meters) high, whose humidity is supplied essentially by rain.

Reduviidae: a family of hemipteran insects, generally equipped with a rigid, needle-like mouthpiece or rostrum: see Photo 53.

rostrum: the rigid, piercing mouthpiece of certain hemipteran bugs, cicadas and other insects: see Photo 139.

secondary forest: forest consisting of low trees and shrubs that grow where the initial or primary forest has been cut or burned.

Satyridae: a large family of butterflies; generally somber in color. They frequent low vegetation near the forest floor, where they are often camou-flaged: see Photo 112.

Saturniidae: family of large moths, generally characterized by circular wing-patterns resembling false eyes; some have long "tails"(long tail-like projections or extensions of the hind-wings): see Photos 118 and 119.

sphinx moths: large family of robust, fast-flying moths from the Sphingidae family whose caterpillars are said to resemble a sphinx: see Photo 174.

stick insects: phasmids whose long, thin bodies resemble sticks: see Photo 3.

substrate: the underlying surface against which an insect is camouflaged

tropical forest: a forest that includes both rain forests and cloud forests and is synonymous with "jungle."

Wasmannian mimicry: imitation permitting certain insects, notably beetles, to penetrate termite and ant colonies, where they are accepted by the hosts.

SOURCES

Bates, H.W. *Contributions to an insect fauna of the Amazon Valley: Lepidoptera, Heliconiidae.* Linnean Society Transactions 23. London, 1862.

Müller, F. *Ituna and Thyridia: a remarkable case of mimicry in butterflies.* Proceedings, Entomological Society. London, 1879.

O'Toole, C. *Alien Empire.* BBC Books, Worldwide Publishing. London, 1995.

Preston-Mafham, R. and K. (1966). *The Natural History of Insects.* The Crowood Press, Ramsbury, U.K., 1966.

Richards, P.W. *The Tropical Rainforest.* Second Edition. Cambridge University Press, 1996.

Rittenmeyer, M.H. "Insect mimicry." Annual Review of Entomology. 15. London, 1970.

Von Frisch, K. *Architecture animale.* Editions Albin Michel. Paris, 1975.

Wallace, A.R. "Mimicry and protective ressemblance among animals." *Contributions to the Theory of Natural Selection.* Macmillan. London, 1870.

FURTHER READING

Collins, M. *The Last Rain Forests*. Published by Michael Beasley. London, 1990.
   Produced in association with the World Conservation Union, this well-illustrated volume is an excellent review of world forests. Although not devoted directly to insects, this book, written for the non-specialist, gives a good description of jungle habitats.

Hogue, C.L. *Latin American Insects and Entomology*. University of California Press. Berkeley, California, 1993.
   Although not devoted specifically to camouflage and mimicry, this very readable book gives an excellent review of all families of insects and related arthropods.

MacQuitty, M. and L. Mound. *Megabugs: the Natural History Museum Book of Insects*. Riverswift, Random House. London: 1995.
   This beautifully illustrated book, written for non-specialists, includes a chapter on camouflage and other means of protection.

Preston-Mafham, K. *Grasshoppers and Mantids*. Cassel, London, 1990.
   This well-illustrated book includes many examples of camouflage. It also gives a good description of many insect habitats.

Wootton, A. *Insects of the World*. Blandford Press, London, 1993.
   A well-illustrated book covering the basic aspects of insects, including their camouflage and mimicry. It also explains insect structure and classification.

INDEX

Page numbers set in italics indicate photographs.